Two Pedestrians on Bicycles

Graham Barden

Pen Press Publishers Ltd

First published in Great Britain by
Pen Press Publishers Ltd
25 Eastern Place
Brighton
BN2 1GJ

ISBN 978-1-906206-31-4

Printed and bound in the UK

A catalogue record of this book is available from
the British Library

Cover design by Jacqueline Abromeit

Contents

PROLOGUE

Estre Cauncy, a small village in Northern France. We had been riding through the gaunt remains of abandoned mine workings in searing heat for six hours when Mary collapsed. For the past hour, close to exhaustion, she had kept going by sheer willpower. Now she lay semi-conscious by the roadside, her bed a hastily inflated sleeping mat placed in the scant shade of a rickety bus shelter. She needed food, drink and rest but our water was gone and her mouth too dry to eat one of the muesli bars that we carried with us.

Two days into an attempted world bicycle trip. Already beginning to falter and perhaps even fail. What to do now? Find a telephone and attempt to seek help? Not easy with my limited command of the French language. Go knocking on doors for assistance? But how to communicate our present difficulties? Attempt to find a shop to buy drink? No sign of one nearby and anyway, should I leave Mary unsupported in her present condition in a land that is foreign to us and seemingly indifferent to our plight?

But no! From a garden gate a kindly looking woman approaches offering a pitcher of water. A van selling cakes and bread stops alongside and the driver alights, offering help. Desperately needed liquid and re-energising sugar and carbohydrates have arrived as though by grand design, but in reality by acts of human kindness.

Two hours later, rested and recovered, we are again on the road. The going continues to be hilly and hard but within another couple of hours we enter the town of Arras. Spacious squares, framed by imposing stone buildings, call for our attention but first two essential questions have to be answered. Where to sleep and where to find food? The town hall houses an information bureau. There we are given a map showing the route to a campsite close by the centre. On the way a supermarket furnishes supplies. Tired but elated, we clean up and eat. Despite an exhausting day we feel an immense sense of satisfaction and the beginnings of some self-belief in our ability to make further progress, but not before resting, so we decide to explore Arras tomorrow.

Sleep comes easily to us this night.

INTRODUCTION

I had taken early retirement in 1997 at the age of fifty-eight. Dreams of endless leisure soon turned to time on my hands and a future that appeared to stretch aimlessly ahead to the graveyard. I took a part-time job as an ambulance driver for the disabled and began to ride an old bicycle for exercise. The job took me to various centres for the disabled and at one of these I met Mary, my partner-to-be. By this time my interest in cycling had begun to grow and with it an awareness of the bicycle as something more than just an exercise machine. Books by Anne Mustoe and Josie Dew proved to be an inspiration. The former is a head-teacher who had retired at fifty-six. Her leaving present from the pupils of her school was a bicycle, whereupon she did no more than proceed to ride around the world in an easterly direction. Josie Dew is a young cyclist whose books of her international travels are full of incident, gentle humour and inspirational optimism.

I began to research the topic of global travel in earnest but found this such a daunting prospect that I came to the conclusion that short duration trips to individual countries was about all I might ever manage. With this goal in mind I bought a new bicycle and rode a circuit of some five hundred miles into Wales, taking ten days over the trip and wanting more. Mary too began to develop an interest in cycling. She bought a fine bicycle and in September of 2001 we toured for a week in Norfolk. We were hooked. Every day was different. The sights, sounds and smells of the Norfolk countryside beguiled our senses and we were constantly entertained by the approaches of friendly folk, who were curious to know what we were doing riding these heavily-laden bicycles about their county.

Mary and I had by now reached a stage in our relationship when perhaps a little excitement was needed and she, possibly also seeking some confirmation of a life ahead, had picked up on my exploration of world travel. It was November of 2001 when she first expressed an interest and so together we went through the material I had collected. Contained within was the promise of idyllic cycling through beautiful countryside, airline travel, waving palm trees, the beautiful southern hemisphere lands of Australia and New Zealand, the soaring snow peaks of the European Alps and the Rocky Mountains of America, Buddhist temples, exotic wildlife, other peoples and their cultures. Many such romantic images of world travel crowded our minds. From these imaginings were sown the seeds of a world cycling trip. In the New Year they were to flower into reality.

We had scant idea where to begin with plans and preparations for such an apparently ambitious trip. Very little information seemed to be readily available. What books we could find were hopelessly out of date and cycle touring club pamphlets were an enchantment of quaint antiquity but useless. Accounts of the travels of others as published on the Internet were often fascinating but gave very few pointers with regard to first steps. One or two web-sites had 'question and answer' message boards but it seemed that cycle tourists were either a very diverse group of people or mostly insane, for their answers to our questions ranged from the contradictory through the eccentric to the outlandish. Invitations to join the Siberian cycling federation or to climb Mount Kilimanjaro (maybe they mistook 'bike' for 'hike') were not quite what we were looking for. Needless to say, we began to wonder if we might be more than a trifle eccentric ourselves. The reactions of friends did not always help, for some clearly thought we had taken leave of our senses.

Frustrated and confused, we took recourse to basics and addressed the two obvious questions of where? and when? This simple approach led us to draft a route across Europe, the Middle East, the Far East, Australia, New Zealand and the USA. This would give us summer in the northern hemisphere, summer in the southern hemisphere and a third summer back in the northern hemisphere. Three summers and no winter seemed immensely appealing to us, especially as the prevailing winds should aid our passage. Having this basic foundation then led on to questions of distance and time, air travel, entry requirements, politics, language issues, money matters, health-care, insurance, equipment and many others. Almost all of the information we needed we found on the Internet, though we had to make certain modifications due to a growing political crisis in the Middle East and a threat of nuclear war between India and Pakistan.

And so our route was decided upon. It was to be Northern France, Switzerland, Italy, mainland Greece, Turkey, Thailand, Malaysia, Singapore, Australia, New Zealand and the USA. In total, an estimated 12,500 miles through eleven countries and taking us some fifteen months to complete.

The first six months of 2002 were very hectic indeed for, in addition to planning and preparation for the trip, we also had to find time for long weekend training runs on our bicycles and at the same time 'place in suspension' our homes and day-to-day lives in England. By early June we were about as prepared as we ever would be. We held a farewell 'drop-in' party for friends and family. Mary and I spent most of the time fluctuating wildly between tearful or manic behaviour. The fears for our sanity of those close to us must have been confirmed but in truth we were existing on a powerful mixed cocktail of elation and anxiety as we approached 'D' day.

The day of our departure dawned. My eldest son, accompanied by his daughter, drove us in his van to Dover. We travelled in thoughtful silence. What lay ahead of us seemed too enormous to contemplate. With lumps in our throats we boarded the ferry to Calais.

We were on our way at last.

Our first day seemed to pass by in a dream; the next day painful reality was to set in at the roadside in Estre Cauncy.

CHAPTER ONE
THE TOUR-DE-ARSE

The crisis of Mary's episode of exhaustion the day before had not dimmed our optimism as we awoke in Arras to the sound of birdsong and the golden glow of a glorious sunrise. Adjacent to us on the campsite were a man and his wife from New Zealand. Peter and Jane, both retired, were touring Europe for some nine months. They had bought a second hand 'campavan' in Belgium, which they intended to sell before returning to their home in Picton on the south island of their home country. We talked of contact with home. Telephone communication, it seemed, was often imperfect.

"Hello, Dad, hope you're enjoying your trip to Europe. By the way, can you let me have some money, we're a bit short just now."

Here Peter, in an attempt to create the sound of a faulty phone line, gave a more than passable imitation of a steam engine.

"Works fine," said he, "haven't given them a single dollar yet and serves 'em bloody-well right for being such scroungers!"

It was our first taste of dry antipodean humour and a trick we thought we might keep up our sleeves for the future. We exchanged e-mail addresses and were invited to look them up when we arrived in New Zealand. It seemed to us that they had a great deal more confidence in our prospects of ever reaching that distant country than we did.

Arras proved to be a gracious and spacious town with two magnificent open squares enclosed by grandiose stone buildings. Pavement cafés were full of people passing time with ease. Shoppers and passers-by seemed to be in no hurry. We drank coffee and ate croissants in the sunshine. The relaxed atmosphere of this happy place transmitted itself to us and the difficulties of the previous day began to fade in our memories. We were beginning to learn a lesson, which would sustain us many more times in the future. Tomorrow really is another day!

The next morning, in the hope of escaping the heat later in the day, we rose at 5.00 am to leave by 6-00 am. However, wet weather set in and all day we cycled through dripping fields of corn, beet and peas. At regular intervals we passed rain-soaked cemeteries and rode through seedy looking villages bearing the marks of war, the walls of many houses scarred by bullet pockmarks. These were grim reminders of the First World War, for this was the Somme. Feeling compelled to enter a cemetery, we wandered around in the rain reading the inscriptions on the crosses. Perhaps the most poignant were those saying "Known only unto God". These stark reminders of the passing of unnamed dead left us depressed and angry at this senseless loss of life. Between them the British, French and Germans suffered over a million casualties as a result of the fighting on The Somme. In the region of a quarter of a million men were killed. For all this carnage the Allied Forces gained at most eight miles.

At St.Quentin there were clear signs to a well-manicured municipal campsite on the banks of the River Somme. Later, a sparsely equipped and very tired looking touring cyclist arrived, pitched his tent and disappeared within. In marked contrast, two more cyclists rode in and pitched a tent of three-ringed-circus dimensions. Their bicycles were surely the Rolls-Royces of all pedal-powered machines and their matching spandex tights a riot of skin-tight colour. Our attempts at friendly conversation met with a cool response, although we did learn that they were from Holland and taking a two-week holiday. We hoped they did not notice our road-stained attire, and remained silent as to our intentions.

All that night thunderstorms raged, allowing us little sleep. A lull in the rain in the morning gave the opportunity for us to break camp but once on the road the rain recommenced and we struggled along, climbing seemingly endless hills and at regular intervals receiving cold douches of spray from passing lorries. By now we were beginning to develop some impressions of the reality of long-distance cycling and we were wondering when the fun was going to start. Our average distance was over fifty miles a day, with perhaps five to seven hours pedalling, depending on road conditions. Mary was in considerable discomfort from her saddle and attempting all sorts of padding strategies but with no great success. Straw from the roadside was a particularly spectacular failure. I had a persistent pain in my right wrist, which was to trouble me for many months to come. This was nothing like those fantasized balmy days of golden sunshine and easy riding on flat roads that we had dreamed of back home in England.

We arrived, tired and wet, at Laon, a medieval walled hill town with a 13th century cathedral looking like an early version of the Empire State Building. This day we were to learn another invaluable lesson about the remarkable powers of recovery of the human body. A baguette, some Brie, a couple of small beers in the cathedral square and our fatigue melted away. We gazed about us at a wonderland of shops, cafés, bistros and houses, scattered as though by the hand of a giant dice-thrower, amongst a maze of cobbled streets. Those same streets soon saw us circling around in amused frustration as we tried to find our way out of town to a campsite nearby. When we were allocated a damp and rubbish-strewn patch of ground to pitch our tent, it quickly became obvious to us that this place was the home of the local scavenging community. Their caravans were surrounded by various selections of old bedsteads, car tyres, rusting electrical appliances and other such examples of expendability. That night we locked our bicycles securely to a tree. Tucked up in our sleeping bags, we reviewed the day. I learned that for most of it Mary had wept with the sadness of homesickness, her tears and the rain as one.

The next day was my sixty-third birthday. It took us through the Cathedral city of Rheims, where we bumped into the sparsely equipped cyclist we had first seen two days earlier. He was riding from London to Dijon to visit his son, not having ridden his bicycle for many years. It was an ancient machine, equipped with a couple of very dog-eared rear panniers. He himself wore a pair of tattered shorts, a working shirt and a pair of brown brogues. His minimalist approach to cycle touring impressed us greatly, as did his relaxed and easy-going nature, but he seemed to think we were over-equipped so Mary retreated into the cathedral. From within

3

there could be heard the sounds of piped devotional music. She emerged in tears, deeply moved by something intensely private. Outside in the cathedral square a stage was in construction to pay homage to music of another kind, a coming rock concert.

That night on the campsite at Chalons-Sur-Marne we met another traveller, a pilgrim who was journeying on foot to the Christian shrine of Santiago-di-Compostella in Spain. His face wore a dreamily distant stare, and he spent the whole evening sitting cross-legged at the entrance to his tent, gazing at a lighted candle. We preferred the less contemplative option of a birthday picnic feast, washed down with generous quantities of local red wine.

Our journey across northern France continued. At Lac-du-Der we camped on the shore of a gigantic inland lake. It was a remote spot promising peace and quiet. It was not to be, for we were kept awake by a chorus of roaring frogs doing their best to outdo a Wembley crowd on Cup Final day. A group of English carp fishermen were camped by the waterside. They had booked their spot twelve months before and were determined to make the most of it. Seven days a week, twenty-four hours a day, they fished. It was a space-age operation requiring a veritable armoury of electronic aids and many crates of beer. All to no avail, for after three days and nights they had not had a single bite, at least as far as they could remember.

At Chaumont, the temptation to pose for photos beneath a street sign was irresistible in our saddle-sore state. It was called the Tour-de-Arse.

We were entering the area of the Haute Somme, beautifully undulating countryside with larks celebrating in an azure sky. Here dreamed a sun-soaked landscape of scattered woodlands amidst ripening cornfields, like waves of golden hair tied with emerald ribbons. At Gray we crossed the River Somme and entered a colourful maze of medieval streets. We drank cool beers in a pavement café and later enjoyed a riverside evening picnic. It had been a good day. Perhaps the fun was beginning to start at last.

We continued to traverse Northern France, the ground ever rising towards the mountains of The Jura. Historical towns and cities were our refuges for the night. Their cathedrals had seen the crowning of kings, battlefields their assasinations. The ramparts of fortified chateaux watched over the dwellings of townsfolk whose ancestors once did the bidding of their rulers on pain of death. Wars were started on the basis of nothing more than the whim of powerful individuals. Surely modern levels of political sophistication would never allow such a thing to happen again! A thousand years of history echoed down the narrow cobbled streets of these ancient citadels. This was a region pulsating with the triumphs and terrors of burgeoning European Civilisation. What, then, of this rich panoply of history caught our imaginations? Two camels grazing by the roadside provided an intriguing tableau. At Pontalier we were beguiled by a field full of zebras and at Besancon all night entertainment was provided by the rhythmic throbbing of tom-toms. These somewhat un-European manifestations of global diversity are the things that are engraved most indelibly upon our memories.

Leaving Besancon, we began the more serious climbing that was to take us over the range of the Jura Mountains. The route ahead snaked its way ever upwards. Rock-fall from the surrounding mountainsides littered the road, provoking uncomfortable thoughts of a hole in the head. A lung-bursting low-gear slog took us ever upward through thick pine forest, cloaked in mizzling rain. We came upon a small grey stone church standing by the roadside. It marked the Col-de-Jougny; at 3,363 feet it was our highest point to date. It was something of an anti-climax for there was little to see in a swirling mountain mist.

We swept downhill and were surprised to approach a range of official looking buildings. We had arrived at the border with Switzerland. There were no formalities; we simply crossed into our second country and fell weeping into one another's arms. Somehow the tensions of the past few months were unexpectedly released. At that moment we knew that we were really on our way.

CHAPTER TWO
DEAD SPARROWS TO DORMODOSSOLA

The trip to Lausanne was an ecstatic downhill glide through luminous fields of sunflowers, all facing south, their golden faces appearing to mirror our beaming smiles as we passed them by. On a grassy roadside bank we rested beneath a cherry tree laden with fruit, on which we feasted. At Vallorbe, a patisserie was unable to sell us pastries for we had no Swiss Francs. Our research had failed to take account of European politics and we did not know that Switzerland was not a member of the European Economic Union. Somehow the subject of Swiss Economic Policy had not been top of our list of priorities!

The approach to Lausanne was made safe and simple by user-friendly cycle lanes. We negotiated the centre in a child-like state of excited happiness. Riding easily down broad avenues, we descended a series of graceful terraces to the shore of Lake Geneva. We quickly found a well-organised campsite just to the south of the city centre, which fortunately allowed us to pay for our site by debit card.

That evening we enjoyed the luxury of an unladen bike-ride along the lakeside, the mountains of the Chablais on the opposite shore glowing in the evening sun. A visit to an ATM furnished fifty francs and a café meal. Returning to the campsite we mingled with lakeside promenaders interwoven by roller-skaters and roller-bladers, one elderly gentleman performing elegant pirouettes in a mobile reverie of his own. The easy sense of relaxation here seemed a far cry from the frantic rush of the busy Midlands city we had left behind in England some two weeks ago.

The next morning, on the campsite, we met Chris, an Australian from Tasmania. He was touring Europe on his cycle for the summer. A well-travelled young man, he was a mine of useful information about his home country and was able to reassure us with regard to our concerns about airport access and airline transport for our bicycles.

"No worries, dudes, there's always a way."

The rest of the day we spent sight-seeing amongst the avenues of the city which, in the steepness of its hills, is often compared to San Francisco. Wandering the spectacular lakeside city of Lausanne, with its ever-changing mountain panoramas, seemed to us to be a fabulous return for the effort of cycling over five hundred miles to arrive here.

Leaving Lausanne at 6.30 am the next day, we rode along the north-western shore of Lake Geneva. To our left rose vineyard-covered slopes and to our right the mountains of the Chablais loomed across the shining waters of the lake. Ahead lay the magnificent snow-covered peaks of the Dents-du-Midi and nestling before them the City of Montreux, famed for its jazz festival and the European 'It's a Knock-out'. Quite obviously a place rich in the diversity of the cultural experiences it has to offer!

Just beyond Montreux stands Chateau Chillon. The stone ramparts of this medieval fort seeming to gaze unblinkingly across the lake to the ramparts of the mountains on the opposite shore. The rock promontory on which it is built is known to have been inhabited since ancient times, the first written reference to the castle occurring some nine hundred years ago. The Swiss, clearly not given to excessive modesty, like to think the Chateau symbolises their country with its beauty, strength and stability. It has been the inspiration for the narratives of many great writers, perhaps the most famous among them being Lord Byron, who wrote his epic poem 'The Prisoner of Chillon' whilst staying here. Perhaps relaxing after his creative efforts, he almost drowned during a sudden storm, which arose whilst he was out boating on the lake. Gazing at the tranquil beauty of this place, we wondered how this could happen, for ahead the peaks of the Dents-du-Midi were perfectly mirrored in the still waters of the lake.

Passing through Villeneuve at the head of the lake, we made our way up the Rhone Valley, vineyards and apricot orchards flanking the roadside. Suddenly we heard behind us a noise like a swarm of bees growing rapidly louder to the proportions of a squadron of wartime bomber aircraft. To our astonishment, a group of several hundred motorcyclists roared past, taking up every inch of available road-space, their machines of every size and shape, some all gleaming chromium, others like mobile scrap-heaps, their riders an equally varied group. Viking horns and swastikas adorned the helmets of those who could be bothered to wear them. Others were sporting heads of wild, windswept hair or shaven skulls glinting in the sunlight, and one man appeared to be totally naked. Cigarettes were being passed around from rider to rider, and from the erratic progress of this convoy, it seems unlikely that they were smoking tobacco. Sunday recreational pastimes in this part of the world were certainly entertaining.

Drawing closer to Martigny, we were to observe a strange and sometimes frustrating phenomenon, which was to recur on a number of future occasions. On a long stretch of road we found ourselves pedalling hard in a low gear whilst travelling downhill. A cyclist riding in the opposite direction was apparently freewheeling uphill! We figured it must be something to do with the mountainous terrain fooling our eyes, if not our legs. On this occasion the effect was against us. Later we were to greatly enjoy the sensation of seeming to freewheel up the side of a mountain.

From Martigny it was our intention to cross the Alps via the Grand-Saint-Bernard Pass, a prospect we viewed with trepidation for it has an elevation of over 8,000 feet and the road carries much trans-alpine heavy traffic. Somewhat anxiously, we set out early the next morning. The dual carriageway was already thick with lorries and had no hard shoulder. Tons of heavy steel whistling by in close proximity accompanied by clouds of choking fumes proved not to be an enjoyable experience. A pair of sparrows lying dead in the road invoked in us an uncharacteristic bout of superstition, giving us just the excuse we needed to about-face and head up the Rhone Valley to Brig and the Simplon Rail Tunnel into Italy.

CHAPTER THREE
CLOSE ENCOUNTERS OF THE TURD KIND

Feeling somewhat guilty at taking the train through the Alps into Italy, we arrived at the station in Dormodossola to be greeted by torrential rain – conditions not ideal for cycling. We soon encountered a problem that was to plague us throughout our Italian travels, that of navigation. Civic coffers seemed not to extend to the expense of the erection of signposts in this country and our lack of Italian language skills did not help matters. Discussion along the lines of "Which way?" and "Buggered if I know!" were equally fruitless, until I remembered the compass tucked into my bar-bag. A bearing from the map, a swift prayer and off we went in a south-easterly direction, possibly heading for Lake Maggiore.

This day proved not to be the most fun-filled we had yet experienced. Lashed by rain and in poor visibility, the front pannier on Mary's bike struck a high kerb and she took a nasty fall. Cold muscles led her to an agonising attack of cramp and later, eating a lunchtime apple, she broke a front tooth. Patched up with Super Glue, this was not to receive a proper repair until we reached Australia.

It was a miserable pair of cycle travellers who later that day limped into the campground at Scolpio, on the shores of Lake Maggiore. We must have looked as pitiful as we felt, for a Dutch couple camped nearby brought us chairs and hot drinks and a pair from Yorkshire supplied us with a brew of tea. Whilst resting that evening, we were treated to the strange sight of two elderly women strolling happily around the campground, one pushing an empty pushchair, the other pulling an empty dog lead.

"Easier than pushing it," mused Mary.

Our spirits were definitely beginning to rise after a difficult day.

The next morning things got off to a flying start with an easy-rolling, down-wind ride alongside the lake. Manicured villages sporting ornate Italianate architecture and many luxury hotels suggested this area was the playground of the wealthy. However, it was too good to last for the countryside soon became increasingly urbanised and industrial and very busy. Dangerously aggressive drivers, choking fumes and a cacophony of blaring horns came close to producing a cyclist's nightmare. We had intended to take a restful lunch in the great northern Italian city of Milan. However, a maelstrom of snarling traffic and non-existent signposting brought us close to despair. Designated cycle lanes plagued our progress, for they would suddenly come to an end without offering any alternative. We became lost in a maze of squalid high-rise development. Rivers running with raw sewage and serried ranks of prostitutes lining the roadside depressed our spirits. The roads themselves were an obstacle course of pot-holes and everywhere motorists were overtaking, under-taking, shooting red lights, constantly sounding their horns and shouting and swearing at all and sundry. Sixty miles of this urban nightmare saw us fall, weak with exhaustion, into a hotel, there to sweat the night away, not even having the heart or strength to find food. This part of northern Italy seemed a far cry from the images of Venetian splendour and Tuscan rural beauty that we carried in our imaginations.

We rose the next morning to discover that we were at a place called Legnano. Not that we cared, for we wanted nothing more than to escape this grim area of ordinary, everyday Italy. It was not to be. Our journey continued through a rash of light industrial development of the sort you can see surrounding any town in Britain. The road surface continued to resemble that of a tank training ground and the howling, stinking traffic was an assault on the senses. Shrines to the dead, killed on the road, lined the verges, giving us cause to wonder how many of the deceased had been cyclists.

The town of Piacenza gave us an unexpectedly tranquil lunchtime interlude with its quiet squares and walls of ancient buildings adorned with colourful Roman frescos. Here we were engaged in conversation by a local cyclist riding a machine so old it left a trail of rust in the road behind it. He was impeccably dressed in an immaculate suit and seemed to be expressing himself with great eloquence, for he spoke for some fifteen minutes, hardly appearing to draw a single breath. It must have been our loss for we could not understand a single word; yet we felt there had been some important human communication between us. Leaving the town we stopped for ice creams and enjoyed yet another human encounter, this time with a group of middle-aged Italians who chatted volubly to us with the same result. We understood almost nothing of what was said yet it felt good to us and we quit the town in high spirits.

We were heading towards the town of Parma, famed for its cured ham, but some six miles from an imagined spicy feast, the pounding traffic and fading light defeated us. A decrepit trucker's rooming shack refused us a night's accommodation on the grounds of no vacancies, despite the absence of any trucks in the parking lot. In desperation, we headed into an area designated a nature reserve for a night's wild camping. 'Nature reserve' turned out to be something of a misnomer – 'turd reserve' would have been more appropriate, for it was clearly used as an outside loo by all and sundry. Our feelings about this region of Italy were by now becoming less than positive and a night spent in this rubbish and shite-strewn place did nothing to improve them. At least we had no pangs of conscience when choosing a spot for our morning toilet call!

Miserably we set out towards Parma, once again in appalling road and traffic conditions, neither of us wanting to concede but both desperate to avoid further suffering. Reaching Parma in glum silence, our eyes met in mute agreement.

"Sod this, I've had enough of risking my life, what do you say to sussing out the trains and to hell with the ham?"

Came the reply: "I'm not *that* hungry, let's get out of here!"

The station was chaotic and when the train arrived, we saw that the goods van was at the front, even though we had been told to wait at the back. A mad dash along the platform did nothing for the guard's temper, as our boarding manoeuvres delayed the train. At Rimini we were left in hostile isolation as we struggled to unload our bicycles and panniers onto the platform. Well at least we were alive and had now reached one of the most fabled beach resorts of the Italian Adriatic coast: Rimini, jewel of the Adriatic. Some authentic local delights were surely to be sampled here.

Beer and chips at the Lord Nelson pub soon dispelled that fantasy, although they were nice. Twelve miles of ribbon development and a beach buried beneath duckboards were not quite what we had expected to see before we reached a campground at Riccione. At the entrance, Mary staged a dramatic fall from her bike. This was a good start, for the male contingent of the campground staff were most solicitous in administering antiseptic balms and plasters for her injuries. We were shown to a postage stamp-sized piece of ground in the midst of a heaving caravan and canvas metropolis. Introducing ourselves to a Danish family nearby, we noticed that the grandma had her leg roughly bandaged and learned that she had tripped over a tree root. An X-ray had revealed a broken leg. The suggested treatment had been for the family to return to Denmark to have the leg put in plaster. Needless to say, the family did not have too high an opinion of Italy.

"Dirty, smelly and noisy," was their consensus.

We could find little to argue with in that analysis, particularly as an all-night, open-air rave kept us awake until 5-00 am.

A day of rest saw us taking a walk along the duckboard-covered beach, perhaps to dip our toes in the sea. The Adriatic is highly polluted and the subject of a number of multi-lateral projects attempting to address the problem. A long way to go from our perspective, for the sea had a dull and lifeless look to it, with not a seabird in sight; and despite the crowded seashore, few of the holiday-makers seemed inclined to bathe in the dubious waters. We deemed it prudent not to take a paddle on this occasion.

The following day, from Riccione, we set out along the Adriatic coast. The going was easy, with flat roads and a helpful tail wind. This at least offered some compensation, for the coastline was grossly overdeveloped and the towns desperately difficult to navigate. There were some rural sections along our route and here fields of golden sunflowers, sweet corn and vines offered some relief from relentless urbanisation. However, the sewage-filled rivers flowing through this area did tend to lead us into morbid speculation about the nuances of flavour present in the local wines.

After staying a night at Senigallia, we set out for our next objective of the town of Porto-St-Elpidio. On the way we passed through Ancona, an important Adriatic port and, like all ports, pulsing with the mysterious breath of faraway places. A serpentine climbing road took us out of Ancona into the kind of classically beautiful scenery we had pictured in our imaginations. This was a landscape of rolling hills, the lines of which might have been drawn by an artist's hand, their slopes adorned by golden garlands of sunflower fields and fringed by manes of cypress trees. Here and there were hilltops crowned by a village pot-pourri of stone houses, topped by lofty church towers.

Porto-St-Elpidio proved to be an undistinguished town but the campground was spacious and the evening entertainment hilarious. A camp concert was the source of our amusement. Language was no barrier to our enjoyment, for the games played by the campers needed no interpretation and nothing more than a broad mind to appreciate. Bawdy gyrations were performed with bananas and oranges and a game of musical underwear, as distinct from musical chairs, should not have been allowed a public showing. An English seaside holiday camp had nothing on this, and we crept into our sleeping bags, our ribs aching from so much laughter and thinking that maybe Italy wasn't such a bad place after all.

Tedious campground bureaucracy delayed our departure the next morning and already the heat of the day was beginning to make itself felt. Once on the road it was hot, some 33 degrees centigrade. Pounding traffic added to the unpleasantness, as did the towns we had to negotiate, for these were the sort of places that could only engender sympathy for the residents.

That night we camped at the village of Pineto. The local church had a set of bells that chimed out one of those ice-cream sellers' tunes. Amusing, but only if you don't mind being awoken every quarter of an hour to the strains of 'Just one cornetto'.

Cycling through the town of Pescara the next day, we were touched by the generosity of a street fruit-seller who would accept no payment for a bag of nectarines. A man on a scooter pulled alongside us:

"Where are you from?"

"Err, England."

"Where are you going?"

"Err, around the world."

He nodded indifferently and rode on.

Climbing a hill we saw a group of *caribineri* by the roadside. They had pistols at their belts and some were carrying short, menacing looking rifles slung over their shoulders. We feared the worse but instead received shouts of encouragement and a round of applause. We rode through an endless corridor of featureless olive groves. At sixty miles we chose to pass by a campground for we were just short of one thousand miles and had the foolish ambition to sleep on this milestone of our journey. Another twenty-seven miles further on, we fell exhausted but happy into a grubby 'camp-ghetto' in Vasto, 1,039 miles under our wheels.

Pausing for lunch in the town of Termoli the next day, we were greatly impressed by a 6th century fort poised on a rock above the harbour. Perhaps only the Italians would have thought to crown this piece of antiquity with a 20th century, windowless concrete shed adorned with clusters of aerials. This certainly made for an interesting contrast in architectural styles. Fortified by a delicious watermelon, we continued to the town of Campo Marino and 'camping pineto'. Here the local campers were accommodated in rusting remnants of caravans and a couple living beneath sheets of polythene. Our modern, lightweight nylon tent looked like a palace in comparison. This had been a short day, just twenty-five miles, so we had time to rest on the beach. Conveniently littered human detritus soon enabled us to scavenge enough furniture to enjoy a comfortable siesta.

From Campo Marino our next objective was the town of Foggia. Fields of corn, tomatoes, vines and olive groves lined the road. Seated at the entrance tracks to each olive grove at regular intervals were women who were definitely not olive pickers – this some twenty miles before the town. Later we were able to form some estimation of the probable prosperity of the places we were approaching from the numbers and frequency of prostitutes at the roadside. Foggia certainly came way down the table of wealth for the first sight that greeted us was a *favela*. Neither of us had ever seen the evidence of poverty on this scale: a heaving and squalid conglomeration of shacks constructed from wood, polythene, cardboard and corrugated iron. Incongruously, the occasional satellite dish stood proudly above these structures, while the rest of the town was seedy and unwelcoming.

Feeling depressed, we decided we could not stay in this place and, in the hope of better things, left for the next town. In blazing heat we cycled a further twenty miles to Cerignola. Here a friendly policeman directed us to a motel on the road out of town. Its somewhat shabby looks concealed reasonable comfort. Our bicycles were housed in the kitchen and we spent an interesting few minutes chatting to the proprietor at check-in. By sign and halting attempts at each other's language, we learned that the owner had lived there for some forty years, having built the place up from a roadside shack to its present state of advanced shackdom. At dinner he waited on us attentively, presenting us with the choice of tagliatelli, macaroni or spaghetti – all *à la Bolognaise*. If he had wanted to reinforce any stereotypical notions we might have held about Italians as pasta eaters, he was doing very well. It was far from easy for us to show respect for the menu by pretending indecision whilst keeping straight faces, but somehow we managed it. With full stomachs we took to our bed in stifling heat and slept uneasily to the tune of a noisy air-conditioning unit.

Accommodation difficulties were to feature highly on the following day. Having ridden some forty miles in oppressive heat, we were unable to find lodgings of any kind. Eventually we were forced to settle for a stony beach just short of the town of Molfetta. A 'scrape' in the pebbles and a sheet of cardboard scavenged by Mary was to be our bed that night. In the evening two fishermen arrived. Their method was to wade far into the shallow sea and lay out an arc of net. Returning to the beach they then proceeded to throw stones close to the shore to drive any sheltering fish out to sea and into the net. They were patient men, and they needed to be, for in two hours of backbreaking work they captured but one fish not much bigger than a minnow:

"*Piscoli piccolini*," they told us with pride and indeed it was very small. We eyed it with some envy for we had nothing to eat.

15

Hungry and uncomfortable, we attempted to sleep but soon there began the racket of the inevitable open-air rave, this coming from the town some four miles distant across a wide bay. Dozing fitfully and twitching uneasily on our bed of stones, we were soon to discover another reason for our discomfort. We felt a tickling in the neck and then in the nostril and ear. Flashing a torch we discovered that the area was crawling with blind white shrimps, which had erupted from their daytime hiding place in the stones. Convulsive thrashing around on our part did nothing to deter these creatures, which seemed to have a biological drive to enter every orifice of our bodies. No food, no bed, a shrieking serenade of 'House' and 'Acid' music and a plague of shrimps hell-bent on invading our bodies. We did not sleep well that night.

But we were learning. Despair had not set in for we knew by now that each day dawned anew and in the morning we were greeted by a beautiful sunrise. One-man fishing boats dotted the bay, silhouetted in the fiery ocean reflections of the ascending sun. A breakfast of cakes in Molfetta and we made good progress, riding sixty-six miles that day to reach the 'Dune Village' campground near the town of Fassano. That night we slept the sleep of the truly knackered.

Excited, we arose the next morning with the prospect of reaching the port of Brindisi at the southern tip of Italy, the departure point for the ferry to Greece. It proved to be a tough thirty-mile ride. A searing head-wind reduced us to walking pace; we could barely make four miles per hour on the flat. Eventually reaching Brindisi, we found our way with difficulty through heavy traffic to the port area. Here we encountered a commercial free-for-all in a jungle of competing ticket suppliers. Perhaps we were becoming more 'streetwise' as travellers for Mary unhesitatingly charmed a testosterone-laden hawker, who eagerly helped us to procure tickets to Igoumenitsa for sixty euros. We later learned from another cycle traveller that he had paid the same amount just for himself.

With time on our hands we found an internet terminal, intending to look for local information. We found this translation:

"Procedure for the confidence of the assignment of advising finalised to the planning realisation and management of a plan for activity of aimed guideline and stage formed to you near the institutes you drained to us advanced of the territory."

Just as well we were about to leave Italy!

We watched fascinated as passengers began to gather to catch the 20-00 hours overnight ferry to Greece. Armies of young backpackers of all nationalities were arriving in racially sorted, guided busloads, police and sniffer dogs circulating amongst them. An older pair of backpackers told us they were from San Fransisco and were attempting to re-live their experience of European travel in the 'hippy' period of the sixties. Two very bored looking teenagers nearby turned out to be their children – clearly not quite on the same wavelength as Mum and Dad.

Another cycle traveller joined us on a machine, all but invisible under a mountainous load of gear. He was a Belgian globetrotter on his way to Greece, Turkey, Iran, China and Korea. Apart from the usual array of panniers, his cycle was hung with a variety of stuff bags and his butterfly handlebars sporting a panel of instruments, just two of which were a Global Positioning System and mobile phone. He had just retired from a high-powered executive post with a large European communications company and was relaying news of his progress by means of his dazzling array of technology. He was an impressive man, gifted in his communication skills, speaking several languages and brimming over with self-confidence. We left 'gadget-man', Mary's nickname for him, with a promise to get together on the ferry. By this time he was deep in one-sided conversation with the American couple, who now looked as bored as their children.

Re-united with our Belgian friend, we boarded the ferryboat 'Penelope', bound for the port of Igoumenitsa on the western shore of the Greek mainland. We were to sleep on the deck, disdaining the comfort of a cabin for the overnight journey. With bicycles strapped to a bulkhead below decks we roamed the upper decks looking for a corner to sleep that night. We found it on the foredeck and prepared our ground-mats and sleeping bags in a sheltered corner. Our companion was by now circulating amongst other deck travellers, conversing freely in French, Polish, and Bulgarian.

"Watch out for the Bulgarian lorry drivers," said he, "they will steal anything that isn't nailed down."

Lacking nails and joking about their effect on our air mats, we had to take the risk. Bedding down, we both had difficulty in sleeping. A heady cocktail of anxiety and excitement saw us pacing the decks more than once that night. It was a delicious time, too wonderful by far to be disturbed by slumber.

CHAPTER FOUR
THE WILD DOGS OF KATARA

A sunrise radiant with the promise of a new land saw the 'Penelope' cruising the Aegean Sea between the Greek mainland and the island of Corfu. We watched the seemingly impenetrable coastline mountains suddenly dividing, like a commanded 'open sesame', to reveal a sinuous passage into the port of Igoumenitsa. Disembarking, we posed with our Belgian friend for parting photographs, as he was heading immediately east towards Istanbul whilst we had decided to tarry for a day. We said our farewells to this wonderful man whose company we had greatly enjoyed, then began to drink in the atmosphere of our new surroundings.

The process of entering a new country, we had by now learned, can be quite a challenging one for an independent traveller. Always there are two crucial questions to be answered: where to go to eat and sleep? Sounds simple and indeed it is – if you are in the tender care of a tour company. If not, then the most basic tasks, which we take for granted in our day-to-day lives, can be difficult to accomplish and there is not much time before a brain-fogging hunger sets in. Finding where to go to acquire a map when you don't have a map to find where to go can be more than a little awkward. That first attempt at communication in an unfamiliar language is fraught with the potential for misunderstanding. We were carrying phrase books. Now it is true they are not at all helpful in terms of language translation, but they are a useful clue to your helplessness for the native population and we were rapidly learning that a helpless appearance is the most powerful tool to be had in finding what we needed. No need to be at all pro-active, just standing around looking bemused, which came easily to us, always resulted in some kindly person coming to our aid.

Well, nearly always, but not on this occasion. So plan B, another fine strategy, had to be implemented. Buy something from the nearest shop or café, since they always have useful local knowledge and often have a smattering of other languages. Of course this takes money and fortunately we already had euros. Later our confidence was to grow to the extent that even money wasn't an essential prerequisite for a new landfall. On this occasion a harbour-side café furnished us with delicious iced coffees and directions to a map-shop and food shops. Greece was clearly going to be a doddle.

We wandered the port on our bicycles amongst gently flowing traffic, including the odd donkey cart. Life here seemed to be a restful business with peaceful cafés and small groups of people appearing to have nothing more to do than stand chatting in the street. In this place we felt we could relax in the comfort of a rich gift of time. Even the seven-mile ride to the campground over a lung-bursting coastal ridge in the wrong direction could not disturb our optimistic mood. The campground did not disappoint. We were directed to our own individual terrace and pitched our tent overlooking a beach softly lapped by the tranquil Aegean Sea.

The next day I was to face the greatest challenge I had yet been confronted with – cutting Mary's hair. Thinking that hairdressers might not always be available on the road, I had been persuaded to take some lessons in this art before leaving England and now the time had come. Comb and scissors in hand, I began nervously snipping at Mary's elegant blonde tresses. Beginner's luck maybe, but the operation turned out to be a reasonable success, although my half-severed thumb seemed a high price to pay for my partner's good grooming.

Refreshed and coiffured, we left Igoumenitsa at 6-00 am. It was the 18th July. Our plan was to ride east towards the Pindos Mountains. Climbing began in earnest as we zig-zagged up a precipitous mountain road for some twenty miles. To our astonishment, the occupants of passing vehicles were shouting words of encouragement and even applauding as they passed us by. We were both feeling fit, climbing strongly and enjoying ourselves hugely. In glorious wooded mountain country we climbed some three thousand feet that day, eventually to plunge downhill into the city of Ioannina where a lakeside campground afforded us a well-earned night's sleep.

Deciding to take another rest, and hungry for new experiences, we spent the next day exploring Ioannina. The city is beautifully situated at a height of four hundred and eighty metres on the west coast of the Pamvotida Lake. Founded in the 6th century AD by the Emperor Justinian, it has a chequered history. Perhaps one of the most interesting periods was the reign of Ali Pasha in the 18th century. Apparently a bit of a local tyrant and fed-up with Islamic rule, he turned his face towards Europe and threw his hand in with the English. Quite understandably his Turkish boss, Suleman the Great, was a bit cheesed off with this and had poor Ali beheaded.

Wandering around, we were to discover a fascinating old Turkish quarter and meandered enthralled through a maze of alleyways in the Bazaar. Carpets and Shisha pipes were displayed in abundance, clearly intended to net the tourist euro. In a wayside taverna we savoured a lunch of Greek salad washed down with cool beers. The owner, a handsome young Greek, would not allow us to pay.

Later, whilst shopping in a supermarket for our evening meal, Mary and I had our first row – something to do with the crucial issue of potato chips but maybe the bigger issues of tiredness and stress lay behind this apparently trivial 'trigger' incident. That night we discovered that Italy had no monopoly on all-night, outdoor raves, and we rose the next morning, unrefreshed, to the music of Dire Straits.

We were heading up the Katara pass, at five thousand five hundred feet, the highest surfaced road in Greece and brilliantly engineered. For us on our bicycles it was an unrelenting low-gear climb, the twisting road often 'carved' out of solid rock, traversing cliff faces with precipitous unfenced drops, too close to our wheels for comfort. After some forty miles of wild mountain countryside we found ourselves far above the town of Metsovo. Close to exhaustion and with no accommodation in sight, we could find no flat ground to pitch a tent. Finding an off-road depression between two thorn bushes, we lined it with bracken and settled down for the night. The sky above us as we lay was an all but overwhelming blaze of heavenly light from the moon and stars. Awe-struck and feeling very small, we drifted into a fitful sleep, plagued by the ever-present insects of the night and the spectres of our own imaginations.

We rise at dawn to a dew-soaked morning and make our way towards the road. Suddenly we hear a menacing growling and find ourselves encircled by a pack of wild dogs. They are closing in on us in a frighteningly co-ordinated attack. One of them, a large and menacing wolf-like creature, makes a ferocious charge. A frantically swung pannier halts the advance of this terrifying animal. It backs off but threatens to attack again and the rest of the pack appears to be gaining courage from this assault. Desperation leads us to a moment of inexplicable inspiration.

"Good morning, ladies and gentlemen, this doesn't seem to be a very sociable way to begin the day."

Starting a conversation appears to be the very last thing they expect and seems to take them by surprise. More by luck than judgement we have seized the initiative. A couple of early morning motorists provide a further diversion and the dogs retreat down the mountainside, though not before taking out their frustration by snapping at the tyres of the passing cars.

Badly shaken, we take off as fast as we can, fear lending strength to our legs as we breast the Katara pass in the thin morning air. We sit for awhile. All around are wooded mountains, garlanded in golden mist, lit by the light of the early morning sun. A chapel, no more than tin-roofed garden shed topped with a cross, serves as a reminder of the faith of humans. A thankful silence blesses this timeless moment. We have survived.

Never had we received such powerful confirmation of the principle 'what goes up must come down' than as we swooped and whooped downhill for thirty-eight miles to Meteora and were welcomed at the campground by the owner, a rotund man wearing green plaid trousers, a purple shirt and a big black moustache. He did not like Germans but the British were OK. We received a gift of 'Greek delight', same as Turkish but with a more acceptable name to a Greek. In the vine-bedecked restaurant we ate moussaka washed down with half a litre of retsina. Here we met Mike and Laura, who had spent the last five years establishing a school in

Uganda. Returning briefly to their home in England, but feeling like strangers in their own land, they were now living in Prague where they were teaching English. They seemed to be people of boundless charitable spirit and splendidly relaxing company. The tent next to ours housed an Italian couple. They were dressing to go out and she was in charge of the wardrobe department. To gain her approval he made more appearances than a performer in a five-minute version of the complete works of Shakespeare. People-watching has always been the finest of entertainments.

Meteora stands upon the Thessalanian plain amidst a monumental group of four hundred metre high rock towers. Crowning several of these towers is a number of monasteries founded in the 15th and 16th centuries. Seeming to reach towards the heavens in stony supplication, some are so inaccessible that supplies and people can only reach them by chain hoist or innumerable stairs. Climbing vertiginously to one of them the next day, we met Graham and his wife from Chesterfield.

"Eee... Bloody Hell!" Graham exclaimed, on learning that we had cycled there from England, and promptly assembled the whole busload from his tour for photos and a round of applause. Embarrassed, we slid off downhill to the campground and more soothing retsina.

We had originally intended to head north from Meteora but an inspection of the map suggested to us that we might find easier going if we continued to ride east across the plain of Thessalonika to Larissa. This proved to be the case. Tobacco plantations and melon fields lined the road, the stalls of local melon vendors an irresistible draw for us passing cyclists.

Leaving Larissa, the road took us to the northeast into the teeth of an increasing head-wind. Lunch adjacent to a rubbish tip meant that we were able to scavenge enough furniture to enjoy a comfortable siesta, and we needed it. We were riding a broad valley, Mount Olympus looming majestically to the southeast. If there is a goddess of wind up there then she was working overtime that day. Although the slope of the road was with us, so strong was the gale that opposed us that we could not ride against it and were forced to push our bicycles downhill. So much for the easier going!

Eventually we entered the Trembi Gorge, the wind eased and we cruised through a spectacular rock-bound defile to Platamanos on the coast of the Gulf of Thessalonika.

At Camping Kalami we were treated with great kindness, the site handyman taking Mary on an excursion to bring us a full set of plastic dining table and chairs for our evening meal. As we dined in the light of glow-worms, he kept returning to us at regular intervals, checking if we were OK with a friendly thumbs-up sign. It seemed that word of our travels had spread for we were soon joined by a young Greek who already knew of our journey. He was, however, much more curious to know what news we had of Manchester United. This was the first of many occasions that we were to receive such an enquiry. We were to learn that a mention of Man U and a smile were the best international passports to friendship we had. Greece was proving to be a wonderfully welcoming country.

Following a rest day at Platamanos, we continued the next day in heavy rain, the first we had seen for three weeks. After some forty miles we halted at Methoni, a fishing village straight out of the brochures. A tempting patch of grass was framed by a tranquil harbour floating a kaleidoscope of colourful boats. What an idyllic place to camp but it had a municipial look to it, conjuring up mental images of a displeased harbour-master. Four miles away, and the wrong side of a big hill, we found the local campground. No reception, a few decrepit tents and toilets to forget in a hurry. To complete the picture, two men and a woman camped alongside us. They turned out to be Bulgarian lorry drivers and cheerful, hearty folk they were too. We shared our washing line with them and made them a brew for they appeared to possess only a tent. When we left the next morning they had stolen nothing from us.

A tail-wind and easy riding took us quickly to Thessaloniki, Greece's second major city after Athens. Climbing steeply on the road out, we stopped for refreshment at a *kantina*. These are the Greek answer to our own lay-by burger vans. Soon our lamb cutlets were sizzling on a genuine charcoal-fired barbecue, with Vangelis and his assistant son Christos making us feel very welcome. Group photos were insisted on and then Vangelis drew me aside to issue some advice:

"Watch out for bad peoples in the towns, not Greeks but bad peoples." And he added in a whisper, "Foreigners from the east."

Forewarned but unenlightened, we continued on our way, resting that night at the town of Asprovalta and also the following day, for we were pinned down by violent thunderstorms for another twenty-four hours.

As we rode east from Asprovalta, a panoramic view of the island of Thassos began to open up ahead. It was to prove an irresistible draw to us as it grew ever more distinct in our vision during the next two days' cycling. Stopping overnight at Kavala, the next day we turned south and found ourselves riding through a billiard table flat landscape of reed-covered marshland with occasional fields of corn and beans. This was the delta of the River Nestos, an internationally important sanctuary for wildlife. A windy place too, as we battled head-down against the sea breeze to reach the port of Keramoti and the short-haul ferry to Thassos. A campground with only the most rudimentary of facilities was to be our overnight accommodation, the only compensation being a beach picnic washed down with a giant bottle of retsina. Never did a sunset look so glorious.

The mountains of Thassos ahead seemed to reach for the sky from their island fastness as the ferry closed with the land the next day. Gulls tracked the ship, diving to snatch flying fish from the air as they were disturbed by the passage of the boat. The scattered houses of the town of Thassos swam into colourful focus as we drew nearer to the shore to alight, entranced, on the dockside. A tour party was gathering to leave and we began chatting to a couple from Sheffield. Linda and Stuart were returning home after a fortnight's holiday on the island.

"Cycling around Thassos, are you?"

"Err, well, a bit more than that."

"Greece then?"

"Err, well, a bit more than that."

Because of people's reactions we were becoming reserved in our answers to such enquiries but eventually we allowed them to wring it out of us.

"Err, well, we're hoping to ride around the world"

Once again we found ourselves the subject of attention. Photos were taken and e-mail addresses exchanged. We were to remain in friendly contact with Linda and Stuart for the rest of our journey.

We had intended our trip to Thassos to be a 'holiday' ride around the island. Setting out in a clockwise direction, we were soon to be disillusioned for the road climbed steeply for one thousand feet, bringing Mary to tears of exasperation and exhaustion by the time we made the summit of the climb. Plunging downhill at break-neck speed and overtaking a motorcyclist on the way, we reached the ocean and a beach campground. The next day we had to face another steep climb and so the pattern was established for most of our circuit of Thassos. We were riding a switchback coastal road with long one-in-ten gradients and in thirty-five degrees centigrade daytime temperatures. Not quite what we had envisaged as a holiday and so it was with some relief that we arrived back at the port of Thassos after four days and seventy-nine miles of cycling. Nevertheless, the beauty of the coastline and mountains of this island would stay in our memories for a long time to come.

Returning to Keramoti, we were entertained at the quayside by a family out for a day's fishing. Refreshed by copious quantities of beer and with Mum, the beginner, doing much better than Dad, the 'expert', they spent a great deal more time bickering than they did fishing. Our night's sleep was barely worthy of that description. Back at the very basic campground, it had filled up with members of the Greek 'alternative' culture. Oppressive heat and the sounds of music along with rhythmic grunting and groaning kept us awake for most of the night.

Knackered, we set out the next day to cross the Nestos River delta. The headwaters of the river originate in the highlands of Bulgaria. It races through the mountains in a southeasterly direction for some two hundred miles or so before dispersing into the Greek coastal flatlands. The delta is a haven for innumerable species of birds. Although drainage and agriculture is beginning to threaten this habitat, we saw nothing but a vast expanse of wetlands, whispering reeds stretching as far as the eye could see. Passing Lake Vistonis, the road took a narrow isthmus of land between the lake and the sea, an asphalt tightrope spanning a vast watery space. Here and there were monasteries appearing to float in the water, so low were the islands on which they were built. Arriving at the tranquil village of Fanari, we spent the next two days making up for the holiday we had missed on Thassos.

Setting out refreshed, we were heading for Alexandroupoli and beyond, the border with Turkey. Along the roadside Mary discovered delicious wild figs upon which we feasted. A stiff climb ensued after the town of Komitini, our toils eased by the encouragement of lorry drivers waving and tooting the horns of their vehicles. A glorious free-wheel to Alexandroupoli followed. We were allowed to camp in the courtyard of a beachside hotel. Word of our travels must have been spreading for the staff already knew where we had come from and where we were heading.

We appeared to be the main entertainment at the Hotel Santa Rosa. Camped on a patch of grass in the centre of a square of hotel apartments, we were ideally situated to give everyone a grandstand view of our activities. And not just as a spectator sport either. Kids were eager to play with us and most of all to ride our bikes, disappearing to who-knows-where on our precious machines. Quite a crowd gathered to watch my second attempt at cutting Mary's hair but performance nerves set in and the resulting mess would have made Wurzel Gummidge green with envy (and Mary red with embarrassment). All in the interests of good international relationships and at least we felt we were doing our bit for England.

Alexandroupoli takes its name from Alexander the Great, who passed this way in the 3rd century BC, on his way to conquer the then known world. Said to be one of the greatest generals in history, he didn't do too badly either, ranging as far afield as India before his death in 323 BC. He probably stood on the very same harbour-side where we found the town market, a colourful mass of stalls with no obvious attempt at organisation and selling everything from pomegranates to piss-pots. The women stall holders wore gaudy headscarves and many men balanced fezzes on their heads. One such rather decrepit individual addressed us at length in his own language. Although we could not understand the words we clearly got the message, for his face broke into a beaming smile when we pressed a coin into his hand.

From Alexandroupoli the countryside had the appearance of a neglected no-man's land. Passing through the village of Feres we half expected to see Clint Eastwood stalking down the street, so frontier-like was the atmosphere, but instead of saloons there were dozens of front yards filled with cars long past their best. We were unable to discover the reason for this rusting display but it definitely had the look of some sort of racket. Nearing the border a great convoy of army vehicles laden with unsmiling troops passed us by. We were beginning to think we had beaten the media to the next outbreak of hostilities between Greece and Turkey!

The road to the border was an ultra-modern motorway but unlike anything we had ever seen, for it was totally deserted. No traffic! How then had it come to pass that hundreds of trucks were queuing to enter as we approached the border post? A mystery we were unable to resolve and just a little unsettling.

A narrow bridge over the Evros River had to be crossed to reach the border complex. It was crawling with armed soldiers, and we were waved over without being shot, which seemed like a good start. And indeed it was, for the scene before us was one of happy chaos. There were people milling around everywhere, all trying to complete border formalities with no real indication of where to go and what to do. More by luck than judgement we managed to obtain visas (two ten-pound notes sterling did the trick), and we then had to present our visas with our passports to the border police. Mary's tall, blonde looks were attracting a lot of attention and the individual checking us through seemed determined to make the most of it.

"Lilian." (This is Mary's middle name). He rolled it around his tongue with relish and called us back. "Lilian!" And again, practising his pronunciation: "Lilian."

We were eventually released into the unknown of the mysterious east. It was Friday the 9th of August and we had ridden 2,010 miles to cross the border between Greece and Turkey.

CHAPTER FIVE
TURKISH DELIGHT

Cranes and Egrets soared above flat wetlands stretching before us. One-person corrugated-iron toilets lined the road and from time to time we heard a curious mewing sound. Mary reckoned tortoises were making this noise. I couldn't see how, for the only ones visible were dead, lying crushed on the carriageway and all very close to the edge. Clearly a slow walking speed is a marked disadvantage for a tortoise when attempting to cross the road. The terrain became hilly, the road undulating through uncultivated scrubland. Once again motorists were tooting their horns and waving to us as they passed by. Close to a village we bought a melon from a terrified looking boy selling fruit by the roadside. A cycle tourist, looking like he was straight out of the Tour-de-France, stopped to talk to us in his native tongue. We think he was from Germany. He shot off ahead on his own personal breakaway as we approached the town of Kesan with little idea of what to expect.

The road into Kesan climbed steeply through military barracks guarded by battalions of armed soldiers. The dark interiors of open fronted workshops between crumbling blocks of flats presented a picture of dusty dereliction as we neared the town centre. Quite suddenly a green space opened up. Here were lawns and fountains and imposing buildings, amongst them a towering mosque. Standing with our bicycles, we were wondering what to do next when we heard shouts from nearby. We were being called and beckoned by a group of men, women and children sitting outside a block of flats by the roadside.

Me, all suspicion: "This looks a bit dodgy, I wonder what their angle is."

Mary, all curiosity: "There's only one way to find out"

Off she went, with me tagging along behind. Reaching the group we were offered chairs on the pavement and the word 'chay' was constantly repeated. Phrase book in hand, we worked out that this meant tea and indeed it was. Served in small glasses, sweet with no milk, it was delicious. This was our first taste of a universal ritual welcome when meeting with Turkish people – taking tea together. Much laughter ensued as we rooted through the phrase book with our newly made friends in an attempt at communication.

"What is your name?"

"Where are you from?"

"Where are you going?"

"How old are you?"

They all seemed to know these words of English and our answers were always greeted with amazement. This was a wonderful introduction to Turkish hospitality, which continued with us being escorted to a hotel where our accommodation, quoted on a scribbled piece of paper, was to be twenty million liras. This sounded a lot of money but the hotelier obviously mistook our attempts to understand the currency as a bargaining ploy and immediately reduced the cost to ten million. Thus we learned another valuable lesson: all prices are negotiable in Turkey and this was less than £5 sterling!

All but overwhelmed by the warmth of our welcome, we set out to explore the town and find food. The mosque seemed to be an obvious first objective for a visit. Concerned not to upset sensibilities and having in mind practices of covering the head and taking off shoes, we hovered tentatively at the entrance. We need not have worried, for the building had been converted into a supermarket.

Finding a café and armed with the trusty phrase book we asked for "*Iki chay lutfen*" ("Two teas please"). And it worked, for two glasses of the delicious drink appeared before us. Entering a nearby restaurant, we were entertained like royalty and enjoyed superb meals of *iskembi* (lamb in yoghurt) and *kebabs* accompanied by salad and giant pieces of naan-type bread.

Strolling the town that evening was a fascinating experience for us. The streets were full of relaxed and contented looking people. We took more *chay* in a café. Groups of young women wearing beautiful long dresses, their heads covered by brightly coloured headscarves, were escorted by chaperones. Across the road on a hotel lawn was a wedding party. Throbbing drums drove on a band of musicians playing long-necked, lute-like instruments and sinuously melodic pipes. Women circled with languid grace to the insistent rhythms of the music and everywhere floated the sound of happy chatter and laughter. We were really beginning to like Turkey and the Turkish people.

Our morning snack before leaving Kesan was a couple of *simmits* brought from a street vendor wheeling his charcoal-fired trolley. *Simmits* are bread rings shaped like dohnuts and covered with sesame seeds. Thus powered up with carbohydrates, we set out for the Gallipoli Peninsula, the Gulf of Saroz ahead and the blue waters of the Sea of Marmaris glinting over the narrow neck of the peninsula. Alongside the road were crumbling concrete pill-boxes, remnants of the 'great' battle that took place here from the spring of 1915 to January 1916. The big idea was to quickly defeat the Turks and gain access to the vulnerable flanks of Germany and Austria-Hungary. The British generals thought they could do the job in seventy-two hours; the Turks, however, had other ideas. The battle raged for two hundred and fifty-nine days; 500,000 men were landed there, 300,000 of whom became casualties. Amongst those who were to suffer the most were the Australian and New Zealand Army Corps, commonly known as the ANZACS. For the Australians, their entry into world politics received a baptism of blood. For the British it was yet another fiasco in a war full of them. For the Turks it was a great victory. Their commanding general, Mustapha Kemal (later to be called Kemal Attaturk), was to become the father of modern Turkey.

The town of Gallipoli was a cheerful place, with a busy harbour and street fair on the quayside. Not so our 'hotel', where we were forced to carry our panniers and bicycles up three flights of concrete stairs to a room of unbelievable squalor. The walls of the only shower were dripping green slime. In the corner was the 'toilet', a hole in the ground. A curtain of water from a broken cistern had resulted in the production of a semi-circular 'earth-works' of faeces deposited by those unwilling to squat under a waterfall when evacuating their bowels. Armour-plated cockroaches were everywhere, the hotel towels proving to be a useful form of defence, for they hung rigid on rusty nails. Unwashed, we headed for the nearest café, there to eat and use the toilet facilities.

The coastal road along the northwest shore of the Dardanelles first led us through a market garden landscape, early morning tractors and trailers carrying dozens of women and children on their way to work in the fields. Wild fig trees provided us with a breakfast supplement. Camped on the forecourt lawn of a garage was a pair of young Swiss cyclists on their way to Pakistan, India, China and Russia. Exchanging information for future reference, we made a mental note of their accommodation for the night.

Wooded undulations and sweeping bays overlooked the busy seaway to our left as we rode into Kildubahir at the narrowest point of the straits. Here stands an imposing fort, built in the shape of a cloverleaf by Sultan Mehemet in 1462. On the other side of the water, at Canakkle, stands its counterpart. Together they have controlled this crucial gateway between Europe and the east for hundreds of years. As we sat drinking cream soda in a café, a square-rigger sailed majestically by and, roaring overhead, a formation of historic bi-planes. Across the straits, in the city of Canakkle, a forest of soaring minarets beckoned us towards the mysterious east.

Crossing on the ferry, we were led from a tourist information office to a *panysion*. Our guide turned out to be the owner, one of those people who seem to be unable to look a fellow human in the eye. He plied us with delicious glasses of apple tea and showed us to a clean and comfortable room. That evening we ate *doner kebabs* at the stall of a street food vendor. These are not renowned for their hygienic practices and are the subject of many Turkish jokes. Well-fed, we were drawn to the sound of a musical performance on the harbour-side. Hundreds of people were dancing in the street to the driving rhythms of a local band playing traditional instruments. 'Heavy Metal' had nothing on this! Back at the *panysion* I too was dancing, but with stomach cramps, which preceded a night punctuated by many explosive visits to the toilet.

Dawn saw us awoken to the eerie sound of amplified calls to prayer from the minarets of the city's many mosques. Hilly terrain and a searing head-wind opposed our progress and now I had begun to vomit. After only seven miles, we called it quits and pulled into a convenient campground to recover. It was crowded and grubby, the shower being a single standpipe on the beach. I slept for most of that day and the night. In the morning Mary too was feeling queazy but, not wishing to spend another night in squalor, we set out on a mountainous coast road. We had our first punctured tyre and stopped in the shade of a tree in the yard of a cement works for a repair, where one of the staff brought us a table and chairs and a pitcher of water.

Moving on, we stopped at a village café for *chay*. Soon a large crowd gathered around us, some eager to practise their English, others just to stare. The son of the owner was studying English at Ezine University and saw us as a heaven-sent opportunity for him to show off in front of his family. We were not allowed to pay and left to a round of warm handshakes, escorted from the village by a guard of honour of boys on bicycles. What a wonderfully hospitable people the Turks were proving to be.

We were taking a little frequented route around the Aegean coastline, way off of any known tourist track. For the next couple of days we bounced along rough roads, up and down murderously steep hills, and with Mary attempting to fight off sickness, more than once there came the words, "What the hell are we doing here?"

And the reply: "Buggered if I know!"

The road wove its way through crumbling villages, local residents squatting idly in the dust; the only means of transport seemed to be the donkey for we saw not a single car. Ahead on a hilltop there loomed what appeared to be a giant industrial complex. Drawing closer we realised they were ancient buildings on a grand scale. They would have to wait as, exhausted, we descended seven hundred metres to search for accommodation.

A dusty road led to a very down-market Turkish holiday beach. Dubious-looking campgrounds dotted amongst frowsy hotels. With an impeccable sense of bad timing, we decided to exchange hard words and set off in opposite directions, me heading for the North Pole and Mary heading for Antarctica. Contriving to bump into each other after a face-saving interval of time, we settled upon a redundant olive grove masquerading as a campground. As we collapsed wearily onto a convenient chair at the entrance, the chair, inconveniently, also collapsed, dumping me in a heap on the ground. The tension was broken, the watching Turks, risking hernias in fits of laughter, soon rallied to our aid and thereafter treated us as honoured guests.

Pitching our tent on a prime patch of bare earth in the shade of a wrecked car and watched by an audience of curious chickens, our eyes met. No need to voice the question. In perfect unison came the answer: "Buggered if I know!"

But the Turks came to our rescue, producing folk remedies to help with Mary's sickness. Some rescue! And so, the next day, I had to cycle forty miles of mountain road to the nearest town to find a dispensary. A hilarious pantomime of body language trying to indicate diarrhoea and sickness led to the purchase of a box of appropriately coloured green-brown pills. And they worked! A night's sleep, a day's rest and we were able to head to the structure of rickety wooden poles and mouldering reeds serving as the camp restaurant. The meaning of the spoken menu escaped us so we were shown into the kitchen, there to point at a couple of fishes from amongst the assortment of dead things – some of them for quite a long time, by the look of them – waiting their turn to be consumed.

Waiting for our fish, our curiosity was aroused by some food being delivered to a table nearby. The diners, noticing this, insisted on giving us their meal of *gozleme*, rolled pancakes filled with cream cheese, flavoured with herbs and totally delicious. A staple item in the Turkish cuisine, rolled out to a diameter of some three feet and cooked on a wood-fired hot plate of equal size, they were to become our favourite food whilst in Turkey. The principal donor of this treat turned out to be the daughter of the family, who actually owned the campground. Aged about fourteen, she had a natural grace and beauty that would have illuminated the catwalk of the most sophisticated fashion-house in the world. Her brother, a bronzed and handsome young man, served at the bar, Mum and Dad watched benignly over proceedings whilst Grandad, muttering, collected the empties and Grandma flitted around like a dark moth in the dim light of oil lamps. Our fish proved to be delicious and was followed by two varieties of figs, brought to us by Grandma, who showed us that the green ones should be peeled and the black ones eaten with the skin on. Touched by the kindness and generosity of these lovely people, we retired contentedly to our tent for the night.

Fully recovered, we climbed the hill to the community of Assos. Blissfully untouched by tourism, it is a fascinating place. A tiny stone village surrounds the ancient town. Founded in the 6th century BC, Greek, Roman, Byzantine and Ottoman buildings stand alongside each other like old friends. Here and there they seem to embrace as though the monumental structures of succeeding empires are expressing a timeless historical unity. Crowning the hill is the Temple of Athena, its Doric columns standing like sentinels over this historic town, and seeming to gaze watchfully at the island of Lesbos some ten kilometres offshore. St. Paul came here to preach in 59 AD. and Aristotle opened a school of philosophy here in 377 BC, teaching in it until 374 BC. As for Picasso, he was still there – at least his double was, for the chief guide could have been the painter himself, so close was the resemblance (and he had newspaper cuttings to prove it). He also had a taste for tall, blonde women, as Mary discovered from his intimate stance when she posed with him for a photograph.

The early morning dew, shining like teardrops in the low light of dawn, seemed to express our parting sadness as we left our friends at Assos the next day. Riding along the north shore of the Gulf of Edremit to Burhaniye, we found our way to a beachside hotel where we were allowed to camp on the lawn. Staying a day, we discovered the town to be a Turkish version of Clacton-on-Sea, swarming with Turkish holidaymakers enjoying the bars, cafés and splendid beach.

The coastline of the Gulf of Edremit was clearly a major attraction for the Turkish holidaymaker and Ayvalik, our next port of call, was no exception. Cradled within the shelter of a sweeping bay, dotted with a myriad of tiny islands, it is a beautiful place. The colourful harbour serves as the departure point for a fleet of pleasure craft plying the bay and its islands, with boatloads of day-trippers. The vessels themselves are magnificent examples of the traditional boat-builder's art, all polished wood and gleaming brass.

In a vine-bedecked alleyway we sat at a wayside café and ate our evening meal. The cook wore a very grubby apron draped about his well-rounded figure. On his upper lip quivered a huge moustache, forever mobile with his constant laughter and in his mouth an equally mobile cigarette, showering ash like confetti upon all before him. We were showered with a variety of dishes, most of which we hadn't ordered, and none of which we were asked to pay for. At a table nearby sat a couple bowed down with the weight of gold they were wearing, throwing scraps of food to a pack of alley cats. From a group of bantering men gales of laughter swirled about the night air. The tough times of a few days earlier soon faded into insignificance in the passage of this joyous evening.

Ayvalik continued to bless us with its benign treasures. A boat trip for a day took us to idyllic uninhabited islands, where crystal clear waters were the playgrounds for our fellow passengers. Whole families were leaping with wild enthusiasm into the sea at every opportunity. A lunch of tiny fish, fried whole, was served, followed by cool slices of refreshing watermelon. The captain gave us special attention, practising his few words of English, and the Turkish families expressed their fellowship with us through gifts of nuts and sweets. Back at the campground we conversed long and earnestly with a well-educated young man from Istanbul about the history, culture, politics and economy of his home country. At a nearby restaurant we ate our evening meal on a candle-lit deck built over the sea and chatted to the owner, the retired captain of a world cruise liner. *Chay* and sign language chat with our campground neighbours rounded off a day to remember.

Two days' ride from Ayvalik we reached Izmir, Turkey's third largest city and second largest port. The city is built around a circular bay. We were greeted by the promise of sweeping palm-lined promenades, backed by tree-lined avenues and green parks, as we arrived and found ourselves a comfortable and cheap hotel in an old quarter of the city. Legend has it that Izmir was founded by the Amazons who, we were surprised to learn, are not South American in origin but came from North East Anatolia to establish a settlement here some five thousand years ago. Spending three days in Izmir, we were constantly being welcomed by the local inhabitants with enthusiastic hellos, handshakes and street conversations. The city is a gold-mine of ancient buildings and has a veritable Aladdin's Cave of a bazaar in the old Jewish quarter known as the 'Kemaralti'. Its main shopping boulevards are lined with expensive boutiques, glass-clad skyscrapers towering above broad squares housing imposing civic monuments, striving to impress.

A custom unique to this region, of which Izmir is the centre, is that of camel-wrestling. Images of North American cowboys wrestling bulls or brawny Australians locked in unarmed combat with crocodiles sprang to our minds when first we heard of this 'sport'. What lunatic would be so brave as to wrestle a camel? But no, on investigating further we learned that the camels wrestle each other. The fighters, all male camels, have their own special techniques and skills learned after years of experience. Trainers groom their animals for battle and a board of referees ensure that the rules of combat are followed. Champions can become famous like boxers or footballers, their reward an endless supply of lady camels. (For the camels, that is, not the boxers and footballers!)

Izmir is also a city of contrasts. Leaving the smart shopping area to walk up a steep hill to visit the *kadiefekale* (castle on a hill), we passed through an area of decaying dwellings with effluent running down the alleyways and heaps of rotting garbage piled in the streets. On our way we gathered an entourage of chattering children all eager to show us the way and some of them holding out their hands, palm upwards, in a universal gesture of need. Many of these children could be seen begging about the streets in the city centre and many others working until late at night as food vendors or street cleaners.

Children in Turkey are obliged to undertake only eight years of statutory education and there is little or no means of enforcing even this basic minimum. As a result some, usually from the poorest families, receive a very limited education and thus seem to be trapped in a circle of poverty that is very difficult for them to escape. For Mary and me it was an unsettling experience to be confronted with this evidence of child poverty and we found ourselves repeatedly wrestling with feelings of inadequacy and guilt for doing no more than press a few coins into small hands, well aware that we were really attempting to deal with our own discomfort rather than contribute in any effective way towards a solution to this problem.

From Izmir we rode eastwards towards Cesme. A boisterous head-wind and a dire road surface opposed our progress and we therefore decided to turn southward along the coast. Reaching Gumuldur, we entered a seedy looking campground. To go or to stay? Our uncertainty must have been very obvious.

"Welcome to Turkey, I can help you." It was definitely a statement, not a question.

A man with an air of quiet authority separated himself from a group playing cards beneath a rush canopy. Introducing himself as Un and taking us under his wing, he moved his car to make a space for us to pitch our tent and made arrangements for us to eat after first showing us the shower. We were treated like VIPs. A meal was prepared for us and when we had finished eating we were visited by a constant stream of young guests asking the familiar questions:

"What is your name?"

"Where are you from?"

"Where are you going?"

"How old are you?"

Un and his wife invited us to join them for *chay* at their caravan. Un's wife spoke no English so he acted as interpreter on her behalf. We learned that he was a retired Turkish Army Lieutenant Colonel with a pension sufficiently large for him to be able to afford a caravan in which he and his wife spent most of the summer months. Drinking *chay* and eating almonds and figs, we spent the evening sharing stories and discussing Turkey. Un had the kind of easy grace that gave us the confidence to raise questions about Islam, the role of women in Turkey, the poverty we had seen, the Kurds and other such possibly contentious issues. His answers were those of a thoughtful, well-balanced and thoroughly worldly man. The Islamic religion, he said, was nominal only for many Turkish people. He recognised the political power wielded by men in Turkey but at home the power lay with the women. Yes, there was poverty but the Turks were working hard to modernise their economy.

His view on the Kurdish issue was that violence begat violence. We had talked late into the night and our tiredness was beginning to show but we were not allowed to crawl into our tent until Un's wife had presented Mary with a delicate china bracelet. They then gave us a calling card, with an invitation to visit and to phone if we encountered any problems whilst in Turkey. This unforgettable evening ended with the delightful Turkish custom of four-cheek kissing. Bristly but nice!

Riding south the next day through tangerine orchards and pomegranate groves, we camped at Pamucak. On site was a 'rollende hotel', a converted lorry housing forty-two coffin-like sleeping compartments, fourteen units along its length and stacked three high. It was packed with German tourists, living like battery hens and all possessing the same pale, light-starved appearance. Our attention was caught by a mewing sound, which proved not to be the campground cat but a female tortoise being aggressively courted by a much smaller male. As they warmed to the task, we thought that Flamenco castanets had nothing on this pair.

The following day we cycled to the ancient city of Ephesus, said to be the best-preserved classical city on the Mediterranean and the best place in the world to get the feel of what life was like in Roman times. Founded circa 1500 BC, the city as we see it today was built by the Romans around about 300 BC and had a population of some 250,000. St. Paul is said to have preached here in 43 AD and Anthony and Cleopatra wintered here in 188 AD. Much of the city is still standing, with a sweeping arc of an amphitheatre and an imposing library. Stone columns line the very same streets that were walked by the Romans and it is indeed possible to imagine yourself back in those ancient times. At least it would have been were it not for the hordes of tourists swarming all over the place. Inching shoulder to shoulder with hundreds of fellow visitors down a roughly paved roman street, we heard a voice behind us:

"I could break my sodding leg and end up in bloody hospital walking down here and where's that bloke waving his pink thing in the air?"

We hoped that she meant their tour guide with his rolled up programme.

Riding eastward and heading inland away from tourist 'honey pots', we passed through the city of Aydin, a centre of the local cotton industry. We had wondered what those fields of potato-like plants had been but now, approaching the end of August, the first 'fluff' of the developing cotton harvest was making them easy to identify. We were riding up the fertile valley of the Menderes River, its broad expanse enclosed between ranges of three thousand metre high mountains. At Buharkent we spent yet another night in a very questionable hotel. Filthy it may have been but we enjoyed a lively evening in the shabby café beneath, drinking *raki* and singing with the villagers while a local man practised his seduction techniques on Mary. She seemed quite flattered.

Arriving at the town of Denizli the next day we were 'trawled' by a man introducing himself as Hassan Ali, the owner of a hotel at the nearby village of Pamukkle. He gave us his card and, since we had intended going there anyway, headed in that direction with every intention of finding our own accommodation. Approaching the village we were met by a young man riding a rusting wreck of a bicycle. He introduced himself as Ali and offered to guide us to a campground. Tired and taking the easy option, we followed Ali, only to arrive, much to our surprise, at the hotel of Hassan Ali, where we were invited to camp on the hotel lawn. It proved to be a good decision, for Hassan Ali turned out to be a wonderfully humanistic man, with a splendidly laid-back temperament and seemingly boundless generosity. His wife took care of most of the day-to-day running of the hotel and restaurant while he fulfilled a management role and Ali junior ran around as everyone's 'dogsbody'.

An anarchist and libertarian, Hassan Ali took us on a night-time illicit excursion to see one of the most astonishing natural wonders in Turkey. This is a two-hundred metre high cliff of calcium carbonate. It is formed from the solidified mineral deposits of hot springs coursing down the hillside. They have produced a succession of snow-white terraces adorned by scallop-shaped basins filled with water of the purest aquamarine. Above them hang implausible stalactites and petrified waterfalls. The whole forms an *al fresco* fairy grotto beyond even the imagination of a Tolkein on acid. By daytime it crawls with a heaving mass of gawping tourists paying exorbitant entrance fees. We saw it for free and frolicked in the hot pools in the eerie light of the moon. The Romans too saw this place as a prime frolicking site and in 190 BC built a spa town at the top of the cliff. It is still there – they built well, those folks. No doubt tourism was as big a money-spinner then as it is today.

Hassan Ali arranged a visit for us to the mountain resort of Egirdir, a half-day bus ride away. Turkish buses are air-conditioned and luxurious, offering steward service of food and drink. Travelling in comfort, we arrived at Egirdir to be met by Hussein, one of Hassan Ali's 'brothers'. The Turkish practice of brotherhood seems to go beyond that of family relationships to include friends, business contacts and others, to suit. This 'brother', a nervous and twitchy man, kept a cheap and cheerful *panysion* with stunning views over the surrounding lake and mountains. He and his father were also fishermen and supplied locally caught bass for that night's dinner. In the manner of Turkish *panysions*, we ate the meal with the family, Mum and Dad smiling but silent and their son unable to sit still long enough for any conversation to take place. As a meeting of hearts and minds the meal was not the greatest of successes, but the food was good.

Next day, visiting a mountain village nearby, we sat at a café perched precariously on the edge of a beetling cliff. Far below Lake Egidir stretched to the horizon. Mountains lined the shoreline and the town, built on a long narrow peninsula, seemed to float on the surface of the lake. Beneath the rush-thatched canopy of the café we ate *gozleme* washed down by *ayran*. This latter was our first introduction to a creamy yoghurt drink, which was to become our regular energy supplement when on the road.

We spent a restful three days at Egirdir. Our time was passed wandering the streets, strolling around the local market and sitting by the lakeside, watching the comings and goings of the fishing boats. It was a tranquil place with a languid pace of life offering us some much needed compensation from the perpetual motion of life on the road.

Returning to Hassan Ali's hotel, we found we had been designated 'family' and accordingly were introduced to a number of our 'brothers', who had come to try out their English language skills on us. However, we felt an invitation to a circumcision ceremony was taking filial intimacy just a little too far for comfort and so we left (in Mary's words, "cut and run") to travel south towards the Mediterranean coast.

We rode a wide valley through high and wild mountain country of almost limitless horizon, feeling both inspired and intimidated at the same time. With little or no signs of human habitation, the sense of space was exhilarating but also anxiety-provoking, given our need for food and shelter. Resting at the roadside, we were suddenly surprised to see a donkey cart appear from the surrounding wilderness. Driven by a small boy, it was dominated by the presence of a sun-dried old woman sitting on top of a load of grapes. We exchanged smiles but no words; the joy of human fellowship was expressed by the gift of an enormous bunch of grapes.

Beginning to think we might have to camp wild in this remote country, we rounded a sweeping bend only to come upon a roadside restaurant, seemingly in the middle of nowhere. Rain was threatening and we were tired after seventy-six miles of cycling. To our relief, a young man we took to be the owner gave us smiling permission to pitch our tent in an adjoining paddock. Rain began to fall in earnest and we were invited into the restaurant, there to eat and spend the night.

The restaurant was in the style of eastern Turkey, furnished with knee-high round tables and large, brightly coloured cushions for resting and sleeping. Ornately woven carpets covered the walls, which were hung with unfamiliar musical instruments, and glass-globed Shisha pipes stood in the corners waiting to be smoked. The women of the household made us welcome with glasses of *chay* and happy exchanges in sign language. The men were working in the kitchen and about the restaurant. We ate an excellent meal of lamb and were soon after joined by the young man, Denise, who had welcomed us. He had a smattering of English and told us he was helping his friend, the restaurant owner, whilst waiting to do his stint of national service. We learned that this is an obligation placed by the government on all young men, although the wealthy are able to purchase a release. Denise had a degree in Geology but was unable to find associated work. This was a lament of the young we were to hear on more than one occasion. However, this evening was to be no lament but a celebration in our honour. The restaurant was closed and more young men began to arrive. Yoghurt and fruit appeared along with several bottles of *raki* and the carousing began in earnest. My memory of the rest of that night is dim but Mary tells me we had a lot of fun, although she found the final episode of underwear-clad, cavorting men a little hard to manage and was relieved when we all fell asleep on the floor.

A series of four-cheek farewell kisses and we set off the next day to continue riding through glorious mountain country, scarcely noticing the highest pass of Comak Gecidi at 4,970 feet. From here we rode easily downhill to Korkutelli but, finding this to be an unwelcoming town, continued through to a 'Petrol Ofisi' gas-station where our request to camp on the forecourt grass resulted in not just a place to pitch our tent, but use of the toilets and shower and the provision of table, chairs and blankets for our night's sleep. The proprietor and his wife even remained open a little late to prepare us a café meal. The Moslem tradition of hospitality to strangers was certainly given the most powerful confirmation by the kindness of the garage proprietor and his wife.

Still in high and wild country, we stopped the following day at a Nomadic tent pitched by the roadside. About the size of a holiday caravan, it was constructed of a timber frame and covered in thick black hessian with liberal reinforcement of corrugated iron and polythene sheeting. Outside sat a traditionally dressed woman wearing a heavily embroidered blouse, thick woven skirt and flower patterned headscarf. With a smile, she beckoned us into the tent. To our surprise, seated on the cushions inside were a group of stony-faced tourists, none of whom offered any reply to our greeting or indeed spoke to each other. They turned out to be a party of Germans who were busying themselves taking photographs, for which they were charged a fee. We had not come to Turkey to patronise the local people so sat uncomfortably until the pointers and shooters departed in a minibus.

There was no doubt in our minds that this set-up had been contrived to net tourist cash and we now waited our turn. Perhaps it was our coating of traveller's dust or maybe the fact that we too were nomads and had arrived under our own steam, but once again we were the lucky recipients of touching kindness and hospitality. Refreshing us with delicious herbal tea, Mum, her two daughters and Grandmother, using sign language, did their best to give us an impression of nomadic life. As usual they laughed joyously at our answers to the now familiar questions and did their best to answer ours. It was a truly delightful interlude, and our tentatively offered donation was smilingly declined. The innate goodness of the ordinary Turkish people was making an increasingly fine impression on us.

Level riding on a barren high plain now gave way to a sweeping, lorry overtaking descent, through pine forests, into the Mediterranean resort of Antalya. We spent a couple of days in this pleasant but somewhat 'touristy' town before heading in a westward direction along the coast. Another night on the forecourt of a 'Petrol Ofisi' garage then took us into an area of intensive market gardening. Serried ranks of polytunnels dominated the landscape and at Komluca, giant civic monuments of plastic vegetables announced to all and sundry the source of the town's wealth. At Kale ranks of ramshackle greenhouses lined the road to a camping spot at a very dubious beachside restaurant with a James Dean lookalike waiter, *al fresco* toilet and a hosepipe shower. Almost deserted, it was not difficult to see why.

Kas, our next port of call, was a pleasant coastal resort and our accommodation a 'beckpeckers' (Australian spelling) *panysion* featuring cold food that may once have been hot. This section of the Turkish Mediterranean coast was challenging us with the most arduous cycling we had yet encountered. Agonizingly rough road surfaces and a lung-bursting roller coaster of a coastal mountain road, combined with daytime temperatures approaching forty degrees centigrade, were beginning to take their toll on us.

The village of Patara claims to be the birthplace of Santa Claus, but for us it was difficult to see any historical link at all between the snowy environment commonly inhabited by Santa and this faraway Mediterranean village. Local legend has it that St Nicholas was born here but quite how he made it to the North Pole is not made clear. Could the seductive glint of the tourist lira be playing some part here?

Passing through some unnamed, mud-brick hamlet the next day we were stoned by a couple of boys, who hurled a handful of sizable rocks in our direction. It was a discomforting experience, for these urchins seemed to really mean us harm. It was only the intervention of a passing man that saved the situation, for I was outraged and just in the process of picking up boulders to return fire. This was probably quite an unwise thing to do. Just as well the incident was nipped in the bud. 'English Tourist Stones Turkish Children' would not have made comfortable headline reading in the press.

Tough going continued on the road to the resort of Fethiye. The Knights of St John built a castle here back in the times of the Crusaders. It is now in ruins and so was our backpackers' hostel. It was a squalid dump with a hostile guardian and our room grubbier than a sumo wrestler's jock-strap. Well, one must take the rough with the smooth but at the moment there were too many of those 'buggered if I know' days for comfort.

Four lung-bursting climbs of over three-hundred and fifty metres, each time descending to sea level, made for a hard day's riding after Fethiye. We could find no accommodation at the town of Koycegiz and two garages politely refused our requests to camp. The light was failing, as were our legs. The unappealing possibility of a bush camp was looming for we had heard that ferocious wild pigs haunted the surrounding scrubland. A somewhat fearful urgency lent strength to our pedalling. Another refusal at a garage, but at least this time a compensatory escort to a nearby outdoor restaurant, where we were given permission to camp in the gloom of surrounding trees. The owner too seemed to be a gloomy man (me under my breath: "miserable bastard!"). How wrong I was! We were brought coffee, picnic table and chairs and a portable lamp. He prepared us a splendid meal of *kofte* (spicy meatballs) and treated us with the utmost kindness and consideration.

The dew of the next morning was clearly a heaven-sent refresher for the local wildlife, luminous green frogs leaping all around us like circus gymnasts, one extrovert executing a double somersault into the toilet bowl as an encore. Another, obviously with ambitions to travel, popped out of Mary's front pannier about twenty miles down the road.

The next couple of nights saw us accommodated in questionable hotels. The first, at Yatagan, had the plumbing reversed with hot water coming out of the cold tap and vice-versa – not at all unusual in Turkey but this place had excelled itself with a hot flushing toilet. The next, at Milas, the Krap Hotel, had a self-registering system, as the keeper was unable to read or write. The register read like a galactic roll of honour with previous guests such as 'Batman', 'Darth Vader' and 'Luke Skywalker'. The central lobby was reminiscent of Alcatraz, a gloomy concrete rectangle with the barred windows of filthy rooms all around. At one end the gap left by a missing French window opened directly onto a lethal two-storey drop, for the balcony had fallen off. Some guests clearly could not even afford a room and simply slept on the lobby floor. I had to stand guard as Mary washed up amidst the slime and marine life of 'the facilities', for there was no door and this was an all-male establishment. For some reason Mary disagreed with my description of the Krap Hotel as "homely" and such excellent value at £4 a night for the two of us.

Turkey, forever a country of contrasts, saw us spend the next night camped in the pomegranate orchard of a magnificently situated campground on the shores of a beautiful mountain-fast lake near Pinacik. We ate an excellent dinner in the vine-bedecked restaurant, had a tranquil night's sleep and enjoyed a superb breakfast. Bliss – and all for twenty-three million lira (£8)! It was the 22nd of September; we had ridden 3,252 miles through France, Switzerland, Italy, Greece and Turkey and were now heading for a family rendezvous and holiday at the resort of Altinkum.

Family stuff is never that interesting to those not involved but it was good to see all four of our respective sons and daughters with sundry wives and partners and all four of my grandchildren. Altinkum proved to be a jolly place, a 'little England' in Turkey. There was loads of beer and chips and all sorts of things English, some of which we enjoyed and some of which might have been better not exported. It was an emotional parting when they all left, for we knew it would be almost a year before we would see each other again.

Leaving Altinkum two weeks later, we had three weeks remaining before taking a Turkish Airlines flight from Istanbul to Bangkok.

Our plan was to ride to Izmir, then explore the possibility of sailing up the Aegean coast and through the Dardenelles to Istanbul. Miles of cotton fields lined the road as we cycled northwards. Polythene-tented shanty towns, the temporary dwellings of itinerant families of cotton pickers, crowded the margins of the fields. Recent rains had left the occupants mopping up their homes rather than picking cotton, but this did not prevent them from finding the time to greet us enthusiastically. This was the human face of a huge industry, which accounts for over one third of Turkish exports. Every year millions of metric tons find their way to markets abroad. We were riding through the Aegean Region Co-operative, consisting of dozens of grower co-ops representing some sixty-five thousand cotton growers, most of whom seemed to be standing waving at the roadside as we passed.

Approaching Izmir and missing our families, our spirits were a little low. Even Turkey seemed less than appealing as we rode into the dusty town of Ayrancilar. Tired and hungry and feeling a little sad, we stopped at the stall of a fruit-seller. He sent to a nearby stall for a gift of *chay* and sat us on a couple of up-turned fruit boxes, where we ate apples and dates. We had no common language but, as we left, the warmth of his gaze and the firmness and sincerity of his parting handshakes had the most remarkable effect on us. Suddenly our spirits were lifted; with that simple act he had restored our belief in ourselves, the greatness of Turkey and its people. If there are such beings as angels, then he was certainly one of them.

Back at Izmir we were able to book a ferry passage to Istanbul for the 13th of October and change our flight date to Thailand to the 26th of October. Riding to the ferry terminal, a passing car clipped one of Mary's panniers and knocked her to the ground. Shaken and with a bruised elbow and knee, she bravely re-mounted her bicycle and rode on. This was not a good start to our journey to Istanbul and things did not improve for, on the ferry, we were both struck by stomach upsets, making the overnight journey a pretty unpleasant experience for us both.

Feeling ill and depressed, we alighted at Istanbul in no mood to explore further than to find somewhere to lay our heads. A campground directly beneath the flight path of departing aircraft from the international airport was to be our noisesome home for the next twelve days.

History would have it that Byzantium, as Istanbul was first called, was founded in 677 BC. Apparently the Greek cities to the west were becoming a mite overcrowded. An enterprising colonist called Byas upped stumps and led an expedition to set up a colony on the European side of the Bosphorous. Didn't think to ask the locals, but then what colonists ever do? The place prospered so much that, three hundred years later, the Emperor of Rome, Constantine the Great, shipped the capital of the Roman Empire to Byzantium. With a name like that, the emperor was clearly not a modest man and he promptly renamed the place Constantinople. It stayed that way until 1928, when Istanbul became the city's official name. In the intervening 2,300 years quite a lot had happened until the city became the fascinating mixture of contrasting cultures that we see today. Turkey is forever wrestling with a half-Asian, half-European identity, and nowhere is this more powerfully reflected than in Istanbul, with its unique blend of east and west.

The campground was a marshalling point for a number of international travellers, amongst them Martin and Birgit who had cycled from Austria through Hungary, Rumania and Bulgaria. They were floaty tie-dye clothing, dangling crystals and green tea people. It was their plan to ride through Iran and onward through Turkmenistan, Uzbekistan and beyond. They seemed to have a fine sense of adventure and a casually open-ended attitude to the future.

Richard and Thierry were from France and were planning to cycle a similar route but then to continue to China and Russia and return to their home country using the Trans-Siberian railway to bring them back towards Europe. They seemed determined and well organised with a serious sense of purpose.

Carol and Peter were from Canada. They were touring the world by motorcycle and taking a very similar route to our own. They were a worldly pair: Carol clever and articulate and Peter more taciturn with a quiet strength. It was Carol and Peter who inadvertently first sowed the seeds of a major change of plan for us – that of crossing Canada rather than America, if ever we got that far.

As our journey continued, through e-mail contact and word of mouth, we followed the progress of our fellow travellers.

Birgit and Martin were able only to obtain a short-term visa for Iran and were forced to fly south to Pakistan. By this time the Iraq crisis was resulting in some anti-western feeling in the Islamic world. In Pakistan they were obliged to have two cars and an eight-policeman escort, sleeping in police stations. They continued through northern India into Nepal. Birgit was by this time pregnant but still riding over fourteen thousand foot mountain passes. From there they returned to their home in Austria and became the proud parents of a baby daughter.

Richard and Thierry split up, with Richard returning home early. Thierry continued but again the politics of the region meant he was unable to obtain visas for Usbekistan and Turkmenistan. He too ended up in Nepal.

We were to meet up with Peter and Carol again in Australia, and stay with them at their home in the Rocky Mountains of Canada. After many adventures travelling through Thailand, Malaysia, Australia and New Zealand, they completed their circumnavigation.

We could not stay in Istanbul without a visit to the Blue Mosque. This is a four hundred-year-old Islamic marvel of decorative art, its name being derived from the blue tiles that cover its walls. Here we met a young American composer and his wife. He was on his way to Cyprus to give music lectures, and they were hotfoot from a nearby museum. With wide-eyed wonder, they told us of a display of the Prophet Mohammed's shoes and the hair from his head. We scarcely dared look at each other for fear that our amused cynicism might show.

Later, we took ourselves to the Grand Bazaar. It is a wondrous maze of ancient streets and alleyways, its traders all dedicated to the extraction of the tourist dollar. Fascinating place though it may have been, we had had our fill of bazaars and quickly scuttled out into the Egyptian spice market nearby. Amongst a superabundance of the usual tourist baubles, spice-vendors' stalls were thin on the ground. Egypt appeared to be little in evidence here.

Just below the 'spice market', on the southern shore of the Golden Horn, stands the Yeni Cami, another imposing mosque built in 1663. The interior was a beautifully meditative mixture of Islamic symbolism, the whole having a quiet devotional atmosphere of serene worship. Not all were devout, however, for amongst the prostrating worshippers was a young man muttering into his mobile phone. Irreverent speculation led us to wonder who he might be speaking to.

A night-time stroll sees us making our way back to the train station through an old part of the city. We notice what we take to be two prostitutes standing in shadow. In a male voice, one of them says something we cannot understand. "No thank you," seems to be the most appropriate answer.

Suddenly one steps forward, grasps from behind a gold chain that Mary has round her neck and, with looped fingers, begins to tighten it. Mary, with remarkable calmness, says, "Please let go." But he continues to tighten his stranglehold. I grasp his fingers and attempt to disentangle them from the chain. A difficult situation is beginning to develop, all three of us locked together in an impasse. It must be broken. A side-handed chop to the man's arm causes him to release his grip, whereupon he reaches down and, in a single one-handed movement, produces a dark object. He raises it threateningly aloft and with a click reveals the blade of a flick-knife, glinting in the streetlight. We all stand frozen, a grim tableau of latent violence, the air filled with unresolved tension. From the shadows comes the voice of the man's companion and, in a moment, as if by mutual agreement, the dangerous connection between us is broken. The knife is lowered and we walk on, trembling but in one piece.

A trip on the Bosphorus ferry was to be our counterbalance to this rather unpleasant experience. This traverses the length of the straits, from the city-centre quayside to the Black Sea. It was a marvellous day, a fascinating mixture of East and West, past and present, splendour and simplicity. Along the shores modern skyscrapers tower above ancient palaces, elegant villas, neat fishing villages and stone fortresses. The whole is given a soaring sky-frame of the over-arching Bosphorus Bridge. When not gazing at the sights we took time to learn the difficult skill of shelling sunflower seeds with our teeth.

As we returned, so did the sun return to earth, the progression of its light from gold to red to purple pulling down a final indigo curtain upon the glorious scene before us until a multitude of city lights transformed the night into urban luminosity.

The evening before our departure we took a stroll from the campground along the shore of the Sea of Marmaris. A splendid promenade followed the shoreline, fringed by manicured lawns and backed by luxury apartments. Promenaders ambled gently along and fisherman lined the shore. A blood-red sunset led theatrical lighting to the scene whilst the glowing 'con-trails' of aircraft seemed to point towards far-away eastern places. That night we shared a celebration meal with Peter, Carol, Richard and Thierry, as it was Peter's birthday. We would soon go our separate ways.

It was now the 25th of October; and we had cycled 3,427 miles, 1,417 of them in Turkey. Tomorrow would see us heading for the airport and Thailand.

CHAPTER SIX
THAI WAIS

Istanbul international airport was all hustle and bustle as we prepared our bicycles for transportation. Taking off the pedals, turning the handlebars, wrapping the chains and deflating the tyres was all that was required by Turkish Airlines. This minimal operation still drew a substantial crowd of onlookers and I have to admit, the experience of being the centre of attention of an international group of well-wishers was not at all unpleasant.

Eventually we were allowed to board the A310 Airbus bound for Bangkok. The flight was to take us over the Indian sub-continent and as dawn was breaking the aircraft flew over the delta of the Ganges River. From above it looked like a gigantic tobacco leaf, coloured a rich brown with a myriad of branching veins. For us it was a pointer to the coming mysteries of faraway eastern countries.

At Bangkok Airport we once more gathered a crowd of spectators, this time to watch us re-assemble our machines. We had to assume that advice and support were being offered but in a musical language quite beyond our understanding. Rebuilding the bikes was not as easy as breaking them down, for the baggage handlers had done their worst. Various fittings were bent, the most problematical being a buckled front wheel on Mary's bike. Fortunately it was not beyond some arrival lounge straightening but doing this, and pumping up the tyres in oppressive heat and humidity, was no joke, although the assembled spectators seemed to find it entertaining.

Outside the airport was a two-storey expressway, a cyclist's death-trap of sixteen lanes of thunderous traffic. Scuttling back inside we sought the help of the staff at a TAT (Thai Association of Tourism) kiosk who, with brisk efficiency, arranged for us to stay at the Tong Moon Hotel near the city centre and advised an estate car taxi to get us there. Sound advice indeed, for the traffic on the expressway seemed unhindered by any notions of speed limits or indeed any other rules of the road. Through this terrifying chaos our taxi-driver, driving with all the skill of a Grand Prix racing driver, somehow delivered us safely to the hotel.

Breakfast the next morning was served amongst the potted plants of the glass-walled dining room. Outside, the overhead expressway provided a roof for dozens of street dwellers sleeping on the ground, their few possessions strewn around them. There are estimated to be some ten thousand of these unfortunate folk, many of them children, living on the streets of Bangkok. Walking to the city centre shopping area of Siam Street, we were to see many such people yet never felt under any threat, despite the very obvious differences between us, the wealthy westerners, and them, the dispossessed.

A short walk brought us to the MBK centre, a huge, ultra-modern, seven-storey shopping mall, where we were able to obtain a *Lonely Planet* guide to Thailand and a lunch of shredded raw pork and chillies. Here in the heart of Bangkok, we wandered beneath soaring skyscrapers, through glass and chromium malls and along overhead pedestrian walkways spanning between elegant boutiques – all the trappings of a thoroughly modern and prosperous city. At a busy intersection, beneath an overhead monorail, stood an ornate pavilion-like structure painted in a dazzling variety of bright colours. This was the 'Spirit House' for the MBK shopping mall. All Thai dwellings and many other buildings have these. They are the home of the spirits of deceased past occupants, who might haunt their former homes were it not for the provision of these special places of comfort. Regular offerings of food, drink and flowers ensure a pleasant and spirit-friendly environment. In this Buddhist country, such colourful manifestations of belief play an important part in everyday life.

In the centre of this very same junction, standing and signalling to the traffic from a raised dais stood a traffic policeman. He wore a protective mask over his mouth – a sensible man, for the air was thick with the choking fumes from a surrounding confusion of trucks, cars, small motorcycles and *tuk-tuks*. These *tuk-tuks* – rickety three-wheeled mini-cabs, constructed like rickshaws and powered by two-stroke engines – are the prime offenders in helping to produce what is said to be the worst atmospheric pollution in the world. Gaudily decorated to attract attention, they are driven by grinning madmen and not recommended, for if the passengers do not fall victim to some horrendous crash, then the pollution will surely get them. Pollution in the city is in fact a political hot potato, the undelivered promises of past politicians to solve this problem having led to many a fall from grace and favour.

We were beginning to think an early departure from Bangkok was on the cards, for the frantic pace of the city was not greatly to our taste. However, troubled by body-clock adjustment and anxiety at setting out unsupported in a country so alien to us, we rested for another couple of days before taking the next leap into the unknown.

The only accounts we had been able to find of people cycling in Thailand had them taking the train out of Bangkok to avoid some of the most congested and dangerous roads in the world. Maybe we were becoming over-confident, but we decided to ride straight out of the city centre, heading south for Highway 35. It proved to be the most extreme test of our riding and navigational skills we had yet encountered. Bottom of the pecking order as far as wheeled transport goes, we found ourselves struggling along the margins of traffic-choked roads in clouds of stinking fumes. Road signs in a script beyond our understanding were of no help. A policeman studied our map upside-down before waving vaguely at the sky. A young man stepped into the road to halt traffic for us and we crossed to a gallery of beaming smiles. Others we asked for help by pointing at our objective on the map showed an eager and touching willingness to assist us with pointing arms, until we began to recognise some streets we had seen before. We were going around in circles. In the end it was our compass that saved the day. A southerly bearing, a big slice of luck and we found Highway 35 as it exited the city. It had taken us three hours to cycle nine miles.

This was our first experience of tropical conditions. Even in this, the cool season, the temperature was around thirty-six degrees centigrade and the atmosphere was oppressively humid. Long-sleeved shirts, gloves and head-cloths were necessary to protect us from the burning sun. However, the going was easy on the wide shoulder of a flat road with no wind, and we were not short of encouragement, constantly receiving friendly shouts and waves from people at the roadside. Cafés and the stalls of fruit- and noodle-sellers lined the road. Garlanded spirit houses were everywhere and here and there exotic temples hove into view, a visual riot of colour and decoration. Ever present was the dense green canopy of the jungle. Everything was either standing or growing in water. The reed-thatched houses, cafés and traders' stalls were all constructed of wood, standing on stilts and reached by raised slatted walkways.

Stopping near a grove of banana trees, we came upon a troop of rhesus monkeys frolicking in a stinking roadside stream. A small crowd of onlookers gathered as the monkeys shinned up trees and dived into the murk. A branch broke under one, causing it to fall, Buster Keaton-style, into the water. Another swung lazily from overhead power cables before dropping nonchalantly into the stream. These were no circus-trained performers; they were wild monkeys playing around for the sheer joy of it. It was impromptu slapstick entertainment of the very highest order.

Coming along the road towards us we saw a tall figure on a loaded touring bicycle. He introduced himself as Peter Wulff from Holland and the keeper of a famed cycling website known as 'Trento's Web Pages'. It was his first trip to Thailand and, like us, he was trying to meet the challenge of finding places to eat and sleep on his first day's travel. He had not, however, ridden out of Bangkok, but had taken the bus to the outskirts. It seemed important to him that he find really cheap accommodation and ride his statutory one hundred kilometres a day. Not having done so, he rode on.

Reaching Samut Sakhon, our first ventures with the phrase book were successful in helping us to find a motel. Outside, two elephants sauntered along the road in the company of their keeper. Inside we found a plain but clean air-conditioned room. Later that night, walking down the unlit road in pitch darkness, we stumbled upon a 'Tom-Yam' restaurant. We had no idea what that meant but, driven by starvation; we entered an uncovered yard and sat down at a stone table. No need to struggle with any menu, for all diners were supplied with their own individual table-top braziers complete with conical lid, the fire burning within heating a surrounding trough of boiling water. Instructed by the staff and other diners, who crowded around to help us, we selected a range of chopped-up meats, fish, vegetables and herbs. Instead of DIY this was CIY (cook-it-yourself). The meat and fish were either seared on the hot lid, the juices dripping into the trough, or boiled in the trough with the vegetables and herbs thrown in to provide a delicious stew of self-determined flavour. Eaten with hand-pinched balls of rice and washed down with excellent Thai beer, it was a superb meal. Our first day on the road in Thailand had certainly been full of incident.

Leaving the next day at 7-00am, we enjoyed easy riding on the wide shoulder of the highway. The surface was good and other road users a model of consideration. They needed to be, for we were not alone. A steady flow of traffic on the main carriageway passed us by. An equally steady stream of traffic poured along the shoulder but against the direction of the main flow. Thus we found ourselves with vehicles coming up from behind and ahead. Interesting, and just a little unnerving as we met buses, motorcycles, mopeds, cars and carts coming in the opposite direction – with no apparent rules as to which side to pass. In tribute to the easy-going nature of the Thais, there was much give and take, the 'system' all seeming to work very well.

It was not long before we found ourselves riding through miles of saltpans with water levels ranging from flooded to dry, the process being controlled by windmill-driven pumps constructed from bamboo with canvas and woven reed sails. The hunched figures of workers toiled in the pans, lifting the dry salt with long-handled wooden shovels. It was a grey day and oppressively hot, the windmills looming over the scene like alien beings on watch as their human slaves laboured beneath them. It was an eerie yet starkly beautiful landscape.

A gradual green transformation took place as we began to ride past coconut groves, banana plantations and through rice paddy fields. The stalls of garland sellers, fruit vendors and others lined the roadside, their wares the product of the watery landscape they inhabit: fish and rolled-up reeds stuffed with fish meat; ducks, plucked and cooked hanging in rows, bagged in polythene.

And then there were the facial expressions of the people we passed. Initially uncertain, they – every one of them – lit up in beaming smiles in answer to ours and so our smiling passage continued to a gas-station-cum-restaurant, where we ate delicious dishes of chicken and lime-green beans with eggs.

Riding westward, there began to appear before us hills, which we had only previously seen represented in oriental paintings and which we had thought were an artist's stylistic exaggeration. But they were for real, impossibly steep and ragged-edged from rich forestation. These hills continued to draw our eyes like magnets towards them as we turned south onto Highway 4 towards Phetchaburi. Snakes lay coiled on the warm hard-top of the road shoulder, making us wonder who was at the most risk – us from being bitten or the snakes from being crushed by passing traffic. We were, however, forgetting the Buddhist reverence for life: no one would knowingly hurt the snakes, but would the snakes knowingly hurt us? Cattle wandered about unsupervised and here and there water buffalo were wallowing in roadside pools of muddy water.

A light tail-wind was aiding our passage and we were making good time, which was just as well for we were beginning to understand the true meaning of tropical heat as the noonday sun threatened to grill us alive. We reached Phetchaburi not a moment too soon. At a set of traffic lights, monkeys were waiting to cross the road and, with the good sense to observe the Highway Code, they looked both ways and did not cross until it was safe to do so. A friendly policeman directed us towards the centre of town, where we adopted the café strategy in the hope of finding accommodation. Drinking iced coffee, we were joined by a passer-by who spoke a little English.

"Welcome to Thailand, where are you from?" he beamed, followed by "Where are you going?" and the inevitable "How old are you?" Exchanging family details and generally chatting, it was a delightful episode of contact between people from widely differing cultures. The essentials were always the same, and always reinforced our common humanity. The man directed us to a cheap and cheerful guesthouse; never was the liquid therapy of cool showers so welcome.

Walking the town and marvelling at the exotic architecture of its several *wats* (Buddhist temples), we came upon a street market. Densely packed stalls were selling everything from bamboo sunshades to bullet-proof vests. We bought green-skinned oranges and a large pink fruit with a hint of artichoke in their shape. The oranges delivered a fruity 'hit' of near-orgasmic intensity, though the pink fruit was a gastronomic enigma. Mary detected a trace of gooseberry; I thought there was a hint of sherbet. Surely this was a combination of flavours guaranteed to deliver a fat profit for a western drinks conglomerate?

At the guesthouse restaurant, we sat in the cooling draft from an open window overlooking a river. The lights of a night market reflected in the dark waters below. The Thai food had a delicious authenticity never achieved by Thai restaurants in England and the cool Singha beer was nectar to our parched throats. The night wasn't so good though, for the walls of our room were a thin wooden partition and the couple next door enthusiastic practitioners of horizontal folk dancing.

Next morning we rose at 5-30am for an early start in an attempt to avoid the midday sun later in the day. Buddhist monks, saffron-robed and shaven-headed, were walking barefoot in the streets with begging bowls in hand.

"Good morning," said one in perfect English.

Back on Highway 4 we were greeted with the now familiar smiles, waves, applause and even, on one occasion, a salute. A passing cyclist gave us water and a woman on a moped stopped and talked volubly to us in Thai, seemingly oblivious to our incomprehension. We marvelled at the jungle landscape, quite unable to identify the huge plants and trees growing in the forest, other than giant bamboos and coconut and banana trees. Buses passed, covered in gaudily painted scenes, complementing the startling blue roofs of roadside dwellings. Seemingly impossibly decorated *wats* stood at the jungle edge, the graceful curvature of their roofs appearing to reflect the sinuous shapes of the trees and plants around them. This was a world so unfamiliar to us as to leave us breathless with wonder.

At Hua Hin we found ourselves a comfortable hotel with a clean air-conditioned room. The local night-market was a marvel of food stalls of every possible kind. We ate duck soup at one stall, mussel omelettes at another and finished off with banana fritters and refreshing lime drinks. All this at a cost of 110 bahts (about £2). Small wonder that the Thais seem to do very little cooking at home, either eating at the stalls of food hawkers or carrying their food home in polythene bags.

After a day's meandering the streets of Hua Hin, we rose the following day at 5-00 am as this was to be a long day – in the region of sixty miles. It was the 3rd of November and we had now cycled a total of 3,551 miles. As we rode, the countryside became a little more open. There were up-market golf courses and sports resorts with elegantly lawned grounds. Roadside fruit-sellers continued to be an irresistible draw for us, their stalls stocked with mountains of pineapples, mangoes and monster bunches of 'lady-finger' bananas, very tiny and very sweet. We chose to experiment with kumquats. We had seen hotel signs banning guests from bringing these fruits onto their premises. The reason? They have an incredibly persistent and foul smell, reminiscent of rotting potatoes mixed with raw sewage, but they have a deliciously sweet custard-like flavour that was much to our taste.

Sixty-one miles in the burning tropical heat passed pretty easily; we must have been growing acclimatised. A steep hill crowned by an imposing *wat* marked our approach to Prachuap Khiri Khan, a coastal town perched on the shores of the Gulf of Thailand. This semi-enclosed sea is about the size of the Mediterranean and is bordered by the nations of Cambodia, Malaysia, Vietnam and Thailand. It is a shallow sea with a mean depth of about 150 feet and, like so many of the seas of the world, it suffers from problems of over-fishing and pollution. The results of these problems were very evident in the abandoned boat wharfs lining the shore. The presence of one or two holiday hotels suggested attempts to bring life back to the local economy but overall the place had a somewhat downmarket look to it. As did our 'hotel', where our room above a garage was reached by a staircase through an obstacle course of half-repaired vehicles and scattered tools. But it had a shower and a bed, complete with resident cockroaches, and was a bargain at 180 bhats (less than £3).

We strolled to the *wat,* buying peanuts for the temple monkeys on the way. The monkeys proved to be thieves, one snatching the whole bag of nuts from Mary's hand, and mean too, for the thief shared not a one with his hairy brethren. They were an ugly and vicious lot, haranguing us all the way up the four hundred and twenty-five steps to the temple and attempting to steal Mary's handbag when we got there. The temple itself was protected by a high, barbed wire-topped anti-monkey wall and was pretty decrepit, despite only having been built in 1922 by a Thai king. The view was memorable though: beaches to the north and south stretched to the horizon. Inland, a bright green patchwork of rice paddy fields was punctuated by coconut and banana groves and here and there, rearing skyward, steep tree-covered crags.

Later, by the beach, we met Tracey from America; she had a boyfriend somewhere nearby. She had bought a bicycle in Bangkok and planned to ride to Singapore (1,600 miles to the south), then fly to Australia and back to the USA by December, and all in the space of three weeks. Superwoman! She told us of an American friend who had been spat on and abused whilst in Malaysia, events in the Middle East apparently having resulted in some anti-western feeling in the Moslem world. We too were riding to Singapore and Tracey worked very hard to give us the impression that she would like to ride with us. We hoped she found our hastily invented excuses convincing, for we had little experience of working as bodyguards.

We had considered the issue of risk, because just a month earlier there had been a terrible bomb explosion in Bali, killing over two hundred people. Thus we sought to minimise any danger by taking what we thought to be sensible precautions. This was where our *Lonely Planet* guide came into its own. As guide books go it was full of inaccuracies, but nevertheless it gave some descriptions of popular travellers' accommodation, bars, restaurants etc. Working on the basis that these were the most likely targets, we reckoned all we needed to do was to avoid these places and find our own. As a result we discovered many unlisted hotels, mostly Chinese, always cheap and adequate for our needs.

Coconut plantations lined the road as we headed for our next destination of Than Sakae. We were to learn that this is the primary product of the area. The coconut is a truly bountiful plant. The juice is drunk and the flesh eaten or made into coconut milk, while the shells are used to make kitchenware, musical instruments and all sorts of other objects. The milk goes into curries, sweets, desserts and drinks, and the outer fibres are used as fuel, for thatching roofs and stuffing mattresses. Oil is made from the flesh and sugar from the seedpods. Housing, cooking, eating, drinking, sleeping, fuel and entertainment – all human needs are met by the amazing coconut. Can there be any downside? Well, yes: occasionally a nut falls on somebody's head and kills them.

At Than Sakae our effortless appearance of bemusement resulted in the kind assistance of Jane, a local woman who spoke good English. She directed us to a beachside hotel and a restaurant nearby but added, "I can teach you to cook Thai-style."

She had a sharp sense of humour. At the restaurant we ate *kuaytiaw naam*, noodle soup with meat and veg. Other diners crowded around to watch us struggle with chopsticks (eating soup with them is not easy) and to pose, giggling, for group photos.

The hotel was cheap and had a few unpaying guests scuttling about the floors and walls. We were fascinated to watch a hunting spider. It would wait for a fly to settle, stalk it and pounce, then proceed to empty the hapless creature of its innards. Tracey from the day before had turned up at the hotel claiming to have her boyfriend with her; he apparently had the good sense to travel by train. We were to see Tracey again but never any 'trace' of the boyfriend.

We took a short ride to a nearby fishing village. A dusty road wound its way through open-fronted, reed-thatched houses. Long wooden boats were pulled up on the beach amidst ranks of fish-drying racks. Loin-clothed and sari-clad people were everywhere, sitting in shade, eating, drinking and chatting and greeting us with enthusiastic 'hellos' and broad smiles as we passed. The population is highly visible in Thailand, much of day-to-day life appearing to take place out of doors. To us it seemed like a refreshingly open culture.

The next morning, Jane of the day before turned up on her mini motorcycle to see us off and advise us on how to reach our objective of the day, the town of Bang Saphon. The north-easterly trade wind was doing its stuff and took us easily there with time to spare.

Mary had a problem with her spectacle frames and we therefore sought out an optician's in the hope of a repair. The staff, two young women and a young man, welcomed us with the Thai greeting and also farewell: "Sawaat-di-Cap." They could not have been more helpful. We were sat down and brought hot fruit drinks while the problem was being attended to. New designer frames, costing a quarter of those in the UK, were provided and the lenses mounted free of charge. As we left we were honoured with more "Sawaat-di-caps" and the most elegant of *wais* performed in unison.

The Thai custom of the *wai* is a graceful bow performed with the hands held together, prayer-like, in front of the body. Both the elevation of the hands and the depth of the bow have to be customised to suit the estimated age of the recipient. Thus, to a younger person, the hands are held low and the bow is shallow. To an older person the hands are held higher and the bow is lower. For us the hands were very high and the bow was very low. It is a beautiful gesture and one we were delighted to return.

Some ten miles south of Bang Saphon, we found the Suan Luang resort, a set of grass-covered huts built on stilts in a beachside coconut plantation with a small eating-house. Our hut was cool and welcoming with a roof-fan and shower. A deserted beach ran for many miles to the north and south. Dining in the eating-house, we met a young couple from the Netherlands, in Thailand for a fortnight's holiday. He was collecting beetles for a friend and had one or two in specimen jars. This caught the attention of the waitress, who promptly disappeared behind the scenes to return with a selection of live creepy-crawlies. We hoped they had not been collected from the kitchen.

The next day we hired a 50cc motorcycle and set out to find an inland waterfall marked on our map. Heading into the hills, up an unsealed road, we passed through fields of pineapples. We had thought they grew on trees but they were growing in rows of single fruit, like fields of turnips. The folk here were dressed in sarongs and saris and had much darker skins than we had yet seen amongst the Thai people. The way became a rough and rutted earth track with here and there bendy, single-plank bridges to be crossed. This was becoming a motorcycle scramble course as we rode deeper and deeper into impossibly thick jungle. Strange inhuman calls filled the air and brightly coloured giant butterflies flitted all around.

Determined to find our waterfall, we pressed on until suddenly the jungle opened up into a clearing. A wooden building had troops, armed with rifles, standing on guard. Apparently alarmed by our appearance, a lean and wiry man wearing a loincloth slunk into the jungle. We had happened upon the frontier with Myanmar, once known as Burma. This has long been an arena for border disputes and the happy hunting ground of drug smugglers. The soldiers turned not a hair but we still thought it wise to give up on the waterfall, and turned back to the main road. Back at Suan Luang Mary burnt her calf on the hot exhaust of the motorcycle. This injury was to give her much pain and discomfort.

A 5-00 am start next day saw us en route to Chumphon, facing a sixty-four mile ride. The road wound its way through afforested hill-country, before sweeping down to a watery landscape of rice paddies surrounding our destination. Finding a cheap Chinese hotel, we ate an indifferent meal at a nearby restaurant then fell into bed, for we were tired after the exertions of the day.

Having been pinned down in Chumphon for a day by torrential rain, we left the next day to a comedy of errors. I dropped our compass and had to return to search for it. Despite finding this crucial navigational aid, we then set off in exactly the opposite direction from that which we had intended. More by luck than judgement we arrived at the town of Lang Sau. Deploying our now well-honed skill of looking lost and confused, we were soon signalled in the direction of a concrete chalet-town calling itself a hotel. This was way off any tourist track but the receptionist spoke good English, for she had lived and studied in Tewkesbury, Gloucester. Our attempts to find food were not very successful; a grubby café served us salty portions of chicken skin and bone and, heading for the stalls of street food hawkers, we found they were closed. We went to bed hungry.

Throughout most of the next day rain dogged our progress. This was rain like we had never seen before – at times so torrential that there scarcely seemed to be enough space between the raindrops to catch a breath. But it was so refreshing, no need to don waterproofs, just enjoy a warm shower on the move. Stopping at a garage for food, we discovered a pharmacist's shop next-door, complete with resident doctor. The burn on Mary's leg was refusing to heal and had become nastily septic. This was professionally dressed with great skill and she was given a four-day course of antibiotics. The cost? Seventy bahts (about £1), and as we left, the doctor and pharmacist stood and waved us off.

Riding on, we were passed by a motorcyclist with a monkey for a pillion passenger. The simian clearly took a fancy to Mary, blowing her a series of pouting kisses. Later a pick-up van sailed by with two more monkeys performing gymnastics on the rear framework. A far cry from the M25.

Reaching Chaiya, we headed for the local police station to seek help in finding accommodation. Going far beyond mere directions, they gave us a police escort, a policeman on a moped, to guide us to a hotel. In the entrance lobby, which doubled as the carpark, was a television set adapted for use as a fish tank, while geckos skittered happily across the walls and ceilings of the establishment. A little girl bade us good morning, despite it being late afternoon, and she continued to do so for the rest of our stay, no matter what time of the day or night.

Wandering the streets, we stopped at the stall of a street pancake-seller. Expertly he hand-threw a pat of dough until it became wafer-thin. Breaking an egg on top, he rolled and fried the whole thing, adding something green and sticky from a tin and finally sprinkling it all with sugar. A mouth-watering performance indeed but no immediate satisfaction was to be had. Dissatisfied with the result of his first effort, the man threw it away and proceeded to prepare another, this time outrageously parading his skill to the gallery (us). Food and entertainment all in one go.

Still hungry, we found a food market and, following local practice, carried off our plastic bags filled with a variety of veggie and meaty items to the hotel. Something of a deterrent to our enjoyment of this feast had been the millions of flies circulating above and upon the food at the market, but starvation won the day and sitting in the car park beside the TV-cum-fish tank, we ate our fill.

Chaiya is one of the oldest cities in Thailand. It was a regional capital from the 8th to the 10th centuries and is also the birthplace of Thailand's most famous monk, Buddhadasa Bhikku. Born in 1906, he was no religious zealot; his philosophy had amazing diversity, with Zen, Taoist and Christian elements thrown in, as well as the traditional Thai Therevada Buddhism. He founded one of Thailand's greatest places of worship, Wat Suan Mokkaphalaram, near to Chaiya. Today this *wat* spreads over a hundred and twenty hectares, with huts, a spiritual theatre, library and museum. Our objective, however, was Wat Phaborommathat, an ancient temple on the outskirts of Chaiya, built in 757 AD.

In the heat of the next morning we decided to take a Sawngthaew to the *wat*. These are open-backed pick-up vans, and passengers sit on wooden benches in the back. There are no timetables; you simply sit onboard a waiting vehicle until the driver decides it is worth his while to take off. Receiving a smiling nod to our queried, "Wat Phaborommathat?", off we went. Our pronunciation must have been improving for we were dropped off at the temple after a ride of about two kilometres.

The *wat* was built in the form of a rectangular courtyard surrounding a *chedi*, a stepped pyramidal structure like a stack of boxes growing ever smaller. The whole was decorated by stone images of grimacing, gargoyle-like creatures. The 'courtyard' perimeter was a cloister with rows of Buddha images sitting in contemplative poses. A deep meditative silence hung over this tranquil place.

Surrounding the *wat* were a number of wooden buildings. There was a library equipped with banks of computers. Elsewhere were accommodation blocks, dining hall and various classrooms. Saffron-robed, shaven-headed monks were moving about; most were very young, some perhaps only ten or eleven years old. A group leaving a classroom played happily with a wooden hoop and one vaulted nimbly through an open window into the dark interior of a building. This was an impressive cocktail of ancient and modern, learning and worship, devotion and play, and all taking place in an atmosphere of vigorous joy.

The 2,500-year-old religion of Buddhism is thought to have come to Thailand from Southern Nepal around 300 BC. It is as much a system of thought as a religion. Today there is not the traditional devotion to the faith, but the Buddhist philosophy of simplicity and moderation seems to be enshrined in the peaceful and tolerant way the Thai people lead their lives. And if the jolly behaviour of the monks we saw is anything to go by, then it is fun.

Fun was certainly our fate as we rode south towards our next objective of Surat Thani. Stopping at a roadside stall for fruit, we spent a wonderful half-hour in sign-language hilarity with the family of the owner. We ate a juicy sweet grapefruit and were given deep-fried battered buns with a sweet filling. As ever, Mary's blonde hair attracted much attention, as did my shaved head. I think I may have been the subject of 'monk jokes' but the universal language of laughter gave us all the understanding that was needed.

Way off the tourist trail, we passed through a mangrove forest and rubber plantations began to appear with spiral-grooved tree trunks and half-coconut sap-collectors. Approaching Surat Thani, we stopped at a garage for cold drinks and the prospect of directions to a hotel. The forecourt staff were running around excitedly, laughing and gesticulating. By now we were used to becoming a travelling sideshow and played outrageously to the crowd, much to their amusement. It worked and we soon found our way to a friendly Chinese hotel.

"This isn't quite so much fun as it was," Mary suddenly said during our second evening in Surat Thani. What a relief it was to hear this, for she had hit the mark spot on. We had stayed two days in Surat Thani and found it difficult to occupy our time. Thais fetch their evening meal from the street food vendors and then go straight home. By 6-00pm it was dark and the street life had evaporated. Our hotel room had a TV but it was perhaps as well that we were unable to understand the language, for the programmes appeared to be a mind-numbing blend of soaps, game shows and endless advertisements – a veritable home from home but offering little comfort. It was a world with which we could not communicate, nor could we with our homes, for we were experiencing great difficulties with the local telephone system. Feeling isolated in a culture very alien to us, and unable to connect with our own, we were feeling lonely and homesick. And it was wet, two days of torrential downpour – raining in Surat Thani as it was in our hearts. The winds of euphoria had ceased to blow.

The northeast trade winds continued, however, and helped us on the way to our next destination of Sichon. En route we passed a large fenced compound that resembled our own cattle markets. But instead of cattle it was full of back-packers, all rucksacks and carefully arranged untidiness. It was a curious phenomenon this. We had seen them being herded at Brindisi in Southern Italy; here they were corralled, waiting for buses to take them to their next destination. Independence, initiative, self-determination, flexibility and resilience – we came to the conclusion that none of these qualities are necessary to be a modern-day backpacker.

Sichon provided us with an interesting hotel. The 'en-suite' housed a 'shower' that was, in reality, a pipe sticking out of the wall and a wash-basin that simply discharged its contents onto the feet of the user. They both drained into a hole in the corner which also served as the toilet. Shower-water, shaving-water and shit all flowed across the floor and down the same aperture and you could, if you wished, perform all three functions simultaneously. By your average western standards this system might be seen as just a little un-hygienic but it all seemed to work very well and gave me a certain moist satisfaction in the economy of its functioning.

Due to recent heavy rain the local police-station yard doubled as a sports-ground and paddling pool. It was packed with children greeting us with chirrupy "hello/goodbyes", all in one breath. Developers had caught the whiff of a profit here, but soon abandoned the scent, leaving the unattractive frame of a half-built tourist hotel behind them. Later, a bowl of noodles, a dubious bottle of red wine, drip-drip plumbing and roaring roof-fan led to deeply meaningful looks between Mary and me and the now familiar chorus of "Buggered if I know!"

After a damp but swift morning session in the ablutions cubicle, we assembled our bikes and panniers in the hotel lobby, only to find ourselves locked in. Some energetic rattling of the barrier gates eventually awoke the guardian, who sleepily released us to ride southerly into a burning sun to Nakhon Si Thammarat where we found a comfortable hotel.

Nakhon Si Thammarat is the capital of the southern Thailand province that bears the same name. It is the 'gateway' city to the Khao Lueng National Park, a region of afforested mountains and the abode of many tigers and elephants. Thai shadow play and classical dance drama originated in Nakhon; it is the home of Khun Suchart Subsin, the acknowledged world master of shadow puppetry. One of Thailand's oldest temples, Wat Phra Mahathat, dating back to 757 AD, also stands here. The city is a great provincial capital and for us the 'springboard' launching us toward the border with Malaysia, which was now only four days' ride away.

We spent two days in Nakhon doing the 'touristy thing' and Mary had her fifty-eighth birthday, which we celebrated with a cake especially iced by a local bakery. It was the 18th of November and we had cycled 3,975 miles, 548 of them in Thailand.

We were riding along the coast of the Gulf of Thailand before turning south at Songkla towards Malaysia and the opposite coast of the Indian Ocean. Thailand has a Muslim population of some 5.5 per cent, nearly all of them living in this area. Evidence of the faith of the local people could be seen in mini-mosques standing by the roadside at regular intervals – evidence also of the political troubles of the area, for government troops were scattered everywhere on the streets.

Fishing is the main economic activity, not so much in the ocean as in the many fish lagoons, which dominate the flat landscape. Fishermen were hand-casting their nets with great skill to catch considerable quantities of the local delicacy, black tiger shrimps. Groups of people, the women wearing headscarves, were busy at tables sorting and sizing the shrimps. Everywhere we received smiles, waves and shouts of encouragement until we reached the town of Ranot for an overnight stop.

Ranot could not be described as the most exciting of towns. It was surrounded by flooded paddy fields, its houses standing proud of the water on stilts. Obviously a 'froggy' paradise, for these cheeky amphibians were hopping around everywhere. We found a 'resort' scarcely worthy of that name but at least our grass hut on stilts made it difficult for the frogs to join us in bed.

We were lucky for we had arrived at the time of the annual light festival known as 'Loi Krathong'. Flowers formed like cups or contained in cup-shaped leaves hold candles and coins and are floated away wherever there is water. As they drift downstream, they take with them the owner's misfortunes and carry away all the sins and calamities of the past year. The citizens of Ranot certainly had the best of intentions but the lighted floats were not really prepared to co-operate, many of them scarce leaving the shore, others getting stuck and most plunged into darkness as their candles went out. Darkness meant that we were unable to find food and so were forced to dine on crisp sandwiches that night. Torrential overnight rain at least silenced the chorus of serenading frogs.

An easy ride in persistent rain took us to Songkla. The town has a splendid beach, its northern end graced by a famed statue, that of the 'golden mermaid'. Made of bronze, she is depicted squeezing water from her hair in a tribute to a Hindu-Buddhist earth goddess. She is treated as a shrine, her visitors bedecking her with coloured cloth and rubbing her breasts for good luck. The temptation was not to be resisted.

Just offshore in the South China Sea stood the Cat and the Rat islands, sheltering a flotilla of fishing boats. The only reason we could discover for the names of these islands was that one is bigger than the other. Songkla also has a magnificent museum, built in 1900, and a delight of Sino-Portugese architecture. We spent a few happy hours wandering its quiet balconies and terraces. Cool breezes fanned the air as we moved from gallery to gallery, marvelling at the collection of 7th to 9th century paintings, sculpture, ceramics and furniture.

Hat Yai was to be our next port of call and the last major town before the Malaysian border. On the way there we again met the Dutchman Peter Wulff. He was so full of enthusiasm about Thailand that he had decided to ride back to Bangkok rather than carry on to Malaysia. Bidding farewell to Peter, we continued easily to Hat Yai, where we obtained some Malaysian currency, ringitts, at six to the pound, before heading to the border with Thailand the following day.

The road to the border was undulating, lined with rubber plantations and dotted with factories associated with the rubber industry. Approaching the border, we rode into a town that was somewhat euphemistically called 'Garden City'. Deciding to cross into Malaysia the following day, we found a reasonable Chinese hotel, but at a somewhat inflated price. Wandering the town, we soon learned that this place specialised in meeting every possible human craving. Strip joints, 'massage parlours', pubs, clubs and scantily dressed women all lined the one street. It seems that a favourable exchange rate for Malaysia had released market forces with a vengeance to provide the fleshpots of a burgeoning frontier town.

It was November 24th. Tomorrow we were to enter Malaysia. We had one day to spare on our one-month visitor's visa, having now ridden 722 miles in Thailand and 4,181 miles in total.

CHAPTER SEVEN
MUGGED IN MELAKA

Cyclists, perhaps more than most other travellers, come into intimate contact with their surroundings. This intimacy can bring great rewards but also great challenges. The stimulus of a new environment brings both excitement and anxiety and thus it was with such mixed feelings that we approached the border between Thailand and Malaysia. Apart from the usual basic day-to-day living questions, we also had concerns that we were entering a Moslem country. Westerners were being warned to exercise caution in such countries, and we also had to consider that there had been the devastating explosion of a terrorist bomb in neighbouring Indonesia just six weeks before. The Thai officials stamping our departure documents did not help with their uncharacteristically gloomy expressions, but entry formalities were completed with easy friendliness by the Malaysian authorities and we received a warm "Welcome to Malaysia" from the man stamping our passports and were soon on our way.

Not for the first time, we were amazed at the difference made by crossing an unseen line on a map. People, often of the same race, can suddenly be speaking in a different tongue and have a quite different culture, but here there were few people to be seen. In contrast to Thailand, the layout of the highway was formal and the margins wide and neatly maintained. Well ordered rubber plantations and rice paddy fields characterised the surrounding countryside, the whole seeming to distance the traveller from the day-to-day life of the people.

Arriving at the outskirts of our destination of Alor Setar, we stopped to ask a passer-by the way to the city centre. He was dressed in a colourfully embroidered tunic, his face long and angular, almond eyes twinkling merrily and wispy beard gently oscillating in sympathy with the movement of his jaw. He directed us to a group of tall buildings in the distance. A spacious square with a monumental fountain and surrounding civic buildings greeted us when we arrived at the heart of the city. At one side stood the Zahir Mosque, one of the largest and grandest in Malaysia. A Thai Temple stood gracefully nearby and towering over all was an elegant, ultra-modern telecommunications tower. We were surprised to see so much evidence of westernisation in the presence of such fast food outlets as KFC, Burger King, MacDonalds and Pizza Hut, all promising gastronomic monotony.

Finding a couple of hotels on opposite sides of the road, we were about to toss a coin when a car pulled up alongside and from the window in impeccable English someone called, "Can we help you?"

The car held what appeared to be a family of four Malaysians: Mum, Dad and two children.

"We were wondering which hotel to use."

"The one over there is cheaper but not so good, this one here is better but more expensive. Either way they are both good, welcome to Malaysia and we do hope you enjoy your time here."

We chose the more expensive; it was still only seventy-nine ringitts (about £12) for the two of us and very welcoming, for we were not the first cyclists to visit. On a board at the desk were cycling club stickers. They belonged to a Danish group which, we were told, made an annual occasion of stopping here on their way through Malaysia. With some indelicacy and a broad smile, the receptionist told us: "And they are old like you!"

As befitted our age, bikes and panniers – with us loaded in too – were transported lock, stock and barrel by the hotel lift to our room, the window of which gave a view over the city and surrounding rice paddy fields.

Alor Setar is the capital city of the state of Kedah. Bordering it to the north is the state of Perlis. These two states are the 'rice bowls' of Malaysia. In terms of its people, it is very much a Malay region with few Chinese or Indians. In Malaysia, of the twenty-two million population, fifty-eight per cent of the people are Malay, twenty-six per cent are Chinese, seven per cent are Indian and nine per cent are classed as 'other'. Thus it is a very multi-racial, multi-cultural country but in this region less so. We were not sure what it was about the local culture, but our *Lonely Planet* guide cautioned care in walking the streets of Alor Setar.

Wandering the city later that night, we did so without the slightest anxiety, for there was an atmosphere of peaceful relaxation amongst the crowds of people promenading the city centre. Looking for food, we did not have the courage to use the local street market with its confusion of stalls and unfamiliar foodstuffs, but instead took recourse to MacDonalds to eat burgers, chips and rice porridge. It was full of people, the young women wearing colourful long dresses with tunic tops and matching head coverings. A shopping plaza displayed a multitude of goods and everywhere shoppers merrily rooted through the stall-holders' wares.

Our first day in Malaysia had been a good one.

Scrambled eggs for breakfast next morning, then we were away to the amplified sound of calls to prayer from the city mosques. Highway 1, our route southwards, took us through rice-paddy fields, the flatness of the landscape given drama by rearing limestone hills. The scattered dwellings of small communities were dominated by the bulk of mosques, their minarets seeming to echo the steepness of the hills around them, but many of these places of worship were in a poor state of repair.

To the west of the highway there soon loomed the vast bulk of the mountain Gunung Jerai. At four thousand feet, it dominates the surrounding plains. In an ancient Hindu period it was a sacred mountain and has long been a landmark for ships from India and Indonesia. For us it was a landmark leading us to our destination of Sungai Petani, known locally as 'SP'.

Traffic jams were our welcome but we slid easily through them to find a hotel, described in the guidebook as 'the best of a bad bunch'. With an array of broken windows and colourfully stained bed-sheets, it was a description that could not be argued with. A large shopping plaza housed a Japanese restaurant in which we enjoyed an excellent meal. Sitting on the steps of the Plaza eating ice cream, we watched the world go by, and a fascinating world it was with people of many races going about their business.

On the way back to our hotel we were engaged in conversation by a group of waiting taxi drivers. Said one man, "We are proud of our city and most of all for the way in which the different races live together in harmony. Malays, Chinese, Sikhs, Indians, Japanese and others, we are all happy together."

From their friendly smiles and firm handshakes, we were left in no doubt about our inclusion in that harmony of races.

By now we were riding past RAF Butterworth, complete with the Penang Straits Country Club, all sweeping lawns and courtly buildings in sumptuously cultivated surroundings.

"So this is what we pay our taxes for!"

"Wonder if they would let us camp?"

However, lured by the promise of Penang Island, we took the ferry at Butterworth to cross the Penang Straits to Georgetown. To the south, suspended between ocean and sky, stood the gossamer structure of the Penang Straits Bridge. At nearly ten miles long, it is the longest in South East Asia. To the north loomed the peak of Gunung Jerai, which had been our companion for the past two days. Ahead lay the skyscraper-crenellated skyline of Georgetown.

A two-mile crossing and we alighted at the dock to ride a seafront of elegant colonial buildings fronted by broad lawns bordering the Straits of Penang. Fearsome stone dragons spouted water into the forecourt fountain of our chosen Chinese hotel, while a pillared portico led into a marble-floored entrance hall, a vaulted ceiling soaring above. Beyond the old oak reception desk was a cool atrium with a sunken pool surrounded by potted aspidistras. A marble balustraded staircase led imposingly upwards to our cavernous, wood-panelled bedchamber with marble bathroom. For all this luxury we paid fifty-seven ringitts (about £8) per night for the two of us. Bliss!

The island of Penang was the first British trading post in the Far East. The local boss-man, the Sultan of Kedah, was getting a bit fed up with marauders from afar trying to grab bits of his kingdom so, looking for help, he called in one Sir Francis Light, who just happened to be cruising around offshore, and gave him the island in return for British military assistance in the area. When Sir Francis landed in 1786, the place was uninhabited and covered in dense vegetation. Light is supposed to have loaded a cannon with gold coins and fired it into the tropical forest. In swept all and sundry and, in the mad scramble for gold, they chopped down the jungle. The grateful Sir Francis then said something like, "Help yourselves, lads and lasses, you have cleared the land, now you can have it."

This clever ploy attracted over ten thousand traders and settlers from all over the place. Malays, Indians, Sumatrans and loads of Chinese, they all piled in and got stuck in to give the world the fabulous blend of East and West, old and the new that is Penang today.

Georgetown has preserved much of its Chinese history in its Chinatown, where there remains more Chinese tradition than in either Singapore or Hong Kong. We found ourselves all but overwhelmed by the sights, sounds and smells of this fascinating place. The spirit of the Chinese community is best epitomised in their *kongsi,* or clan formations and clan houses. These are a sort of historical community centre laying on all kinds of support to the local Chinese. Visiting the most famous, the Khoo Kongsi, we marvelled at the rolls of honour. Photographic portraits and gold inlaid text marked the achievements of those past and present, amongst them doctorates, professorships and the like from universities all over the world. Politicians, scientists and other such eminent people seemingly churned out by the hundred.

Little India nearby was a contrasting mixture of spice and sari shops, food-stalls, temples and restaurants. Tamils from the south of India, as well as a significant Sikh community, populate this area. Here we bought samosas and onion bahjias, familiar enough from our hometown in England to bring on a brief attack of homesickness.

The redoubtable Sir Francis, intent on hanging on to his chunk of land, built a huge defence system, which he called Fort Cornwallis. The ramparts and a few blockhouses remain to the present day. Ancient cannons abound; the largest is named 'Seri Rambai', and it is a veritable monster of a blunderbuss. Dating from 1603, today it is famed as a mystical aid for childless women. Apparently, flowers stuffed down its barrel and a prayer or two are all that are required to become pregnant.

Jalang Pelang is the city's main street, where modern hotels, pubs, clubs and bars line the thoroughfare. Drinking cool Chang beers in a wayside bar, we were engaged in conversation by a local man. He had an easy manner and a sophisticated awareness of the world about him.

"I am proud to call myself a moderate Moslem," said he, "and proud of the way we Malays, Chinese and Indians live in harmony."

A native of Malacca, he had a wife and four children living on the mainland and was clearly very proud of his family. We ventured to raise the subject of colonial rule.

"They were great days; we in Malaysia see it as having been a privilege which brought order and prosperity to our country."

Not quite the answer we had expected but it was one we were to hear again and again.

After three days of soaking up the sights, sounds and smells of Penang, it was time to leave. A dawn ride took us through Chinatown, Little India and old colonial Georgetown. We were feeling deep pangs of parting affection. Amongst a crowd of early morning commuters on the ferry, we watched a dramatic sunrise ahead. Sampans drifted silhouetted against a golden morning mist. To the north the familiar peak of Gunung Jerai wore a necklace of cloud and to the south the tracery of the Penang Bridge appeared to float in the air like the arc of a perfectly thrown net. We were spellbound by the beauty of this scene until the sudden rush to leave the ferry jerked us from our reverie.

This reality check was further reinforced when a policeman misdirected us on to an expressway, upon which we were in real danger of losing our lives and were forced to push our bicycles contraflow to the traffic to reach safety. Even so, we were lost and somehow found ourselves heaving our bikes over rough ground and across the lines of a railway. The heat was intense and so it was with some relief that we struggled into the town of Taiping and fell into a cheap hotel. We had cycled sixty-two miles that day. It was the 29th of November and we had now ridden a total of 4,305 miles.

Taiping boasts that its Lake Gardens are the most beautiful in Malaysia. We spent most of the next day sauntering and sitting in these gardens. This collection of lakes and rolling lawns, planted with an abundance of tropical trees, plants and flowers, were a delight. We recognised the turquoise iridescent flash of kingfishers but other brightly coloured birds were unfamiliar to us. Fish were grazing the water-margins of the lakes. Terrapins surfaced from time to time and a three foot long water monitor lizard swam gracefully in a pond crossed by a bridge of impossible curvature. Whist I wandered, Mary spent time chatting to a group of Malay sailors on leave.

"Hello, my name is Popeye," said one of them, obviously a man with a sense of humour. Mary was having an exciting day for she was later invited to join a man feeding the local wild monkeys, one of which had some difficulty in telling the difference between a finger and a banana, and nearly severed one of her digits.

Providing a dramatic backdrop to the gardens were the tree-clad slopes of Bukit Larut, its summit wreathed in a garland of cloud. Formerly Maxwell Hill tea plantation, at an altitude of 3,300 feet, it is the oldest hill station in Malaysia. We set off to board the government Land Rover shuttle to the summit but were unable to find the departure point.

Highway 1 was threading an ingenious path through high, mist-shrouded mountains as we rode towards Kuala Kangsat the next day. Stopping at a ramshackle *kedi kopi* (coffee shop), we ate *roti cani* (pancakes) and drank strong, sweet coffee. This was made using a grubby cloth covering a tennis racket-like frame holding coffee grounds. The boiling mixture from the pan beneath was simply poured repeatedly through the grounds, the resulting brew then sweetened with copious quantities of condensed milk. It was unexpectedly delicious.

Kuala Kangsat was graced, with a restful riverside garden where we lazed in the shade of a huge tree and watched fishermen wading in the river before setting out to find our evening meal. A collection of street hawkers' stalls was all we could discover, so busy as to have no vacant tables. Seeing our plight, a pair invited us to join them at their table. They were a Chinese couple, Hugh and Nan, and they both taught English locally, Nan having spent five years in New Jersey before returning to Malaysia. She felt that Malaysian culture was a little restrictive of women and would have returned to America but for Hugh, who wanted to remain in his home country.

We spent an evening in animated conversation, at the end of which Hugh would not allow us to pay for our meal.

Our next stop was to be Ipoh, so-called 'city of sin'. We never did find out why, for its scattered conglomeration of colonial buildings, shopping malls and fast food outlets seemed anything but sinful, but at least the city provided us with food and a place to sleep.

We were heading towards the Selim River where, in 1942, the Malays, Australians and British, fighting alongside each other, lost a decisive battle to the Japanese. A dull showery day dogged our progress as we rode beneath the towering Cameron Highlands. We had thought we might stop on the way but the towns of Taipah and Bidor were unappealing and so, continuing in a tremendous thunderstorm, we eventually arrived at our destination after a ride of seventy miles. Calling at the local police station, we were directed towards a rest house. Having missed the turn, we were riding aimlessly around when a pursuing policeman pulled alongside. Concerned that we might lose the way, he had followed us in his car and now led us to the rest house. This good Samaritan was Abdul Rahman; he stayed to see that we were securely settled in to what turned out to be the police rest house – and very comfortable it was too. The bathroom was huge, big enough to accommodate our bicycles and the bidet hose long enough to give them a thorough wash down.

The next day we set out intending to stop at a town called Rawang. It proved to be a somewhat seedy place and unpleasantly congested with traffic. Continuing on Highway 1, our eyes were constantly drawn to the dramatic Cameron Highlands to the East, but we could not afford to gaze too much, for road traffic was becoming increasingly dense and dangerous. Selayang, the next prospect for an overnight stop, appeared to have no hotels and so we were committed to going on to the capital city of Kuala Lumpur. This had not been our intention for we had thought we would need to be well rested before tackling this huge metropolis.

Having ridden over sixty miles and feeling weary, we were not in the best of condition to negotiate the multi-lane, multi-layer traffic system leading into the centre of Kuala Lumpur. However, we had no choice but to continue, for we were committed with no options for escape. A broad shoulder gave us a relatively safe haven in which to ride but crossing the exit lanes to continue straight on was an alarming experience.

Somehow, we made it safely to China Town in the heart of the city. Pushing our bicycles through a crowded street market caused much local excitement as we forced our way between the stalls to arrive at the Hotel China Town Inn, where we received the warmest of welcomes. We barely had enough energy left to eat at a nearby street restaurant before falling exhausted into the bed of our windowless room.

Without the familiar visual stimulus of dawning daylight, the bleariness and confusion of morning awakening is definitely cranked up a few points. But we were in Kuala Lumpur, the legendary KL, and eager to see some sights. If any city embodies the spirit of the Asian Tiger, it is this one. In little more than a hundred years, it has grown from nothing to a dynamic metropolis with a population of nearly two million. Although a modern city full of towering skyscrapers, it still retains a great deal of local colour with its Chinatown, Little India, night markets and colonial buildings.

We headed on foot to an area commonly known as the 'golden triangle'. It is a district of commerce and entertainment to which the eye is drawn like a magnet by the sheer scale of its buildings. The Petronas Towers, at 1,453 ft, are claimed to be the world's tallest buildings and the Kuala Lumpur Tower one of the world's tallest telecommunications towers. We could not fail but to be impressed by these mighty structures but found the excitement and colour of Chinatown and its night markets much more to our taste. In one of these Mary bought three watches as family presents: two Rolex and an Omega, normal retail value of all three about £1,800. The cost to us, as esteemed visitors, was 150 ringitts – a bargain at £25, even if they were fakes.

A couple of days in Kuala Lumpur and we were beginning to reach metropolis saturation level. Our next destination had the particular attraction of being the home of the parents of a friend of Mary's, on whom we had been invited to call. The town of Seremban clearly saw few Western travellers for, on arrival, we caused quite a stir when taking coffee in a *kedi kopi*. There was even more of a stir as we kept popping up in the same places whilst searching a labyrinth of streets for the home of our friends.

"Hello, I am Subra, can I help?" This giant of a man with an equally gigantic moustache added, "I am the owner of a car wash and have a friend in Huddersfield."

These were credentials that simply could not be ignored. Sitting us down in the shade of a tree, he set off in his car to find the address we were looking for and, on his return, guided us to our destination.

"Now we are friends," he beamed, "take off your watch, we will exchange so we will always think of each other when checking the time."

It seemed a delightful gesture, especially as my watch was a cheap Swiss Army imitation. We parted with warm handshakes but, on closer inspection of his watch, I reckon Subra got the better deal.

Most of the Malay people we had met used English names; this, we had been told, was for ease of address, since their given names were often long and cumbersome. The 'Lawrences' were no exception and quite the most delightful of people. Their home was typical of many in the area, a maisonette with through lounge and kitchen, and the bedrooms and bathroom off the main part of the house. Mr Lawrence had been a civilian employee in the British Army and talked with great affection of this period of his life. His manners and English were impeccable, showing more than a touch of ancient Eton and Harrow. He and his wife had then owned and run a kindergarten until illness had forced Mr Lawrence's retirement. Two of their daughters were living in London, one a nurse and the other a teacher. The whole family were devout Catholics and deeply committed to their faith.

That evening, various family members gathered for a meal. A couple of nieces turned up, one with her partner. One of the nieces was a teacher and dedicated to her profession. She was an impressive person. At some considerable risk to herself, she had recently donated a portion of her liver to save the life of a three-year-old Chinese girl whom she had never met. In addition to her work, she was pursuing further training and she also found time to work as a prison visitor. She was a young woman with great generosity of heart.

Thanks to God were said by Mr Lawrence before we began our takeaway Chinese meal. It was a dinner to remember, for we were many thousands of miles from the familiar surroundings of our native land. This was a very different world to our own and yet, amidst the warmth and kindness of these hospitable people, we might well have been at home amongst our own families.

The evening entertainment was an epic Hindi film shown on giant screened TV. The dialogue of this film was in Hindi, subtitles were in B'hasa Malay and for our benefit the family members gave simultaneous English translations. It was a hilarious and most entertaining evening.

It was with some sadness that we said our goodbyes the next morning and left to ride Highway 1 to Tampin. This proved to be an undistinguished town with the familiar rash of fast food outlets and little else. Starvation forced us into a KFC and tiredness into a frowsy hotel.

A short day's riding took us to Melaka where we were soon settled into a friendly and cheap Chinese hotel. Taking an introductory stroll, our emerging perception of the town was of a somewhat touristy place looking very much towards the Westerner's dollar. Fish and chips in the 'Kafe Loony Planet' did little to dispel our first impressions.

Melaka stands on the straits of Melaka between Malaysia and Indonesia, in an eminently strategic position. The story goes that a Sumatran prince on the run landed here about six hundred years ago. Hunting for his dinner, he happened upon a mouse deer – not to be trifled with for, single-handed, it took on his pack of dogs and chased them into the river. "A deer with attitude," thought the prince, "must be something in the local water, this could be a good place to form a new empire." So he did and since he was standing in the shade of a Melaka tree at the time, he called the place Melaka, or was it Malacca?

It did well. Sea merchants from China, Java, India and Arabia flocked there, intent on making their fortunes and the place prospered. Needless to say, a few envious European eyes were cast in Melaka's direction and in 1511, in marched the Portuguese, followed by the Dutch in 1641, followed by the British in 1824, followed by the Malay Federation in 1948, followed by the declaration of independence in 1957. In the last five hundred years, half the world has come to Melaka to fight for their piece of the action, and it shows, with bits of old forts and Portuguese, Dutch, Colonial British and Malay influences all around. We decided to stay for a couple of days.

Breakfasting at the 'Loony Planet', we met a couple from New Zealand who had been sailing the world for the past thirty months. They had no time horizon for their trip; sailing was what they did and the world was their home, their native country a dim and distant memory for them. We had only been travelling for some six months but we were beginning to understand the feeling of remoteness from home.

In Chinatown we discovered a mysteriously delicious local delicacy. Mung beans in a sort of sweet green jelly were topped by shaved coconut-flavoured ice with a liquid toffee pour-on – irresistible! A boat trip on the river Sangai Malacca followed. Five centuries of history line the shores of this river. Portuguese, Dutch, Straits Chinese, Indian, Malay and British Colonial buildings crowd the waterfront, as huge four- and five-foot-long water-monitor lizards sunbathe on the verandas of riverside dwellings, or cruise majestically in the murky waters. A corrugated-iron shantytown slouches on stilts out into the river. Modern sanitary systems would have quite spoiled the foetid ambience of this community. It is a film-maker's paradise and the set for more than one adventure movie. Mudskippers crawled and leaped comically upon banks of malodorous slime.

"Yes, it smells," said the Malaysian commentator on the boat (and it did!) "But it is the humans which create this mess, not the animals."

Some things are the same the world over.

The commentator had the looks of Omar Sharif and the voice of Richard Burton. He was a man of magnetic personality, a mine of information and an effortless natural comedian. His public relations job for Malaysia would have persuaded anyone that his country is a paradise on earth and, with an unerring eye on the prospect of a tip, he concentrated most of his efforts on us. As the trip came to an end, he delivered his tour-de-force, a farewell in sixty-three languages. Well worth a tip of five ringitts.

Plying the city streets, forever touting for passengers, were the local tri-shaws. These are three-wheeled, human-powered bicycle-type vehicles, ridden with extraordinary panache by their owners and gaudily decorated in all sorts of themes. There were nautical, military, airborne, operatic, geriatric, Grand Prix, zoo, space age, the muppetts and many others. We started up our own private competition in a concourse of elegance, the winner being a particularly appealing version of the Blackpool Illuminations.

Dinner could be an interesting experience. Another local delicacy seduced our palates: barbecued pork and rice balls, deep-fried in coconut oil. Others were less palatable and one appeared to be the staple diet in Malaysia. A chicken is boiled and, usually with an axe of executioner's dimensions, is hacked to bits. The result is a crunchy mess full of shattered bone and shredded bits of chicken. We found it an impossibly tricky operation to eat this dish but the locals tuck in with relish, stuffing the lot into their mouths and skilfully separating out the lethal bone shards with their tongues and teeth.

More often than we would wish, we had to take recourse to MacDonalds and the like. Maybe the axed-up chicken wasn't that much to the taste of the natives, as these places were always full of locals tucking in enthusiastically to their burgers and fries.

Once, just for a change we sallied forth to eat at 'Gluttons Corner', a supposedly renowned outdoor food market. It was a complicated experience, for there appeared to be no apparent system in place to meet the diners' needs. Individuals would appear and take an order but nothing would happen. The dishes required to make up a meal came from specialist stalls: rice from one, chicken from another, noodles from a third, drinks from yet another, and so on. Eventually we got to our feet and wandered around pointing, but even so we were unable to recognise some of the dishes placed before us. Then, as a finale, we had to act as detectives and circulate amongst the stalls to find out to whom we owed money. We must have looked like fish out of water with our lack of understanding of the local food culture. Fleeing to the security of the 'Loony

Planet', we dined on egg mayonnaise sandwiches washed down with Cambodian Angkor beer.

Melaka at one time had expansionist ambitions with a huge land reclamation scheme. We thought we would take a look at this in the hope of finding a beach. No such luck, for the scheme had been abandoned. At least we caught a glimpse of the South Java Sea and some extensive mud flats, which gave us ample opportunity to observe the comical antics of the local mudskippers. These are fish, about four to eight inches in length, which have taken to the land. They have eyes on stalks on the tops of their heads and powerful pectoral fins, which they use to propel themselves. They can swim, walk, jump and climb, fill their gill chambers up with water to supply a reserve of oxygen and pop their eyes up and down like the periscopes of a submarine. When in the mood for mating, which is often, the male develops a nice golden chin and throat. To show this lot off he does press-ups on his pectoral fins and, leaping into the air, will spread his dorsal fins in an attempt to fly. If he gets lucky he creeps off to his burrow with a female, there to do whatever mudskippers do. These little creatures were wonderfully entertaining to watch.

Mary decided to trawl the side-streets of Melaka, seeking a bakery to buy bread. Suddenly, a male crash-helmeted figure leaped out before her. Her seized her handbag, punched her arm, wrestled the bag violently from her grasp and ran down an alleyway, making his escape on the back of a waiting motorcycle. Now she sits in our hotel room, bruised and trembling with shock. She is the victim of a vicious mugging. We wonder what to do next. Passport, credit cards, driving licence, medical card, travellers' cheques, US dollars, and Malaysian ringitts – all are stolen.

It took us ten days to sort out the consequences of this incident. Police interviews were a farcical pretence at attempted detection of the culprits. Credit card companies were a circus of incompetence, misinformation and downright deceitfulness, and our insurers proved to be worthless. We were forced to return to Kuala Lumpur where the British Consulate worked miracles in providing a same-day replacement passport. A visit to KL Immigration offices was necessary, for Mary had to obtain a new entry stamp before she could be let out of the country. This establishment made our own dreary public service institutions look like the Paris Hilton, operating on the basis of a frenzied scrum with no apparent system and desk clerks who had elevated bureaucratic bullying to a fine art.

We were forced to re-schedule the next leg of our journey. We had to give an address for the forwarding of credit cards, and the only viable one we had was in Sydney, so we needed to change our next destination to Australia and not New Zealand, as we had intended. This could not be done until we arrived in Singapore where there were airline offices.

Marooned in Melaka, we wandered listlessly around the city for ten days, growing increasingly concerned, for time was running out for us to reach Singapore in order to make to make arrangements to fly to Australia. The owner of our Chinese hotel was a great support, allowing us to stay on at a reduced rate and giving us unlimited and crucial access to the hotel telephone. Incompetent to the last, the credit card companies sent us a double ration of three-month duration temporary cards; the long-term ones were supposed to await us in Sydney. From the insurance company, to whom we had paid premiums of some £1600, we heard nothing. We were very glad to leave Melaka.

Even a slalom course of road-works could not daunt our enthusiastic push to the south towards Singapore, but a long stretch of hilly expressway in burning heat soon slowed our progress. Mary had a bout of heat exhaustion and I suffered an agonising attack of cramp. A raging thunderstorm broke about us and we were very fortunate to find a roadside shelter where we both fell asleep, oblivious to the discomfort of lying on bare floorboards amidst the noise and turmoil of the storm. We arrived, after eighty-three miles, and very tired, at the town of Ayer Hitam.

It was little more than a shantytown; apparently owing its existence to the presence of a popular tourist-bus rest area on the fringe of the town. Amidst the grubby collection of shacks making up this community there was the incongruous sight of dozens of pottery, fruit and flower stalls but not much in the way of accommodation, and the townsfolk did not seem to be the most welcoming of people, giving only unhelpful grunts to our enquiries about hotels. A house-to-house search on our part eventually yielded an unpromising Chinese hotel standing in a scrap-yard. The entrance was a door-less hole in the wall with a narrow staircase leading up into the gloom. The upstairs lobby doubled as a sitting room cum washroom-cum-dining area and, on our arrival, as a bike park. Too tired to care, we flopped onto a very questionable bed to sleep the sleep of pure exhaustion.

A dull start to the next day saw us heading for the border town of Johor Bahru. The highway cut its way through mist-shrouded jungle, with here and there a sentinel monkey sitting at the roadside, curiously observing our passage. A dilapidated *kedi kopi* furnished us a late breakfast of pancakes and coffee before we began to approach the outskirts of our destination for the day. Clouds were gathering above and traffic thronged the road. Merging roads forced dangerous lane changes on us and suddenly the heavens opened. Just in time, we were able to join hordes of motorcyclists sheltering under a bridge whilst a violent storm raged about us. Such was the force and volume of the tropical rain as to halt all traffic.

The storm abated and we continued on our way towards a scattering of high-rise buildings. Huge and threatening cliff-like faces of decaying high-rise tenements loomed over the road and all about us were the signs of carelessness that seem to be an inevitable characteristic of all border towns. The gloomy sight of dark, canyon-like streets and tall buildings rearing oppressively above greeted us in the centre of Johor Bahru. Everywhere there were the signs of dodgy border commerce, for this town is a magnet for rich Singaporeans seeking cut-price pleasures of the exotic kind. Our hotel resembled a concrete chicken-house, offering hourly rates, cockroaches as big as hamsters and a constant procession of furtive men and women.

Apparently Johor Bahru offers the visitor heritage attractions, colourful culture, delectable local cuisine and exciting recreational activities. It certainly does that. Snake-based preparations offering penis enlargement can be bought from street-vendors. (For anyone who is interested, I can tell you it tasted awful and doesn't work!) Love-oil can be obtained from spiritual healers and the barber's shops do not offer haircuts! An indifferent meal in a food-market, followed by a night of cavorting cockroaches, dispelled any regrets we might have had about leaving Malaysia.

We had cycled 607 miles down the Malaysian peninsula and from Bangkok to Johor Bahru, a total of 1,329 miles. It was the 21st of December. Overall we had ridden 4,756 miles in just over seven months.

CHAPTER EIGHT
SINGAPOREAN XMAS

Passports stamped on exit and we rode the unspectacular one-kilometre-long causeway across the Straits of Singapore, as ever stimulated by the heady bittersweet sensations of leaving one country to enter another. Entry formalities were quickly and efficiently completed and traffic was halted for us by a Singaporean policeman to allow us access to a cycleway, thus avoiding the expressway into the city. This soon came to an end and by default we found ourselves riding the broad shoulder of the expressway itself. Although not dangerous to our lives, there might well have been great danger to our wallets, for it was our understanding that cyclists were not allowed on this road and Singapore uses the powerful deterrent of substantial on-the-spot fines for such offences.

Smoking in public places, jaywalking, parking bicycles on the pavement, the importation, or even possession, of chewing gum – all are frowned upon and attract heavy fines. A frightening reminder of Singapore's draconian deterrent culture was printed on our customs cards: "Possession or importation of drugs is punishable by death". Thus when I was forced to dismount for a roadside wee, my trembling knees owed more than a little to the fear of the number of offences I might be committing, possibly enough to land me in jail.

Undetected and relieved, we rode comfortably into the heart of the city to find a hotel close by Little India. We found ourselves in a traffic free area amidst shopping malls and food courts. Alongside the hotel were two temples, one Hindu and the other Chinese, indicative perhaps of the freedom of worship enjoyed by the multi-cultural society of Singapore. Of the four million population, seventy-six per cent are Chinese. Malays account for some fourteen per cent and the remainder are Indians and others. Religions are predominantly Buddhism, Islam, Hinduism and Christianity.

Consumerism may or may not qualify as a religion but the city of Singapore is certainly a shrine to the big spenders of this world, making their pilgrimages here to worship at the futuristic shopping malls and elegant boutiques that line the city's main shopping venue of Orchard Street. The primary commercial area of Raffles Place, a giant concrete forest of towering skyscrapers, is a glittering tribute to the country's prosperity, which has one of the highest per capita incomes in the world.

We were not exactly rolling in cash so most of our shopping was of the window-gazing variety, but the local Marks and Spencer's did resolve for us a seven-month-long source of discomfort – cycle-unfriendly underwear. Yet despite all the commercial 'glitz' of the city, many of the basics were not expensive. Our hotel was about £12 per night and a good meal out could be had for about £4 for two. Perhaps our greatest extravagance was a visit to the legendary Raffles Hotel. This potent symbol of colonialism was said by Somerset Maugham to "stand for all the fables of the exotic East". Opened in 1887, it was the haunt of other such literati as Joseph Conrad, Herman Hesse and Noel Coward. There, in a cool atrium beneath an elegant wrought-iron canopy, we drank whisky sours at $15 a throw (about £5).

We were to spend Christmas in Singapore and, whilst turkey and Christmas pud weren't much in evidence, the other trappings of the season shouted out loud on every street corner. Giant Santas, reindeer, fairy lights, Christmas trees and the like were to be seen all around. Failing to find any trace of a traditional 'English' Christmas dinner, we took recourse to a 'Carrefour' supermarket where we bought a mixture of cheeses, ham, salad, bread and wine. Reading the food labels, we saw that we had purchased produce from America, France, Germany, Japan, England, New Zealand, Australia and Singapore. Eight nations, potent evidence of the world as a 'global village' and Singapore as a trading nation second to none.

In 1819, Thomas Stamford Raffles struck a deal with the Sultan of Johor to set up a trading post at Singapore. At that time the place was an all but uninhabited tract of inhospitable swampland and crawling with tigers. The rate of growth was phenomenal. By 1824 the population had reached ten thousand and so it has continued, with the occasional wartime hitch, to the present day. From trading post to trading nation with no natural resources to speak of other than its people. If ever there was a testimony to the rich treasure of human resources, then it is Singapore.

It was time to service bicycles, adjusting, lubricating and replacing parts where necessary. New chains were required, for the second time since leaving England also brake blocks, a new back tyre for my machine and a new cassette (the cluster of cogs at the back). This was fitted at a local bike shop and here we met two young local racing cyclists, Ian and Sean. On returning to our hotel, we received a message to ring Ian, who invited us out for a meal that evening. We wondered what exotic and expensive restaurant Ian might be taking us to when he and Sean arrived to pick us up in a Mercedes. We need not have worried, for we were taken to one of the city's most famous outdoor food-markets, 'The Newton Circle Hawker Centre', there to enjoy a delightful evening.

Ian was a banker and Sean an architect, and both were dedicated racing cyclists. They were fun-loving yet thoughtful young men in their mid-to-late twenties, and both fascinated to learn of our journey to date. They in their turn told us much of their home country. Government claims of zero unemployment and a thriving economy they saw as dishonest attempts to spur on a presently static economic situation. They nevertheless recognised the prosperity of their country but felt this came at the expense of a certain lack of freedom. Ian and Sean were certainly a tribute to the educational system of Singapore and, with their easy grace and confidence, a credit to their country.

In all we were to spend nearly two weeks in Singapore, sorting out flights, exploring a route to the airport, seeing the sights and exploring the city by bicycle. But Singapore lies only ninety miles north of the equator and the unrelenting heat and humidity were beginning to take their toll on us. We both suffered heavy colds for a time. Feeling ill, we ushered in the New Year with a feeble chorus of Waltzing Matilda. We were now ready to leave the amazing monument to capitalism that is Singapore and head for the unknown of Australia.

CHAPTER NINE
FELLED BY A LOG-TRUCK

It was the 5th of January of the new year of 2003. A Chinese festival band of drums, cymbals and flutes were playing to mark some notable event as we left the hotel to ride to Singapore Airport. We arrived in the nick of time to seek the shelter of the terminal buildings, just as a torrential tropical rainstorm began. Checking our distance, we saw that we had cycled a total of 4,812 miles since leaving England in June 2002. This felt like a particularly significant milestone of our journey, for soon we were to cross the equator into the southern hemisphere.

The airline flying us to Australia had supplied us with strong cardboard containers for our bicycles. Some considerable dismantling of the bikes was required to fit them into the boxes. This process drew the familiar crowd of onlookers, though by now we were used to being the centre of attention. Not comfortable as the subjects of idle voyeurism, we had settled on group participation as a defensive strategy. Accordingly, we involved the most curious spectators by giving them tools to hold. A running commentary enlivened proceedings, the whole event turning something of a chore into a cyclist's version of performance art.

Despite this being an overnight flight, we were unable to sleep on the journey. As the plane approached our destination, the vast and wild red interior of the Australian Outback unrolled like a great russet carpet below. Gradually the landscape changed, and some features began to swim into focus. Rivers, hills, forests, fields and homesteads. This was the cultivated hinterland surrounding the city of Melbourne.

It was early morning, the city had not yet awoken but the airport was busy with the hustle and bustle of travellers intent on their own comings and goings. Because of bio-security concerns we had to take our bicycles through quarantine. The tyres of our bicycles received a microscopic inspection whilst we were subject to a detailed cross-examination about our journey to date. In the end we were dismissed with the comment of one official to his colleague:

"Looks like they've been everywhere mate"

Well not quite, but the humour helped.

Bike-rebuilding proved to be as much of a crowd-puller as had been the dismantling, attracting much curiosity and questioning:

"Crikey, couldn't you just have bought a couple of keyrings?"

Already dry antipodean humour was making its presence felt.

Dollars were obtained from an ATM, and information and a map from a kiosk as to the whereabouts of the nearest campground. Not knowing quite what to expect, we set off in search of this desperately needed place to rest. Paul, a local cyclist, soon joined us. Hearing of our objective, he rode most of the way with us as a guide. The temperature quickly rose to 35 degrees and the ride through the northern suburbs of Melbourne was hilly and hard. It was with considerable relief that we arrived at a 'Big 4' campground, there to be escorted to a shady spot to pitch our tent. After a pizza from a nearby takeaway, we fell swiftly into a deep sleep.

The next day we took the tram into the centre of Melbourne. Endless suburbs of spacious bungalows eventually gave way to central high-rise commercial buildings, shops and offices. Melbourne is a very modern city, having grown up only in the last eighty years. Just two per cent of the people live in the actual city, the majority of the three-and-a half million population living in the well-ordered suburban expanse of the metropolitan area. It is a most cosmopolitan place with nearly half of its people having been born overseas. Apart from English, the main languages spoken are Mandarin, Cantonese and Indonesian – proof, if any were needed, that the Australia of today is turning its face very much towards Asia.

The 'gridiron' pattern of Melbourne's streets certainly made our search for information, maps, guides etc an easy one and also made for a very cyclist-friendly city. Designated cycle lanes were a feature of most roads and the state of Victoria has a dedicated cyclist organisation called 'Bike Victoria'. In their offices we took refuge from the 40-degree of heat in the city streets.

Britain is not the only country where the weather is a main topic of conversation. In 'Bike Victoria' we met Brian, a local cyclist, who thought us insane to even think of riding in the present heat.

"Find a shady place, take a couple of tinnies and sit the bugger out," he advised.

He told us that Melbourne had a climate all to itself with wild fluctuations of temperature. Tomorrow, at about 3-00pm, a 'cool change' was said to be coming when a 20-degree drop in the temperature might be expected.

Sitting in a chip-shop close by the campground, we waited for our evening meal of fish and chips. Mary's paper bundle arrived first and I sat and watched hungrily as she tucked into a veritable mountain of food. Mine seemed a long time coming, and soon the shop was clearing up to close. Too late we realised that we had misunderstood; the food was for both of us. Mary had eaten my dinner!

Back at the campground, tucking in to a packet of biscuits, we were joined by a couple bearing a bottle of wine.

"Ay yer dooin?"

Straight out of an Aussie soap, they were a trucker and his wife. Sharing the wine, we learned that they were working their way around the country. He was finding driving jobs and she whatever she could. It had been two-and-a-half years since they left their home in Perth and it was "bladdy gerd".

We were warned of the dangers to cyclists on the Australian roads. With a slightly menacing air, the trucker told us, "We truckers don't like slowing down for cyclists."

(We think: *We don't like dying*)

But they were nice folk really and good company for a campground evening.

Confident in the prediction of the coming 'cool change', we loaded up and cycled into Melbourne for more exploration before catching a bus to clear the environs of the city. Policemen on bicycles kept us company part of the way. These were not the 'sit-up-and-beg' bike, pointy helmet and bicycle-clips variety of copper; high-tech mountain bikes and black, skintight riding gear were their style. Answering the call of duty, they set off in hot pursuit of a young man riding his bike on the pavement.

With time to spare, we explored the south bank of the Yarra River. This area is a magnet for tourists. Broad promenades, lawns, gardens, up-market cafés and restaurants, line the riverbank, the city-centre skyscrapers across the river forming a spectacular backdrop. Sitting in the sun, eating sandwiches and gazing at the view, we quite suddenly began to feel cold. The 'cool change' had arrived just as predicted. It was time to set out on the 1,800-mile leg of our journey to Brisbane.

An obliging driver loaded our bikes, panniers and all, into the luggage trunk of his bus. For a time the road headed south along the eastern shore of the Bass Straits. Inland were rolling hills and woodland. We were heading for the town of Anderson, marked as a circle on our map. Pulling into an area of gravel, complete with pond and broken-down bus-shelter, our driver announced, "Anderson!"

We had arrived. This, the driver told us, was it and it was cold, in the region of 16 degrees.

The cool change had indeed done its stuff, from 40 degrees to 16 degrees in the space of a couple of hours. Shivering, we rode east on an undulating coast road, a tumultuous sea battering at the shore. A collection of low clapboard buildings around a pub turned out to be our objective of the town of Wonthaggi. A caravan site behind the pub was to be our place of rest for the night and the pub our source of an evening meal. But we only just made it, for the bar had stopped serving food when we entered at 7-00pm. The landlady very kindly rekindled the stove and cooked us a fish-and-chip meal, which we were forced to hurry, as the place closed at 8-00 pm. Clearly we were going to have to make some adjustments in this very different culture from the 'open all hours' of Asia, if we were to survive in Australia.

In 1852, one Richard Davies located a coal seam close by Wonthaggi. Loading a 50lb sack of coal on his back, he promptly humped it the ninety miles to Melbourne to collect a £1000 reward offered by governor La Trobe. Mean man, that governor, for he deducted the cost of sinking a shaft on the site before paying out. So began the coal mining industry in South Eastern Australia.

Newcastle in England had its commercial nose put out of joint by this discovery, for from then on the Aussies were able to mine their own. And they did, to the tune of seventeen million tonnes in the fifty-nine years that the mines operated. Today nothing remains but a few relics. Profits from the beef and dairy industries now pay the bills.

Twelve degrees. This couldn't be right, especially as parakeets squawked raucously in the eucalyptus trees as we rode past the following morning. Road signs warned us not to run over koalas and to watch out for leaping kangaroos. These signs put us in serious danger, for we spent all our time gazing around, hoping to spot these creatures, instead of watching where we were going. A garage furnished us with a breakfast of hot sausage rolls and picnic bars and at Fish Creek, a farmyard out-building housed an Internet terminal, where we were able to pick up messages from home, the first for twelve days.

Crossing a ridge, jutting out into the turbulent waters of the Bass Straits, we could see ahead the blue strip of land that is called Wilson's Promontory. The oldest national park in Australia, it was designated as such in 1898, but the Aborigines had been there much longer, around about 6,500 years. It is the southernmost point of the Australian continent; once past here, we would soon be heading north along the eastern coast of the state of Victoria.

At the town of Foster we found a spacious campground and an information centre where a friendly young woman helped us to plan our ongoing route and phoned ahead to book us a spot on the Port Albert Caravan Site, our next destination.

The local pub was typical of many we were to visit in Australia. High tables and stools were all arranged to enable an easy view of a multitude of television screens. These were all showing sporting events such as horse racing, pony-and-trap racing and greyhound racing. Bets could be placed at a counter near the bar and patrons sat with eyes intently focussed on the screens. This was certainly no place for a bit of a natter with your mates, but the cool and light beer was very refreshing.

Back at the campground, pigeon-sized birds with grey and white plumage and a pink breast were performing spectacular aerobatics to the accompaniment of raucous cries. These were galahs, said to be the most familiar and abundant of all Australian parrots. Their aerial stunts are a prelude to roosting and a most entertaining prelude to our own journey into sleep.

We were riding through grass-covered rolling hills, mostly fenced off into fields. Herds of cattle lent a homely appearance to the landscape but the swarms of flies doing their best to devour us were anything but homely. Mary fashioned a cat's cradle of string about her cap; all she needed was a few corks as a finishing touch but this dangling deterrent was amazingly effective.

The cycling was comfortable on a well-surfaced road with a reasonable shoulder and the traffic was light. This was the South Gippsland Highway and well appointed it was too. At regular intervals there were designated 'powernap' and picnic pull-ins complete with free gas-fired barbecues. A flock of bright yellow budgerigars flitted around a pair of black parrots whilst a multi-coloured parakeet watched their antics with interest.

Port Albert's caravan park was sited upon the sweeping arc of a golden beach. Black swans cruised on the calm blue waters of the bay and pelicans flew majestically above in their search of a fish-dinner. We received a friendly welcome from the wife of the owner, whose voice carried the warm lilt of Northern England. She had lived in Australia for more than thirty years, but before then, in the same Nottinghamshire village as Mary. They had even attended the same school, albeit at different times. Happy reminiscences were enjoyed by both.

Port Albert is Victoria's oldest port. In the mid 19th century, European colonists, mostly British, were buzzing like flies around the coast of Australia looking to establish points of entry into the continent. Exploration parties were landing everywhere, no doubt thinking, "This might be a good place for a port", but not in this case. In 1841 a ship called the 'Clonmel' was wrecked here and, since they could hardly sail away, the castaways stayed and named the place after Albert, the consort of Queen Victoria. Whether there is any connection between the consort and a wreck is not clear. They grew rich, for gold was discovered in the hills nearby. Forty years later the railway came, the gold ran out and two-thirds of the population ran out with it. Today the place is still a port but used only by sport fishermen and supply boats for Wilson's Promontory National Park.

We were riding grasslands with scattered clumps of eucalyptus trees stretching as far as the eye could see. Kangaroo warning signs were everywhere but the only ones we saw were lying dead on the road. A huge bird we took to be an emu loped across our path. This countryside seemed largely to be given over to nature, with human settlements nowhere to be seen. A searing head-wind made this a day to endure rather than savour and so it was with relief that we rolled into a spacious campground at the town of Sale. We had ridden fifty-six hard miles and in so doing had broken the 5,000-mile figure to reach a total of 5,049.

On the banks of a *billabong*, beneath the shade of a eucalyptus tree, we pitched our tent. A *billabong* is a river remnant, which has been by-passed by a change of course, leaving it without a current. An Aborigine word, it means 'river without life', but it was far from that here, for the place was alive with large, parrot-like white birds with a fluorescent yellow crest. They lined up in the trees to watch us, passing raucous comments to each other on what they saw. From the sound of their screeching calls they were not that impressed. When they got bored, off they went to perform aerial stunts or just languish, apparently asleep, in the trees. Australian wildlife was certainly proving to be exotic. Close by the campground was an information centre; here we learned that these birds were sulphur-crested-cockatoos and "a bloody pest".

"Supposed to be protected but we shoot the buggers around here."

Enquiring about our journey, the person at the desk said, "Good to see some poms with a bit of go about them, all the bloody fight went out of the poms after the last war."

Sale was a low-rise, ranch-style town arranged in a cross-shape about a central clock tower. A huge board announced the town's facilities, one section devoted to educational resources, charities and similar organisations. This was the first clue we were to have of the amount of charitable and voluntary work that goes on in Australia. Back at the campground we wined and dined handsomely on a supermarket-acquired feast, only to awake, fully clothed, in the middle of the night, half in and half out of our tent. Well, we were very tired, or could it have been the wine?

Australian campgrounds were beginning to impress us. This one was equipped with a covered cooking and dining area complete with electric griddles, microwave ovens, electric kettles and toasters. Remarkably, all these electrical goodies were not chained down, and they were still there! We tried hard to imagine such levels of trust being possible in our own country, but soon gave up.

A roaring easterly gale opposed our progress as we rode towards our next overnight stopping place. At times we were barely able to make 5mph through the uninhabited grass plains of the countryside. Fifty miles of this tough going saw us arrive brain-fogged and rubber-legged at Bairnsdale. It was one of those "buggered if I know" days, but a couple of beers and we soon recovered. Not for the first time we marvelled at the amazing recuperative powers of the human body.

Mercifully, the wind had dropped. There were the 'Tambo' and 'Nicholson' Rivers to cross with a couple of stiff climbs out of their valleys. Crossing a wooded creek, our ears caught the airborne sounds of what seemed like chiming hand-bells, the notes having a random beauty beyond any human imagining. They were the calls of bellbirds. These birds are about the size of a blackbird with greeny-black, plumage. For a very plain bird they produced a most heavenly sound.

Reaching a summit pull-in, we stopped to view the spectacular panorama of lakes, wooded promontories and beaches that were the resort of Lakes Entrance and our home for the night.

We were entering the Snowy River National Park, 98,700 hectares of forest wilderness and mountainous enough to require our lowest gears. Coming in the opposite direction we met a young cyclist from Germany. He was riding from Cairns to Adelaide. We talked of the local hilly terrain.

"You don't need to be a good cyclist to do long bike trips, just a good traveller," he mused.

His words were wise indeed. Lunching in a forest café we chatted to a man from Sydney.

"Good on yer," was his comment when he heard of our trip.

Trivial stuff, you may be thinking and you would be right, for life on the road can, on occasion, be trivial. Not every day can be eventful but there is a magical up-side and we had found it. For those periods when nothing much happened, we had developed our own mantra. It was Pedal, Eat, Sleep. Pedal, Eat, Sleep. Pedal, Eat... and so on and so forth. And there you have it. Life was that simple. Back home, it was all traffic jams in the morning, exhausting work, traffic jams on the way home, dire TV when you get there, petulant children, petulant politicians, credit card debt, soaring cholesterol, a bewildering complexity of life. All had gone. Pedal, Eat, Sleep. Pedal, Eat, Sleep. Transcendental bliss!

Reaching the small town of Orbost, we pitched our tent on a spacious municipal campground. We were soon engaged in conversation with a solo cyclist called Bill. He had a broad Geordie accent, despite having lived in Australia for thirty years. Aged seventy-five, he was on one of his annual touring trips, towing his homemade trailer. He thought nothing of ten-day self-supported trips into the bush, carrying all his supplies.

"Do you know what my crowning ambition is?" he asked us.

"No, what is it?"

"To climb Everest, even if it kills me."

We didn't like to say so, but at his age it probably would.

Camped nearby were Arthur and Maria from Cheshire. They were on a six-month bicycle tour of southern and eastern Australia. Now retired, for the past ten years they had been touring southern hemisphere countries as refugees from the English winter. This year it was south-eastern and eastern Australia. They took us off to the local bowls club to eat. All evening, Maria told Arthur stories of their travels. Now since he was her travelling companion and was there, we figured he probably knew these stories from first-hand experience. Nevertheless, he seemed to be fascinated. During the rushing flow of this torrent of words, trying hard to be well mannered, we did our best to pretend attentiveness. In truth, we had to try much harder to stay awake. Well at least we didn't have to work at keeping a conversation going. At bedtime, heads still buzzing, we crept into our sleeping bags. In the morning Maria and Arthur had gone.

We stayed, and rode the valley of the Snowy River downstream to the coastal village of Marlo. Here, a shimmering aquamarine ocean seemed to stretch embracing fingers around sandy islets, reaching tenderly towards golden beaches in a perfect union of land and sea.

On the way back to Orbost, we met Bill again, wearing a fly-proof net over his head. Hotfoot to the local hardware shop, we duly kitted ourselves out with these netting equivalents of a balaclava without a face-hole. Peals of riotous laughter were not what we expected when we tried out our protective gear that night, especially as the chucklers didn't have the decency to reveal themselves. We need not have been embarrassed; the laughter came from birds perched in the trees. They were laughing kookaburras, a member of the kingfisher family, their laughter being a means of advertising the boundaries of their territories. You have to agree, it is far more hygienic than peeing up a lamp-post.

Several local people had warned us of the strenuous nature of the next leg of our journey. The riding was indeed hard, with viciously steep hills and awkward bends on a twisting mountain road. On a steep and fast descent, an overtaking log-transporter suddenly closed in on me and forced me off the road. I fell heavily, sustaining severe lacerations to my thigh and forearm and splitting my helmet on impact with the ground. Help was on hand in a trice. Passing motorists stopped to pick up debris and two South Gippsland council workers pulled in to administer first aid. The log-transporter did not stop. I do not remember, but Mary tells me my first words were:

"Is me bike all right, for without it we're stuffed."

The panniers had saved the bike from serious damage and probably me too. Nevertheless, badly shaken and with stiffening limbs, I found it a struggle to make the ten miles necessary to reach the township of Cann River.

At the Cann River Valley Bush Nursing Centre we were greeted by Coralie, the 'Bush nurse'. She was the very epitome of kindness and efficiency. We were given cups of coffee and I was sent off to use the centre's shower before Coralie cleaned and dressed my wounds with great tenderness and skill. Antiseptics and dressings were provided for continued treatment and we were invited to call the next day if necessary, even though it was Saturday closing. She was an administering angel indeed.

I had foolishly thought that we would be able to leave Cann River the next day – a gross over-estimation of my powers of recovery, as the next morning, I could barely move. And there was another difficulty. The worst forest fires in living memory surrounded the nearby capital of Canberra. Sunsets were an ominous blood-red, while an ugly grey haze dimmed the sky and ash fell from the heavens, coating all with sticky grime. For a time the road out was closed but in any event we could not have gone on for I went into a mild state of shock and was forced to rest. It was to be six days before we were able to continue our journey.

Brian, the manager of the municipal campground, was a man under siege. Privatisation was looming, his premises were subject to all sorts of examination and he himself was in the frame as a buyer. The air was thick with his resentment of all things commercial and official:

"The world is full of fucking idiots and radical fucking feminists!" he fumed.

Hard to see any connection between feminists and campground privatisation, but the man certainly loved his parrots. He had a redundant freezer cabinet full of bird food and only had to lift the lid to attract flocks of the bright red and green birds, which would hand feed when not pinching the food from the cabinet. These sumptuously coloured birds were king parrots, a totally wild bird that Brian had tamed to sit on his hand and eat. He would miss his birds if he had to leave, but he was off to Sydney for some wheeler-dealing to try and acquire ownership of the site.

Off he went, leaving Beth in charge. She was a local teaching assistant and one-time international volleyball player. A single parent, she had a forlorn loneliness about her and would walk her dog about the campground, thus giving her opportunities to chat with guests. She showed great kindness to us, lending us a chiller cabinet and allowing us use of a caravan. In return, we kept an eye on things when she had to leave to attend to other matters.

This wasn't the only local establishment we found ourselves in charge of. The township had a community centre-cum-library. Jim, the man running the place, was a laid-back, easy-going individual, typical of many Aussies. On our first meeting we had gone there to use an Internet terminal. It was a quiet day, we were the only users and Jim had other things to do.

"Keep an eye on the bloody place would you?" he asked us. "I'm off for a few shakes of a dingo's tail."

And so it was that we ran the Cann River Library, even collecting money from those using the computers. Jim came back two hours later.

"No worries?"

"No worries."

We were charmed by such delightful informality and unhesitating trust.

Across the road was the 'Op Shop'. We were to learn that these could be found all over Australia. They are charity shops run by cross-denominational Christian organisations and for us an invaluable source of cheap second-hand books and clothing.

Other cycle travellers came and went. Bernard from Canada was riding from Brisbane to Cooktown. A German couple were cycling from Brisbane to Melbourne and two young men from Belgium were heading for Alice Springs across the outback. We felt a strong sense of international fellowship with these passing travellers, all of whom had fascinating tales to tell of their journeys.

Our sojourn was continuously enlivened by the presence of the local wildlife. At dusk wallabies could be seen grazing and the possums came out to play. These cheeky creatures were ingenuous scavengers. One stole a banana from under our noses and proceeded to sit on the saddle of a bike to eat it. Another prized off the lid of our borrowed chiller cabinet and took a loaf of bread. The local magpies constantly amused. Australian magpies are a complete mirror-image of those in Britain. The conspicuous black-on-white colouring is reversed and they have short tails. Their voices offer the greatest contrast. Instead of a raucous croak they have a remarkable range of musical calls and warbles and use them in a melodic style that would do justice to a coloratura soprano singer. And every evening we would be quite unable to stop ourselves joining in with the infectious laughter of the kookaburras.

It is said that laughter heals, and if this is so, then the local kookaburras should be available on government health schemes for my wounds healed rapidly and we were able to move on – though not by bicycle. Warned of the dangers of the road ahead, we took the bus out of the mountains to Batemans Bay, a day's ride away.

The journey by bus confirmed our fears. The twisting and mountainous road had no shoulder and was busy with log trucks. The lines of the road reflected the indented coastline of this region. Its beauty was outstanding, the route passing through small coastal townships. Most were situated on river estuaries. Aquamarine necklaces of river and sea threaded tree-maned headlands and islets. Cattle ranches became a feature of the landscape. Here the hand of nature seemed to have woven a tapestry of landscape in mystical harmonisation of hill, tree and pond. A bus window might distance the traveller somewhat from the surroundings but the prospect was nonetheless beautiful for it. This was the far south coast of New South Wales.

Batemans Bay was busy for it was the week of the Australia Day national holiday. Our bus driver took us on an unscheduled tour of the town, looking for a scrap of grass to pitch our tent but without success. The local YHA came to our rescue but the only spot they had available was a bare patch of ground in the recycling and clothes-drying area, cut price in view of flapping washing and stinking rubbish but the hostel had a tranquil veranda and well-equipped kitchen.

Batemans Bay lies on the estuary of the River Clyde, and is famed for its seafood and in particular its oysters, often hailed by connoisseurs as the 'best in the world'. It was not the first time we had heard such a claim but the local chippie certainly did a fine bag of calamari and chips.

The most decrepit looking of bridges crosses the estuary of the River Clyde. Local information has it that it is of a rare lifting span type and, when operating, 'a fascinating marvel of engineering to witness'. We could only think nervously of the need for us to cross it when we left. But it made a marvellous launching place for the helmet, which had saved my life. I had saved the split helmet from my crash and bought a replacement in Bateman's Bay. The time had come for a parting ceremony. Waiting for dark, we crept onto the bridge and from there launched the helmet into the sea with this commemoration, "Helmet, thou hast saved mine life. With eternal gratitude I do commit thee to the deep, the fount of all life. Farewell, brave helmet, farewell."

Unfortunately our tidal calculations were awry, so instead of drifting out into the ocean, the helmet floated upstream to become stuck on a sandbank.

At the information office we bumped into a young Yorkshire man who was cycling from Sydney to Perth. After talking to him we felt a little better about taking the bus for seventy miles, for he seemed to spend more time on the bus than his bike. His experience of the Australian people didn't seem to be that positive either. He reckoned they were unfriendly, to the extent that he had been sworn at and spat on whilst in Sydney. Well, the Aussies do seem to be great cursers, but spitting was something we had not witnessed. Maybe he was in the wrong place at the wrong time.

A hot day was predicted so we rose early to safely negotiate the bridge and set out to travel north on Highway 1. Hills and a head-wind made for slow going and there were no compensatory views. The road was lined with eucalyptus forest, just trees and then more trees. Despite the hard going, we made our stopping place of Ulladulla by 11-00am. The campground was situated on a broad headland overlooking a sweeping bay with a tidy boat harbour sheltering many sport-fishing boats. Tourism was the main industry here and a good place for it.

We stayed for a day and walked the headland coastline. Bay followed bay along the shore. All with broad expanses of golden sand and roaring surf. Many had attendant surfers patiently awaiting the 'big wave'. 'Lobster Jacks' was our favourite. This was a deserted rockbound cove with a fine beach and rock pools to explore. An evening picnic on the beach rounded off the day, but the night was a restless one.

"He's a beaut."

"Bagger won't stend still."

"Thet one's tyking a crep."

Possums were abroad and the Aussie trippers were intent on taking their holiday snaps

The southern coastline of New South Wales is very much the holiday haunt of those who live in the east of Australia. This means most of the people of the country. Of the total population of nearly nineteen million, something like twelve million people live on the eastern side of the country between Melbourne and Sydney and most of them were on holiday. For the Aussies the months of January and February are the peak season. Highway 1, the Princes Highway, was busy and Australian drivers seemed to have scant regard for the safety of cyclists. The riding was not fun, more than once we had a close shave and were beginning to fear for our lives.

To escape the highway we took a secondary road into Sanctuary Point. This township seemed to consist entirely of retirement villages and luxury, live-out-your-days housing. It was a place to die in. Chatting to a local man, he could raise no enthusiasm for the changes that had come to his home township,

"It was dirt roads and shacks in my youth, now it's a bloody morgue."

But he directed us onto a pleasant coastal path, where we rode for a time with an Aussie couple. Thirty years ago, when just eighteen months old, the young man had come from Peterborough with his parents on a £10 assisted passage. His dream of a lifetime was to tour Europe by bicycle. It would be a time yet, for his partner was still in the process of gaining confidence in her bicycle riding. We continued to ride together to the township of Huskisson where we camped on a giant holiday site by the beach.

At Orbost, Maria and Arthur had given us an introduction to the world of Australian clubs. These can be associated with various sports or simply be a social club, but by far the commonest are the RSL – the Returned Servicemen's League Clubs, roughly the equivalent of the British Legion Clubs, but in Australia they are very luxurious. They offer a wide range of food, drink and entertainment and are subsidised, which makes them extremely cheap. The one in Huskisson was no exception. Situated above a small harbour with a magnificent view over a wide arc of beach, the club provided us with a splendid meal.

Without these clubs we should not have eaten as well as we did throughout our time in Australia but we were in the second division when it came to eating. Australians consume veritable mountains of food, far more than is good for the health of any nation. Too many of the adults and children we saw were seriously overweight and the consequences were all too much in evidence. Almost every township had a heart recovery park with an exercise circuit. Almost half of the women and two-thirds of the men are overweight and they have children to match. It has reached the point where folk look out of place if they are *not* fat. Government sources describe obesity rates as being out of control and have reached the status of an epidemic. It is now thought that the dubious distinction of being the world's fattest nation has passed from America to Australia. Those gorgeous bodies you see on the Aussie soaps are very much in a minority. These people are fat. Maybe if more of them rode bicycles...

Riding the valley of the Shoalhaven River, we came across a winery at a small village called Coolangatta. It had a history stretching back to 1822. A Scottish-born surgeon, merchant and explorer called Alexander Berry obviously had friends in the right places. Governor Brisbane, in a fit of generosity, gave him ten thousand acres of land. Since this was a fair bit of soil to turn with a spade, he threw in one hundred convicts for good measure. It did well, expanding to forty thousand acres and remaining in the Berry family until 1912, when it was split up and flogged off. In 1947, a farming family called Bishop stepped in and bought a couple of hundred acres. The old convict village was by then a ruin. The Bishops set out to restore it to its former glory and in 1972 it re-opened, but not really, for we found it a bit of a sham. No wine is made there and the former convict homes have been converted into luxury accommodation serving the golf course where grapes once grew. However, wine for tasting is shipped in, and very pleasant it was too.

The Seven Mile Beach National Park lay immediately to our east. Waves could be heard crashing on the shore, but not seen, due to the intervening dense eucalyptus forest. At a roadside café we ate homemade sausage rolls to die for and listened to the life story of the English owner, a jolly man with more than a trace of a Yorkshire accent. Forty years ago he and his wife had travelled overland on their Lambretta scooter to Singapore. Dumping the scooter, they caught a freighter to Australia. At Brisbane they simply walked off the boat. According to him, "They don't even know I'm here."

Could there have been an element of Aussie straight-faced line-shooting in this story?

After spending a night at the small township of Gerringong, we were forced, the next day, to push our bicycles uphill before rolling easily into the small township of Kiama. Its claim to fame is its waterspout. At the end of a wide headland stands a white stone lighthouse and beneath it lies a submarine cave with a surface vent. Rolling pacific waves surging into the cave are said to produce a column of water soaring some two hundred feet upwards on a good day. This was not one of those days. The ocean was calm and the waterspout a damp squib.

However, we were fortunate enough to meet a local fireman and keen racing cyclist. He directed us onto the Bomba Bikepath. This found its way over breezy promontories, around broad bays, alongside golden sand beaches and through small harbour communities, to Shellharbour. This large township is a huge conglomeration of dormitory estates but the campground was well situated on the shore of an expansive bay.

We stayed for a day whilst Mary explored locally on foot, and I set out to ride to the nearby reserve of Bass Point. Used by Aborigines for sixteen thousand years, it is one of the most important archaeological sites on the coast of New South Wales. Rock paintings can be found and rare flora and fauna may be seen, but not on this occasion, for the reserve was closed due to the risk of fire. Australia was in the middle of a drought and the temperature that day reached 43 degrees. Back at the campground; bike servicing revealed a broken front-shifter cable, the first breakage of the trip. This was easily replaced with a spare.

We were now approaching the urbanised and heavily industrialised territory of Woollongong. A giant steelworks loomed ever closer. Prepared for the possibility of less than pleasant cycling, we were surprised to discover a wonderful bikepath, constructed along the coastline by the Wollongong City Council. Back on a short stretch of road, a local touring cyclist stopped his car to chat with us and directed us onto a continuation of the bikepath. He also advised not to miss 'Rubies' at Bulli Head:

"The best bloody burgers in the whole of Australia!"

They were too: four storeys high and splendidly fortifying, washed down with giant mugs of coffee. As we sat on the deck of 'Rubies' café, watching the blue shimmer of the Pacific Ocean whilst basking in the warm sunlight, we were well content.

But not for long, for our overnight stopping place at Coledale did not turn out to be one of our most enjoyable. An ill-appointed surf club campground had only minimal facilities. The village was no better. We could find no food and had only a few slices of bread and some honey for our evening meal. Late that night a party of young Australians camped nearby. Drinking and shouting went on into the small hours of the night, culminating in one youth using a loud hailer to amplify his cursing and belching. The next day, when returning the facilities key, I wished the guardian a good morning.

"No it fucking isn't," said he, throwing the key deposit of a ten-dollar note to the ground for me to pick up. It was indeed a pleasure to leave this place.

The road ahead followed a narrow coastal strip between high cliffs and a pounding ocean. A long and lung-bursting climb began until we reached a summit viewpoint, known locally as Bald Hill Look-out. This airy place gave a breathtaking view southward along the coast, allowing us to pick out the route of our past two days cycling. Its elevated position had been the site of activities leading to the claim that this was 'the birthplace of flight'. The story goes that aviation pioneer, Lawrence Hargrave, tested box kites on Bald Hill and communicated his findings to the Wright Brothers in America. They promptly incorporated his ideas into their early flying machines. It is still a magnet for aviators, today being the home of hang-gliding and paragliding in Australia.

We were entering the Royal National Park, the second oldest in the world, after Yellowstone in America. In 1994 some ninety-five per cent of the park was burnt in a devastating bushfire season. The evidence of this could still be seen in some fire-blackened tree trunks but Australia's flora have natural adaptations to fire and the life of the park has now largely recovered. We found the rainforest a tranquil world of soaring tree trunks topped by a vaulted canopy of green foliage, the silence broken only by the soft call of forest birds. Emerging into the open, the distant high-rise buildings of Sydney could be seen stretching wide to the north as we cruised easily downhill into the small township of Bundeena.

Bundeena is a quiet backwater lying on the southern shore of a series of bays and inlets known as the Port Hacking Waterway. We spent a pleasant hour there chatting to a couple of Sydney motorcyclists and lounging on the ferry quay before catching the boat to Cronulla. For us this was to be the gateway to the great city of Sydney. But first we had to find a bed for the night and so settled upon a caravan park in the small township of Kurnell. Welcomed by the park owners, we were told that a large party of cyclists were due to arrive later.

In twos and threes this group trickled wearily into the park, where they were accommodated in a bunkhouse close to where we were camped. They were a party from the hundred-year-old Bronte Surf Club, and they had ridden thirty miles that day. For many of them it was their first bicycle ride of any distance. Theirs was a gourmet outing. Steaks were grilled in the park kitchen and the beer and wine flowed freely. It was our great good fortune to be the benefactors of this happy coincidence, for we were invited to join the fun and spent a splendid evening with this most friendly and hospitable group of people. Ours was the privilege to be party to the first ever meeting of the Bronte Surf Club Cycling Section.

This was not the only first to occur at Kurnell for, a kilometre down the road is the site of Captain Cook's landing. We could not miss this historic spot, so we backtracked the next morning to stare in thoughtful wonder at a stone obelisk marking the point where Cook's young midshipman, Isaac Smith, is thought to have leaped ashore on April the 29th, 1770. Cook is said to have named the bay 'Botany Bay' after the many botanists he had on board his ship, *The Endeavour*. Revered as the birthplace of modern Australia, it was the starting point for our journey around Botany Bay into the heart of the city of Sydney.

A short ride through Kurnell brought us to a bike-path following the shore of Botany Bay. The bay was not quite what we had expected. Images of a utopian paradise had planted themselves in our consciousness and it seems the botanists on Cook's *Endeavour* had been of the same mind, thinking this was the new Eden. It appears they were fooled by the greenness of the indigenous vegetation and chose to ignore the fact that the local plants were growing on some of the poorest soils on the continent of Australia. A settling fleet was sent, this time with a few more down-to-earth, hard-nosed colonists in the party. Amongst them was one Arthur Philip, who soon spotted the shortcomings of this place as a settlement and took off for the nearest big gap in the shoreline and in so doing discovered Sydney Harbour.

Although Botany Bay is a fine harbour, the only water is salt; the place is all sand with shallow shores and nowhere to pitch an anchor. It has its uses today though, for this low swampy wasteland houses Sydney Airport, Petro-Chemical works and other such industrial development. Not that pleasing to the eye of the passing cyclist, but the local folk don't seem to care, for the shoreline was a hive of leisure activity. Hardly a beach was without athletic wind-surfers and kite-surfers and the shoreline path was crowded with other cyclists, roller-bladers, joggers and walkers. There was almost a festive atmosphere of easy-going relaxation, for this was a Sunday and the people of Sydney were intent in making the very best of it.

The names of the places on our route unfolded a pageant of early Australian colonisation: Botany Bay, Captain Cook's Way, The Cook River and the Endeavour Bridge. A name of lesser historical resonance was the Shiralee Caravan Park, but it was good enough for us to pitch our tent and there make telephone contact with the son of our friends, who had kindly agreed to receive replacement credit cards for us. By coincidence, our friends were visiting their son and so we rode the southern suburbs of Sydney to his clap-board home. Here we were wined and dined to the extent that we needed a lift back to the campground to ensure our survival. It was raining heavily and our dripping tent had a wet-night dreariness about it. There was more than a hint of pity in the farewells of our hosts as we crawled into our home for the night, but inside it was warm and dry and we were well satisfied for we had arrived at Sydney having cycled 898 miles from Melbourne and 5,710 miles in total.

The next day, armed with our replacement credit cards, we set out to make arrangements with regard to air tickets and of course there was the city to explore. Catching the local train, we headed for the celebrated harbour bridge. Walking across this famous structure and gazing in astonishment at the remarkable architecture of the Opera House, we were both overcome with a mixture of emotions, which seemed beyond any words.

"I can't believe where we are," said Mary, "and we did it on our bikes!"

And that was it: just an overwhelming sense of quite extraordinary disbelief.

Sydney is the oldest city in Australia. People might be forgiven for thinking it is the country's capital, because effectively it is. The first humans came here about fifty thousand years in the past. The next lot arrived about two hundred and fifty years ago in a takeover bid without so much as a by-your-leave. There were several boatloads of British, amongst them seven hundred and thirty male and female convicts and sundry military personnel. The locals never stood a chance and, notwithstanding a few ups and downs, the place has grown ever more prosperous since. Today it is Australia's largest city with a population in the region of four million and has one of the most magnificent natural attractions in the world, Sydney Harbour.

Too often we had found that much vaunted tourist attractions could be something of a disappointment. Travel books, TV travelogues, holiday brochures, tourist handouts, etc – all are selling a fantasy, and the reality rarely lives up to that fantasy. Sydney Harbour and its environs did. The natural beauty of the harbour with its inlets, islets and beaches is perfectly complemented by the soaring lines of the opera house and the dramatic backdrop of the city skyscrapers. The harbour bridge gives solidity to the scene, the whole achieving the most wondrous harmony between the works of nature and the works of man.

Full of anticipation of the joys of further exploration, we first had to get the matter of air tickets out of the way. This proved to be a far more complicated business than we had expected. The next two days we spent sitting in various airline offices and languishing for quite a time in the New Zealand Embassy, checking out entry conditions. We ended up obtaining refunds on tickets which had been miss-sold to us in England and buying round-the-world tickets back to Australia. This was the cheapest way to get us back home to Britain via New Zealand and Canada. It was time to move on. Exploration of the great city of Sydney would have to wait for another day, but at least we had the tickets to return.

Sydney's municipal trains allow the transportation of bicycles free of charge outside of the rush hour and so we were able to convey our loaded bikes with ease into the city centre. We were to catch a ferry from Circular Quay. This collection of boat wharfs sits beautifully sandwiched between the Harbour Bridge and the Opera house. We were heading for Manly on the north shore of the Harbour. The ferryboat took on a marked lean as the passengers all rushed to one side as we passed close by the Opera House. The rest of the harbour did not disappoint as we cruised past numerous bays, inlets and islets to reach our landing place.

From Manly, the road ran close by the famed northern beaches of Sydney. At Freshwater Beach there stood a bronze statue of Duke Kahanamoku, who took to the waves in 1914 and thereby started Australian surfing. At Palm Beach we took a fast and exciting catamaran ferry ride across Pitt Water to Ettalong and from here an undulating road took us to the small resort township of Terrigal for an overnight stop. This was very much a holiday coast for we were approaching a region dedicated to the leisure industry, known as the Great Lakes.

Ever present to the east along this coast there was the Pacific Ocean. To the west there was a succession of lakes. It was a world where water dominated and the land submitted into slender peninsulas and narrow strips of forest and sandbank. A flock of pelicans basked in the sunshine and predatory sea eagles circled lazily overhead.

An excellent reserve at the margin of the road became a memorial cycleway, dedicated to the memory of Darren Smith, a renowned and superb racing cyclist who was killed by a passing motorist in the early 1990s. Sad reflections crowded our minds as we left secondary roads to join the Pacific Highway. This climbed a high and narrow ridge between Lake Macquarie and the ocean. Here we rode, seemingly suspended on a ribbon of road above a blue carpet of lake and sea before sweeping downhill to the township of Swansea, our strip of land now anchored to the waters. At an information office we were given help to plan our route ahead and directed to a campground on the shore of Lake Macquarie. An evening picnic dinner by the lakeside, and we retired happily to our tent.

We were now heading for the city of Newcastle to catch another river ferry to take us on our journey north. On the way we passed a junction to Cardiff and we had come from Swansea. These familiar names reflect the industrial past of this region. Newcastle was a major industrial centre from the 1930s to the 1980s but recession set in and in 1989 the first earthquake in Australia ever to claims lives hit the city. Thirteen people died and there was much destruction. The city was down but not out. With a clear vision of the future, a shift was made towards service industries, tourism and the arts, to make the Newcastle of today the place of the moment. It stands on the arc of a bay on the shore of a broad estuary. A magnificent one hundred and eighty-year-old red-brick cathedral dominates the cityscape and, at the mouth of the estuary stands Fort Scratchley, famed for returning the fire of a Japanese submarine in 1942.

The Japanese might not have invaded then but they certainly have now, for when we arrived at the resort of Nelson's Bay, the citizens of the Land of the Rising Sun were out in force. This township styles itself as the dolphin capital of Australia. No, this is not the seat of dolphin government but the venue for a huge fleet of dolphin-spotting boats and the Japanese had come here in numbers to photograph the aquatic mammals. Whilst on shore they diverted themselves by pointing their video cameras at a couple of strange creatures riding laden bicycles.

Another ferry ride and we arrived at our objective of the day, the township of Jimmy's Beach. A friendly local on the ferry had directed us to a beach campground in a eucalyptus grove.

"Guaranteed to see roos and koala but watch out for the dingoes. Only last week a woman was walking her pet dogs on the beach when the dingoes attacked and ate the buggers as breakfast tucker!"

"What, all of them?"

"Nah, just the bloody dogs."

This sounded ominous but only served to sharpen our desire to see these creatures. We needed a rest anyway, so we decided to stay for a day.

We saw no koalas, kangaroos or dingoes but instead came across a gigantic colony of fruit bats. There were many thousands of them, hanging like alien pods upside down in the trees of a wood. Powerful smells of ammonia and dung assailed our nostrils and their eerie high-pitched calls filled the air as they waited for the night to come.

Commonly known as flying foxes they are widespread in Australia. We had seen them in the centre of Sydney, circling in the light of dusk, but here we were close. They are a very large species of bat and can have a wingspan of up to five feet. Their short jaws and powerful teeth are specially adapted for piercing the rinds of the fruits which are their staple diet. As night begins to fall they set out on foraging trips. These can take them up to thirty miles from their home roost. That night, as dusk fell, we sat gazing upwards in wonder as flocks of these creatures flew majestically overhead in search of food. We dined handsomely at a local Chinese restaurant before settling down for the night.

Our ride continued to traverse a watery world of ocean, lake and forest. Because of the risk of fire, almost all access to this countryside was closed. It was very remote country with almost no sign of human habitation and very little traffic. At a narrow neck in a lake there was a chain ferry crossing. We were the only passengers until, at the last moment, a car arrived. Chatting to the occupants, we learned that they were Ann and Tor from New Brighton, a coastal township some seven hundred miles to the north. They themselves had travelled a great deal and had friends living near to their home who had cycled the length of South America. They invited us to stay with them when we arrived in their area and promised an introduction to their friends. "Never miss the chance of a bed and a bath" is the rough traveller's mantra but perhaps a somewhat distant prospect to count on at this time.

After the ferry crossing the road was unsealed; its uncomfortably corrugated and rough surface made for tough going until we re-joined Highway 1 at the small township of Buladelah. Taking a drink at a garage café, we met Ross and Kay, who were making their way back to their home of Port Macquarie. Like Ann and Tor, they were well travelled and also invited us to stay when we reached their home township. We could almost feel that hot water and those clean sheets caressing our bodies, for they did not live much further to the north. It had been a good day for meeting people but it was not a good night. A huge column of smoke from a forest fire menaced ahead and the local campground was close by the Pacific Highway. As a result, a constant volume of noisy traffic made for a sleepless night.

Drought and tinder-dry bush, a few lightning strikes and possibly some arson had started widespread fires in the south east of Australia. The year before thousands of people had to be evacuated from Sydney and this year, in Canberra, lives had been lost and there was much destruction of property. Forest fires are a terrible natural hazard in Australia and for us a considerable source of anxiety, for they were an unknown quantity and we did not have access to media in the event of warnings.

As we were making ready to leave the next morning, we began chatting to a Danish man who spent the European winters in Australia working as a travelling bee-keeper. He was full of complaints about the negative effect of the current drought on his trade. It was certainly hot and dry, the huge column of smoke arising inland still a threatening presence. This was difficult to reconcile with the world of water we rode that day. Leaving the highway, we joined up with the so-called 'Lakes Way'. The route threaded its way through many lakes to arrive at the township of Tuncurry where we were to spend the night. Here the local bowls club furnished us with an excellent meal of poached snapper washed down with a bottle of sparkling champagne, all at a cost of about £11 sterling.

Travelling the 'Lakes Way' was proving to be a stressful experience. The next day saw us riding nervously along a narrow road, often with no shoulder. From our perspective many motorists and truck drivers were murderously inconsiderate. For long sections we were forced to drag our loaded bicycles along bush and boulder strewn verges. At one point a motorist executed a 'U-turn' to talk to us. He was also a cyclist and very concerned about the risks to our lives on this road. He directed us on to an alternative route that took a quieter road to the highway. Here we felt somewhat safer riding a reasonable shoulder, but our confidence in the good intentions of Australian drivers had taken a serious blow. On that day we felt as though our lives meant nothing to the other road users and were relieved to pull into the township of Laurieton. We had ridden fifty-four nerve-wracking miles and felt that a feast and a few stiff drinks at the local RSL Club had been well earned.

A twenty-five mile ride through flat coastal heathland took us easily to Port Macquarie. Here, in a public square, we were welcomed by a succession of curious folk enquiring of our travels. It felt a bit like giving an audience, as we repeated the same answers to the same questions. We were aware that Port Macquarie had an interesting convict past but we were far more interested in visiting a koala hospital located in the township. As we neared the hospital, Kay, whom we had met with her husband Ross a couple of days before, pulled alongside in her four-by-four. She insisted that we call later and gave us directions to her home. Warmed by the thought of a bed for the night, off we went to see the koalas.

The staff at the koala hospital seemed to embody all that is good in humanity when caring for animals and these furry creatures have such an appealing innocence as to render them quite irresistible. They are very vulnerable to forest fires and road hits and many of the koalas being cared for had suffered terrible injuries. The aim was to return them to the wild but some are so badly hurt as to require care for the rest of their lives.

Fenech was one of these. He had been a great favourite of local fisherman, who would regularly escort him across the road. Twice, when making solo crossings, he had been hit by cars. The second time he suffered many broken bones. These mended but head injuries had rendered him blind, so that long-term care was necessary. He became great friends with another sightless koala; the two of them lived as permanent residents at the hospital, and their fame spread. They appeared in a number of films and droves of people from all over the globe came to visit. Fenech's friend died of leukaemia a few years later but Fenech lived happily on. He would walk in circles, apparently usual behaviour for blind koalas, and use his keen sense of smell to seek out the juiciest tips of gum tree leaves. Loved and admired by all, he died in 1998 at the ripe old age of eighteen. Today, in honour of his memory, one of the hospital yards bears his name.

When first welcomed to Port Macquarie by curious local folk, we had thought that perhaps this township had a warm heart. Our visit to the koala hospital further reinforced that impression; and Ross and Kay gave the final confirmation. They received us with great warmth and quickly put us at our ease. They had both retired from the teaching profession and were now inveterate travellers themselves. They took us on a tour of their hometown before wining and dining us that evening. Hospitality to strangers was second nature to them, to the extent that they kept a visitors' book for guests to sign. We left the next morning to their parting waves, refreshed and uplifted with more than a trace of a lump in our throats at leaving these kind and generous people.

Again we felt at risk from the traffic whist riding a narrow two-lane road towards the Pacific highway. Back on the highway, huge trucks hurtling by at breakneck speeds did nothing to calm our nerves and a succession of roadside shrines dedicated to the memory of the dead victims of crashes did not help. It was with relief that we reached our stopping place of Kempsey. Here at the information office we agreed to pose for photographs and were interviewed for an article to appear in the local newspaper, the Macleay Argus. We never saw the article for we had no forwarding address. It was St Valentine's Day and we had now covered a total of 6,028 miles.

Kempsey lies in the valley of the Macleay River. It was used as the subject town in Thomas Keneally's novel *The Town on the Bend* and is the home of the acclaimed Australian artist Les Graham. Living nearby is the country and western singer Slim Dusty, the composer of the song 'A pub with no beer'. The town certainly seemed to have a little more life and heart than many others we had yet visited for we had begun to form the impression that small-town Australia can be something of a dull place.

We had often found it difficult to discover the 'heart' of many small Australian townships. Fruitless searching of these places had led us to the conclusion that this was because most of them didn't have one. Typically we would find a broad scatter of clapboard bungalows joined by roads with no pavements and no street lights. Only very occasionally would we find a pub, and it was usually closed by 8-00pm. No community centre, no sign of civic life, just beer and television at home and bed by 9-00pm. This seemed to be life in ordinary, everyday Australia – a far cry from that depicted in the Aussie soaps seen on British TV.

However, the next day was anything but dull as we rode the valley of the River Macleay. Dolphins paralleled our course as they swam alongside in the river. Twice we were forced to stop to mend punctures. At the township of Frederickton, I ate a crocodile pie. It tasted like chicken with a flavouring of fish. Coming in the opposite direction, we met Hans and Susanne, touring cyclists from Germany. Susanne was in tears as she told of her experiences on the road in Australia, for she felt that the drivers were so careless that her life was worthless to them. While we were chatting at the roadside, a passing motorist actually stopped to abuse us. We were beginning to think that this was not a cyclist-friendly country and once more were relieved to arrive at our destination for the night, the coastal township of South West Rocks.

Our ride to South West Rocks was an out-and-return diversion for we had heard it was a splendid place. It did not quite live up to that description. The town was a collection of standardised holiday flats and shops which we soon quit to ride to a state recreation area on the nearby headland of Arakoon. Here there was a different kind of development, a prison called Trial Bay Goal. It was built between 1877 and 1886. Its prisoners were employed building a breakwater around the harbour. They can't have done much of a job for their handiwork collapsed in a storm a few years later. The prison closed but was reopened in WW1 to house German detainees. Now a museum, its environs are the haunt of the local kangaroos, and one obligingly came out to pose for our cameras. Right and left profiles, hindquarters, full frontal and quizzical gaze. It was a model kangaroo.

"Well, I'll be a couple of Poms, I'm not the only one then. My name's Quentin, pleased to meet you."

We had stopped for a coffee when he appeared on his bike and made his introduction. Quentin was riding from Cairns to Melbourne. A journalist and broadcaster from Torquay, he was distributing the story of his trip by weekly broadcast to the UK and also by his website. When younger, he had lived and worked in Australia and was revisiting some of his old haunts. We enjoyed his company hugely for he had such ebullience and inspirational optimism that we were sent on our way uplifted and re-energised.

We were following the valley of the Nambucca River and history was repeating itself. Dolphins were swimming in the river alongside and twice we had to stop to repair punctures in Mary's rear tyre before reaching our objective of Nambucca Heads. Here a riverside campground gave us the opportunity for a refreshing swim before retiring to yet another RSL Club, this one set upon a hillside looking out over the Nambucca River. The waters glowed purple in the low light of a setting sun and a myriad of sandy islets were the night refuge of roosting parakeets and lorikeets, chattering in the soft voices of evening. The curtains of night drew gently upon this scene, leaving velvet darkness.

The next day, unpleasant cycling on the rough and narrow shoulder of the highway took us to Coffs Harbour. This township styles itself as Australia's most liveable city but we found it to be a characterless collection of low-rise tourist development, retirement condos and very little else. By the next morning rain had set in so we decided to walk in the wet rather than ride, and visit Mutton Bird Island, which isn't really an island for it is reached by a sea wall. Mutton birds are shearwaters, they nest in underground burrows and the island is said to be home to thousands of them between September and April. Maybe it was the rain but we saw none, the only avian life to enliven our visit to Coffs Harbour being a bedraggled owl sitting on the fence at the campground.

Things were by now becoming a little uncomfortable. Joints had split in our aluminium tent poles and we could not therefore trust our shelter to stay erect. A temporary sleeving repair kept us going but we had lost confidence in the capacity of the tent to keep us dry. This was not good, for heavy rain continued to fall for the next two days. We splashed along the highway, staying for a night on a dismal campground in a forgettable small township. Persistent head-winds drove penetrating rain through our wet weather gear and pounding traffic constantly threatened our lives. Unable to avoid a patch of broken glass on the road shoulder, my bike tyre suffered yet another puncture. Repairing it in the pouring rain and buffeted by the wind from passing vehicles, our eyes met. It was definitely one of those days...

At Grafton the sun came out but we went in, to a caravan on a holiday park, for everything was wet and drying time was needed. Furthermore the road ahead was closed due to flooding and so we had to accept being pinned down until further progress was possible. This gave the opportunity for reflection, some of which was not entirely comfortable.

Almost without exception, person-to-person, the Australian people were some of the kindest and most hospitable folk we had yet met. But put them in a car or truck and they became potential killers. The two German cyclists we had met had suffered a bottle thrown at them from a car window. We were no strangers to abuse hurled from passing vehicles and had been the victims of more close shaves than a female impersonator. We had learned that a section of the youth of Australia measure their car journeys in 'stubbies'. These are small dumpy bottles of beer. Thus a short trip might be a 'one-stubby ride' and a longer one perhaps a 'six-stubby ride'. This was elevating drinking and driving to previously unknown heights and the evidence of this practice was to be seen in the broken glass littering the shoulder of every road and highway. A retired trucker told us that many of his kind used amphetamines to stay awake on the road, thus creating a double whammy of drunken youths and drugged truck drivers. It was small wonder then that the roads were littered with shrines to the dead. It is no exaggeration to state that our days on the road were spent in fear of our lives and this was beginning to colour the whole of our Australian experience.

In the year 2001 there were 1,737 road deaths in Australia. In the same year in the UK, there were 3,443. Taking into account the demographics, in Australia fatality rates are 9.5 deaths per 100,000 population and in the UK, 5.8 deaths per 100,000. On this basis, we were almost twice as likely to be killed on the road in Australia as we were in our own overcrowded country.

Still, life goes on and Grafton was an attractive place in which to while away time. The city lies on the banks of the Clarence River. Richard Craig, an escaped convict, first discovered the area in 1831. For the price of a pardon and nice little handout of £100, he set sail on the cutter *Prince George*, leading a party of loggers to cut the 'red gold', that grew in plenty in the district. The 'red gold' was cedar and its harvest brought the riches on which Grafton is founded. An enlightened city council passed a series of by-laws to ensure the planting of trees and shrubs and the establishment of parks. The result: broad jacaranda tree-lined avenues, expansive parklands and many old buildings, all combining to give the city an air of easy graciousness.

The rain stopped but we were still waiting for flooding to abate in the Clarence River Valley. Two other touring cyclists, riding recumbent bicycles; arrived at the campground; they were Grady and Gretchen, retired police officers from New Mexico, currently touring Australia before moving on to New Zealand. Their bicycles were long and sleek with armchair-like seats slung low between small wheels. They had taken the philosophy of recycling to new heights and had built their home in America using coke cans and old car tyres. Over a bottle of wine, Grady and Gretchen did much to dispel any notions we might have had about hard-nosed, gun-toting police officers. Grady had never drawn his pistol in the thirty-five years of his career and held political views of an unexpected kind. On his home of America:

"What other country in the world would elect the village idiot as its president?"

It was late at night before we went to bed. In the morning we would be leaving, for the floods had abated in the valley of the Clarence River.

The evidence of recent heavy rains was all about us as we rode the flat river valley northwards. Water was everywhere in creeks, ponds and flooded fields. It was a paradise for birds. We saw ibis, egrets, swamp hens, pelicans, sea eagles and, on one occasion, an osprey. A remote ferry crossing took us across the Clarence River. Whilst waiting we met a canoeist specialising in marathons. He had trained on the Clarence for the Murray River event, three hundred miles in five days. Shyly he slipped in a few words of his own world record achievements.

We were now riding through the prosperous sugar cane country of Woodford Island, said to be the largest inland island in the southern hemisphere. Lunching by the Clarence River we watched a small fleet of shrimp trawlers ply the river. They were kept close company by a much bigger fleet of voracious pelicans.

Soon we reached the township of MacLean. Here, pipe bands skirl in the streets, haggis graces the counters of the butchers' shops and even the lamp-posts wear tartan kilts. But no misty highlands here, just fields of towering sugar cane alongside the road until we came to the township of Yamba.

We were to catch a ferry across the river and whilst waiting, we began chatting to a fellow passenger who lived at Iluka on the opposite shore. On that brief acquaintance, he invited us to his home to stay. George was a domestic refugee. A successful farmer, he had three farms in the locality but, fed up with family wrangling, he had left his wife and sons to their bickering and bought a house in Iluka. It is a good place for a retreat, so remote a community as to be referred to in Yamba as 'Siberia'. George gave us tea and the use of his shower before we took him to dinner at the local bowls club.

He was a self-effacing man with a quite remarkable life history. Born in Irkutsk in Russia, when he was aged twelve the Germans took him, his mother and sister to Poland, there to work in a labour camp. He had been a witness to many wartime atrocities but somehow survived to join the Polish Army as a military policeman. Like many displaced persons in the post-war period, he sought a new life and came to Australia. Along with others like him, he suffered vicious discrimination in his new country. He had literally to fight for survival, becoming an all-Australia boxing champion and investing his winnings in the businesses he currently owned.

George was now a cheerful refugee from the stresses of family life and, at seventy-five years of age, as fit as a flea. He took great delight in the local wildlife, hand-feeding a great flock of rainbow parakeets and putting out food for the rabbits. (Maybe not a dedicated animal lover for he had a freezer full of meat from the rabbits he had trapped). He was a man of piercing intelligence and observation with a razor sharp wit and deeply sensitive. He proudly showed us his family albums one of which contained a newspaper cutting from the Leicester Mercury. It was a photograph of his mother who had come to our hometown of Leicester in the post-war period and been welcomed by the city's Lord Mayor. George showed a touching delight in our presence in his home, just as we delighted in his company. In the morning, and not for the first time, we were to experience the pangs of parting sorrow as we said our goodbyes to this quite extraordinary man.

Two National Parks were to be traversed this day, the forests of Bundjalung and the coastal heath land of Broadwater. Australia seems to have more national parks than public toilets, which says much more about all the land there is lying about than any shortage of public facilities. Amidst the forest we found a coffee house-cum-museum called 'Little Italy'. This commemorates the arrival and departure of Italian Immigrants in the region.

Back in 1880, an Italian aristocrat called the Marquis De Rays, a bit of a lineshooter, conned farmers from Veneto in Northern Italy with stories of a Pacific paradise in Australia. He had a vivid imagination as well as a heart of stone. When the expedition arrived, they were dumped on shore and left to get on with it. They found themselves confronted with deprivation, disease, starvation, cannibals and death. The premier of New South Wales heard of this disaster and launched a humanitarian rescue. In April 1881, the rescued settlers arrived in Sydney; out of the original three hundred and forty people, only two hundred and seventeen had survived. These must have been courageous folk, for when they had recovered from their ordeal, they returned to the area to hack a living out of the virgin forest. They were very successful, establishing a three thousand acre settlement, which became a prosperous and self-sufficient community, producing crops in land so poor that no-one else would ever consider cultivating. By the early 20th century the settlers had drifted away to better farming land and the forest once again reigned supreme. The present day coffee shop houses many mementos of this time. For us it was a poignant reminder of the tough and sometimes tragic lives led by the early colonists. As we mused over this story of triumph from tragedy, the rest of our day's ride passed uneventfully, as did our night's camp in a caravan park in the nondescript town of Broadwater.

The next day saw us riding a secondary road alongside the east bank of the Richmond River. This was sugar cane country and from the size and obvious luxury of the plantation houses, a very profitable crop indeed, thanks mostly to a toad from Hawaaii. Introduced into Australia from its native country in 1935, it has thrived on a diet of scarab beetles and in so doing controlled the major pest of the sugar cane plant. This is good, for that was the intention. Not so good are the toxins it carries. Many native animals are poisoned by this amphibian and humans too are injured. It preys on native fauna, eats the food of other reptiles, transmits diseases and even eats small mammals. Now designated a pest, it is called the cane toad and is an immigrant that is in Australia to stay.

Resting at a small settlement with the somewhat grandiose name of Empire Vale, we chatted to a local farmer. An ex-shipwright from Sydney, he had quit the ailing shipyards for the riches of the cane-fields and was doing very nicely indeed. He took us into a tiny wooden shack about the size of a small garden shed, which turned out to be the local post office. There we were introduced to Gary the Postmaster and his golden labrador. Gary had been the keeper of his tiny empire for twenty-eight years. Effectively a community meeting place for the scattered farms of the region, it had been built in 1941 and by the look of it, had not seen a coat of paint since. Gary was a cheerful soul dispensing stamps and sociability in equal measure, and we left his tiny abode with renewed energy to reach a rusting ferryboat at Bluff Point, there to cross the river and enter the township of Ballina.

Founded on the 'red gold' of cedar discovered in the region by the early settlers, Ballina now devotes itself to the harvesting of tourist dollars. Stunning coastal scenery and recreational boating on the Richmond River are the main attractions. For us the local campground and a nearby Chinese restaurant were sufficient. Returning to the campground after eating, we were invited to join a nearby camper for a beer.

Some of you may have read the book *Around Ireland with a Fridge* by Tony Hawks. For a bet he did just that, hitching lifts for himself and his fridge. Whilst he and the fridge had many bizarre and amusing adventures, his electrical companion was but one of those mini affairs and so far as I recall, he never actually used his fridge to keep anything cool. Well, our neighbouring camper was travelling Australia with the real thing, a gleaming white giant double-decker, fully functioning, powered from a campground electrical hook-up and loaded to the gunnels with bottles of ice-cold VB. Darren's (at least we think that was his name) speech was somewhat indistinct. At first we thought it was his Aussie accent but began to conclude it might be the effects of the VB he had imbibed. The evening wore on, with Darren generously dispensing deliciously cool bottles of VB. We understood even less of the conversation now, including our own contributions. I remember thinking it was rude of Mary to fall asleep, although if she had passed out, then that was OK. Somehow we must have found our way back to our own tent, for that is where we awoke in the morning. At Darren's tent there was no sign of life, although his fridge could be heard gently humming. We left quietly to ride to Byron Bay.

A pleasantly undulating coast road took us easily to our objective. Our cyclists guide to Australia informed us that Byron Bay is the much vaunted centre of Australian alternative culture. Everyone came here – 60s' surfers, 70s' hippies, 80s' backpackers and all and sundry since. Laid back it may be but there are pressures. New Age healers may still chant in their gardens of peace but red-necked property dealers are eagerly warming up their bulldozers. The all too familiar low rise sprawl of holiday commercialism gave us as much incentive as we needed to take the road out of town. It must be said however that nearby lay New Brighton where we planned a visit to the home of Ann and Tor, whom we had met several hundred miles further south and with whom we hoped to stay and maybe revisit Byron Bay. Maybe!

We were hungry and so stopped at a grubby gas station which, like most in Australia, did a nice line in fast food. Bacon butties and cappuccino did the trick, as did the bush toilet. The inevitable enquiries about our journey, as always, gave us quite a kick. A chorus of "Good on yer!" and "Enjoy the rest of your trip!" sent us happily on our way. Not that happily though, for, approaching

New Brighton, we were forced to push our laden bicycles up hills so steep that we could manage only a few lung-bursting steps at a time. A terrifying swoop down to the coast took us to a convenience store and a telephone call to Ann and Tor.

Me, tentatively: "Hi, Ann, its Mary and Graham."

We were not forgotten. "Dinkum, where are you?"

"Outside the convenience store."

"Our place is just a hundred metres back south. I'll wait for you outside."

And there was Ann, radiating all the warmth and friendliness we remembered from our first encounter at the Buladelah Ferry nearly three weeks and seven hundred miles ago. We had been a little anxious at the reception we might receive, for our meeting on the chain ferry had lasted only the width of a fifty-metre neck of water. Maybe they were just being nice in their invitation, never expecting us to actually turn up. Maybe they wouldn't even remember who we were. It was me doing most of the worrying, for Mary was invariably more hopeful than I was.

And she was right. We were welcomed with open arms. Tor had been sent to buy supplies and, after storing our gear and cleaning up, we were treated to a splendid meal on the outside decking of Ann and Tor's delightful home on stilts. It was a dreamy sub-tropical night. The Pacific Ocean could be heard caressing the beach at the bottom of the garden. A possum watched wide-eyed from the branches of an overarching gum tree where flying foxes were feeding and fireflies gleamed like distant stars. Tor had come to Australia from Denmark before meeting Ann and both had travelled widely. We found we had much in common. Conversation, wine and time flowed easily and that night we slept the deep sleep of the well content.

The night before we had learned that our hosts were off to 'Brizzy' (Brisbane) the next day to attend a Buddhist lecture and afterwards spend the night with friends.

"No worries, stop over, take one of the cars, make yourselves at home, no need for a house-key, just come and go as you please."

The culture of our home country would never allow such trust as this and we surely would lock our front doors. For all that

Ann and Tor knew, we might steal the car and pilfer their choice possessions. But these dark musings are ones to be ashamed of, considering the gift of such touching hospitality. And gift it was, for in relaxing the next day, we began to realise how tired and jaded we were becoming and how much we were in need of the healing this precious recuperation time allowed.

Later the next day, Ann and Tor returned from Brisbane, elevated by what seems to have been a very worldly take on Buddhism. At dinner, I expressed a view that much of eastern Australia seemed to be covered in somewhat uninteresting eucalyptus forest and appeared to be land beyond any use at all, 'so let's call it a national park'. Perhaps to redress the balance a little, our hosts decided to take us to Byron Bay, a prospect we viewed with some misgivings. We need not have been concerned, for we were first taken to walk up the magnificent hundred-metre heights of the headland of Cape Byron, the most easterly point of the continent (and a national park). Topped by an elegant lighthouse, it was a most magnificent viewpoint. Pod after pod of dolphins surfed the pacific waves far below, whilst sharks circled watchfully around the swirling shadows of shoals of fish.

"A far cry from Swansea Bay!" said the lilting voices of a couple from South Wales, escaping the gloomy winter of the valleys. For us there was to be no escape, for back down the headland, 'boogie boards' were unloaded from the boot of the car and we were escorted on to a glorious sweep of golden beach, populated by golden people. It seems we were to enter the roaring surf and ride monster waves with flimsy bits of polystyrene under our bellies.

"But what about the sharks?"

"No worries."

And it seemed to be so, for all sorts of tasty-looking humans were frolicking happily in the surf. Well it appeared that Tor had a bad leg and Mary really can't swim, so it was down to Ann and me. 'Boogie boarding' turned out to be as much fun as near-drowning can ever be. Maybe Byron Bay was quite a nice place after all.

Back at New Brighton, we were given a telephone introduction to Margy and Lins, friends of Ann and Tor whose home was in the township of Murwillumbah, our next port of call. In Ann and Tor we seemed to have discovered kindred souls and there passed one of those wonderfully effortless, just-being-together evenings, which occur all too rarely and are all the better for it. In the morning we parted, each of us in tears.

The road to Murwillumbah was narrow, shoulder-less and dangerous to cycle. Fortunately we soon turned onto the old highway and enjoyed easy riding through sugar cane plantations and banana groves. Stopping to buy fruit at a roadside store, we were buttonholed by a man wearing a wide-brimmed hat, floral tank-top and leather trousers.

"Take it easy," was his approach to life, "far too many wankers in this world and all in such a bloody rush."

And throwing his leg over his streamlined super-bike, he roared off into the distance.

An arduous climb in intense heat gave us the compensation of a cooling downhill rush into the township of Murwillumbah, its name meaning place of many possums. We soon found the home of Margy and Lins, who were expecting us and with whom we had much in common. They were avid cyclists, having completed a number of worldwide trips, including a six thousand mile ride along the length of South America. Lins was particularly dedicated to his cycling, regularly doing a forty-mile morning sprint on his bike before riding to his work as a child psychologist. On Lins's recommendation, it was this route that would give us a pleasant recreational ride the following day.

Murwillumbah lies in the crater of the Southern Hemisphere's largest extinct shield volcano. The remaining central core of Mount Warning towers six thousand feet above the region. As we rode the valley of the Oxley River the next day, the mountain loomed ahead. This was an area of small homely fields and deciduous woodland giving it the friendly look of the English Shires. Drawn by a roadside sign we decided to visit the advertised 'Hari Krishna' village. Sweeping grasslands and groves of trees sheltering comfortable looking huts gave meditative grace to the landscape. Our first human encounter, however, was not to be with a devotee but with Seigfried from Germany. He camped in the grounds for six months of each year in order to preserve his dual citizenship. For this he paid $35 a week, including food. He too was a cyclist and like us, he did not always find riding the Australian roads a pleasant experience. He told us he had suffered abuse, bottle-throwing, deliberate 'close-cutting' at speed and being told to "fuck off". He perceived "dark undercurrents" in the Australian psyche and certainly, from a cycling perspective, it was not difficult to agree with him.

The Krishna Temple resembled one of those roadside fast food outlets. One-storey sprawl, plenty of glass and built to last not very long. A single hall held no furniture or fittings other than an elaborately decorated shrine to Lord Krishna at one end. Yet it did not lack a devotional atmosphere, bringing to us a sense of calmness we had not expected. Seeming to appear from nowhere came Chris from Sydney. He was dressed in saffron robes, with a shaven head and steady gaze. He was happy to chat to us about his faith. Krishna, we learned, is the one God. All other deities are his reincarnations and worryingly, we are soon due five thousand years of chaos. Chris's perspective upon his faith was by no means idealistic. He related splits in the religion, bids for power and other such human shenanigans. By contrast, he and his fellow devotees do much community work locally whilst internationally a great deal of food aid work is carried out. He had an appealing calmness about him and a touching faith in his one true god , Lord Krishna. Perhaps we had addressed some of our misconceptions about the Krishna people, who just seem to be attempting to make some sense of life in their own chosen terms.

Crossing a low ridge into the valley of the River Tweed, a roadside fruit-selling set-up sold us deliciously frozen, chocolate-covered bananas. Dining that evening with Margy and Lins, they gave us dire warnings about the dangers of attempting to cycle the highway to Brisbane, some ninety miles further north. Respecting their judgement as local cyclists, we accepted their offer of a lift to Nerang, there to take the train to Brisbane's Central Station and change to a local train to Zillmere, a northern suburb of the city and the location of a convenient Big 4 campground.

For any cyclists among you, Brisbane, like Melbourne and Sydney, has a wonderfully cyclist friendly railway system. Stations have lifts where necessary and trains are equipped with roll-on, roll-off access with designated bike parking on board. No need for bookings and all free of charge. Take note, you cyclist-hostile train operators in Britain.

Alighting at Zillmere, we were immediately approached by a Good Samaritan, who led us to her home nearby and fortified us with tea and fruitcake. She and her husband had come to Australia from Hucknall in Nottinghamshire some forty years ago. Ill health had forced Eric out of his employment as a miner and he and his wife had promptly emigrated. Now aged seventy-six, Eric was still a successful marathon runner and proud patriarch to four highly prosperous sons and eight grandchildren. Both Eric and his wife retained their northern accents and boasted the fusion title of 'Ozpoms'. They were typical of many Australians we had met, being either direct or first generational immigrants from Britain and still retaining much of their former sense of national identity.

After a disturbed night on the somewhat dismal Big 4 campground, we took the bus into Brisbane, there to gather essential information to enable our departure for Christchurch in New Zealand. Our journey in Australia had almost come to an end. We had cycled 1,700 miles from Melbourne through Sydney to Brisbane. We had survived often dangerous road conditions to enjoy superb hospitality and the sights sounds and smells of spectacular wild life living in the lands bordering the stunning coastal scenery of the Eastern Australian sea-board. We were due a break and so took the bus one hundred miles north to the so-called 'Sunshine Coast', there to spend a week at the resort of Caloundra with family friends who were escaping the rigours of the English winter.

It was now the 20th of March 2003. We were back in Brisbane preparing to leave for Christchurch. By coincidence Peter and Carol, whom we had met in Istanbul, were stopping over in the city before riding their motorcycle north to Cairns. They too would later be travelling to New Zealand before returning to their home in Canada. We hoped to meet up with them there but first a reunion in Brisbane and much swapping of travellers' tales. We parted with promises to link up in Canada but, as anyone who has joined the travelling community is aware, these partings are tinged with sadness, for such are the vagaries of travel that you know full well you may never meet again.

Setting such sentiments aside, we prepared to leave 'Brizzy' and Australia. We had now ridden our bikes for a total of 6,613 miles in nine months. Still to come were some 1,500 miles in New Zealand and 4,500 miles across Canada. Looked at in this way, it seemed a pretty daunting prospect. However, life on the road had taught us the invaluable lesson of living one day at a time and tomorrow we were heading for one of the remotest and reputedly most beautiful countries in the world.

CHAPTER TEN
44 MILLION SHEEP CAN'T BE WRONG

Our aircraft to New Zealand did not leave Brisbane Airport until 1-30am, thus allowing a leisurely start to the day and an easy meander, mostly along bike-paths, through the northern and eastern suburbs of Brisbane. At the village of Nundah, close by the airport, we stopped for coffee and were joined at our street café table by Eddie and Nan. They were enthusiastic local cyclists, thus no prizes for guessing the main topic of conversation! Like so many Aussies we had met, they had the natural warmth and friendliness typical of almost all their countrymen, which is still the thing we remember the most about Australia.

We were leaving on a high note, which continued with an easy ride to the airport and yet another human encounter, this time with Geoffrey and Rachael, who were semi-retired hoteliers from a town north of Alberta in Canada. Despite being in their eighties, they were dedicated motorcyclists and inveterate travellers who were also flying to Christchurch. They were also inveterate talkers – so it was something of a relief to escape their company when the time came to leave the concourse and check in.

Standing in the queue for the check in desks, we suddenly heard the words:

"We couldn't let you leave Oz without a goodbye!"

It was Eddie and Nan, a self-appointed farewell deputation on behalf of the Australian people. We had never met them before today and spent just twenty minutes in their company yet in the dead of night, they came to see us off. It was a gesture of great generosity of spirit and one that somehow seemed to wipe from the slate all those times we had nearly come to grief at the hands of Australian drivers. As ever, it was the kindness and goodness of people we had met that left by far the most indelible impression.

A half-loaded aircraft, allowing us three seats to ourselves, gave us a comfortable journey. Crossing the North Island of New Zealand at dawn, we were treated to a breathtaking sunrise of crimson and gold, providing a blazing aerial canopy to the dark mystery of snow-capped mountains and purple lakes below. Ground mist on landing and an unfamiliar chill in the mobile access tunnel reminded us that we were deep into the southern hemisphere. Successfully reunited with our bikes and luggage we had to run the gauntlet of Bio-Security. The bicycles, and particularly their tyres, were scrutinised carefully. Fortunately we were forewarned and had scrubbed the lot in the Brisbane Airport toilets before embarking. Our tent did not fare quite so well. Unpacked and unrolled it revealed a dead beetle, to be placed in a specimen jar and taken to laboratories for identification. It was a thorough process and understandably so, for the New Zealand economy is based upon animal husbandry, particularly sheep, and its unique wildlife is a precious asset to the country. Eventually declared clean, we obtained our visas at the entry desks, New Zealand dollars at an ATM and maps and leaflets at the information desk. We had all we needed to ensure our immediate survival and once again set out to savour the uncertainty and excitement of entering a new country.

We soon began to feel at home, for the bungalows and houses of suburban Christchurch, with their neatly kept gardens, might have been those of any comfortable English town. Our chosen campground of 'Meadow Park' turned out to be a large holiday complex with a small corner for itinerant travellers of all kinds. Small wonder, then, that we soon found ourselves in conversation with a couple of fellow travellers, a young Irishman and his American partner, who had been on the road for the past year. They had ridden their bicycles down the West Coast of America, through central and South America to Chile, where they had worked as project leaders for the 'Raleigh' organisation. They had cycled New Zealand for a couple of months and were leaving for Australia the next day. Mutual information-swapping of the kind never seen in the guide books ("Don't go there, it's shite!") kept us happy until we crawled into our tent for a much-needed siesta.

Refreshed, we set out on a preliminary exploration of the city of Christchurch. A pleasant cycle path took us towards the centre, where a cyclist waiting at a set of traffic lights gave us directions. His name was James and he there and then issued us with an invitation to visit him at his home the next day.

Crossing Hagley Park, we cycled along a broad boulevard, passing the fine stone buildings of the Canterbury Museum and turning left to cross the River Avon. Reclining people relaxed on rolling grassy banks as punts negotiated the willow hung tranquillity of the waters. A little further and we entered Cathedral Square. Local publicity blurbs would have it that the square possesses 'elegant simplicity' and that the city itself is characterised by its 'elegant charm'. Well, for once they were not far off the mark. A soaring neo-gothic cathedral dominates the broad expanse of the square, which has an attractive absence of the usual clutter of civic extravaganzas. There was, however, a giant steel sieve, shaped in the form of an ice-cream cone. Maybe it was meant to be art. You know the kind of thing: concrete cows, randomly welded heaps of scrap metal or hundreds of tons of sand dumped in a town hall square to symbolise a holiday beach. Anyway, there wasn't much of this stuff and it was all the better for it. We liked it a lot and the surrounding grid system of broad avenues made it easy for us to find sources of maps, books and guides to enable us to plan our travels in New Zealand. Having completed the essentials, we sat in the square, the late summer sun of March feeling very refreshing after the sub-tropical heat and humidity of Brisbane. So far New Zealand seemed to hold much promise.

Maoris are said to have visited the area of Christchurch some one thousand years ago. Captain Cook sailed up the coast in 1770 and the first four boatloads of English settlers arrived in the period 1850 to 1851. They left their mark, the Christchurch of today being thought of as the most 'English' city in New Zealand. The local economy was founded on primary products and long recognised as 'living off the sheep's back'. Today 'new economy' sectors are emerging and newly arrived immigrants from Europe and the Orient are adding spice to the local culture. Christchurch now has a sizeable population and is claimed to be New Zealand's most attractive city. No doubt the claimants just happen to live in these parts and doubtless are also the ones who voted the place 'one of the most beautiful and liveable cities in the world'. Not the first time did we hear such a claim, and probably not the last, but from our brief acquaintance, it seemed to be quite a nice place.

The next day we visited James as arranged. He and his wife Lucy and their infant daughter live in a comfortable two-storey clapboard house in a quiet suburb of Christchurch. We caught Jimmy in the middle of giving a drumming lesson to a pupil as a diversion from his usual occupation of teaching geography. He turned out to be an energetic advocate of cycling and a mine of information with regards to route options in the South Island. Furthermore, he gave us phone numbers and introductions to relatives and friends whom we might want to stay with during our travels. Once again, the people we had been fortunate to meet were proving to be our most precious resource.

"Guten Tag."

"Good Morning."

It was Klaus and Gretchen, dairy farmers from Heidelberg. They had been cycling New Zealand's South Island for the past three months and were soon to fly back to Germany for the milking season. Yet more swapping of travellers' tales and gathering of useful information. The next day we took breakfast with our new German friends, along with couple from Switzerland who were also soon due to leave, on their way to Vancouver and later back to Europe. We were beginning to feel like we had joined a globe-trotters' convention, not just great fun but also a valuable source of information about our forthcoming journey in New Zealand. Klaus did a nice line in straight-faced wind-ups, which soon got up the noses of our somewhat po-faced companions from Switzerland. An international incident appeared to be looming – time to beat a strategic retreat, and tomorrow set out into the neutral territory of the Canterbury Plains.

The Canterbury Plains are about one hundred and twenty miles long and forty miles wide, bounded on the east by the South Pacific Ocean and on the west by the Southern Alps. The going was flat and the riding easy as we rode south the next day. The growing of wheat and the raising of cattle and sheep seemed to be the main occupations in the area. New Zealand has a population of around forty-four million sheep, as compared to four million people. Needless to say, we saw lots of sheep that day and very few people.

Our ride was uneventful until we crossed the Rakaia River on the longest bridge in New Zealand, which is possibly also the narrowest – in the region of one and a half miles long and so narrow as to require us to dismount and cringe by the parapet as traffic passed. A campground lay on the south side of the river. Here we learned that, for reasons of safety, the owner was in the habit of ferrying cyclists northwards across the bridge in the back of his 4-by-4 when they left. Southward approaching riders were left to take their chance.

We spent that night in a camping cabin: two bunks, sink, kettle and toaster and all for $28 the two of us (about £10). These friendly little wooden huts were to become our havens for the night on many occasions whilst in New Zealand. The campground had a covered kitchen-cum-TV lounge. It was equipped with cookers, both electric and microwave, kettles, toasters, pots and pans and cutlery. These kitchens, we were to learn, are standard in the country, always free of charge and operating entirely on trust.

Rakaia is the self-styled salmon fishing capital of New Zealand and announces that distinction to all and sundry by means of a forty foot high plastic salmon slap bang in the middle of town. It was a handy landmark for our turning point off the H1 onto the H73, otherwise known as Thompson's Track. A light tail-wind and an almost imperceptible gradient meant that we were able to climb a thousand feet without breaking sweat.

Ever closer loomed the Southern Alps until we rolled, starving, into Mount Somers. Food from the general store and directions to the village camping domain answered the always pressing problems of eating and sleeping. We had the camping domain to ourselves. Good grass, bathed in the evening sunlight, coin-operated showers and all for $2 (less than £1), payable to number forty just up the road. Opposite stood a pub; what more could any weary cycle traveller wish for?

A light tail-wind and gentle downward incline eased our southward progress the following day. To our west lay the ever present Southern Alps and behind us, to the north, the dark summit of Mount Somers wore a sombre wreath of cloud. Deer farming was much in evidence here. Corralled in fields about the size of football pitches, they were quite the most beautiful breed we had ever seen. They were as big as the red deer of Scotland, with the faces of angels and the graceful walks of four-legged ballet dancers. A man we met later in a pub told us that they were raised mostly for meat but some were spared for the gun tourists. Mostly American, they come to shoot the deer. Not for them the discomfort of stalking, belly down, in bog and heather. No, they just kill the deer as they graze peacefully in the fields and carry off their trophy antlers to the land of the gun, there to hang proudly above their mantelpieces. Just ask yourself: can there really be any truth at all in this story?

Spotting a diversion to the town of Arundel we could not help but speculate.

"Ivy covered stone cottages."

"Cosy teashops."

"Maybe a towering castle."

It was not to be missed. But when we got there, it was. Just two ramshackle farms and a saw-mill. Maybe our day's objective of the town of Geraldine would be better. And it was, with echoes of an English country town, sporting a park of sweeping lawns and a main street lined with craft shops and cafés. In 1854 one Samuel Hewlings built the first bark hut here. He married a Maori woman and planted a Totara tree to mark the occasion. The tree continues to flourish and so does Geraldine, lying as it does in the midst of a prosperous farming area and coining it from the tourist dollar. Perhaps they flock to see the world's largest jersey, ratified by the Guiness Book of Records, no less, which hangs fetchingly in the window of a local knitwear shop.

Next day steady rain and a crossed head-wind made for hard going as we rode towards the port of Timaru. When we arrived, we discovered that an air fair in honour of one Richard Pearce had drawn in the crowds, filling all the local accommodation. Here is a word about Mr Pearce. A local aviator, he took to the skies under power in March 1902 and in so doing, beat the Wright brothers to it. Anyway, that's the version of aviation history favoured around here. However, his contemporaries saw him as something of a nutter, giving him such unflattering nicknames as 'Bamboo Pearce' and 'Mad Pearce'. He ended his days in a mental institution, unable to cope with a lifetime of rejection. Trailing around Timaru, we might easily have suffered the same fate as we were turned away by numerous keepers of hotels, hostels and flop-houses. Eventually the proprietors of the '334', a backpackers' 'hotel', took pity on us and gave us an unfinished and undecorated attic room, but at least it had a bed.

At breakfast we met Lynda Wysmer, a painter whose home is "wherever I happen to be". She was a New Zealander, claiming English ancestry back to the authoress of 'Lorna Doone'. Born in Timaru, she had lived most of her life in America and was here for an exhibition of her paintings – at eighty years of age, an itinerant artist.

We spent the day half-heartedly exploring Timaru, which we found to be a pleasant enough place with a splendid crescent of beach backed by the magnificent rose gardens of Caroline Park. Back at the 'hotel', we were treated to a preview of Lynda's exhibition with the artist as guide. Inspired by ideas of sub-atomic particles and the cosmos, the paintings were abstract yet somehow wonderfully expressive of their theme. Lynda's niece was present and clearly very proud of her aunt.

"She's very famous in America," she whispered to us, and it was not difficult to see why.

Persistent 'mizzle', a steeply undulating road, a strengthening head-wind and eventually driving rain made for a challenging experience as we rode south towards Waimate, our next day's objective. Such was our evident discomfort when we stopped at a roadside café that the fire was kindled in sympathy for our shivering and bedraggled appearance. An exhausting ten-mile flog took us to Waimate, where we flopped gratefully into a warm camping cabin on the local domain.

In Maori, *waimate* means 'dirty waters'; apparently the valley of the river Waitaki, in which the town is built, was swampy until drained by the early settlers. The area round about is host to the largest number of wallabies in New Zealand, though they are not native to the country, having been brought here from Australia. The animals have thrived and in so doing, played an unwitting and self destructive part in the creation of yet another tourist industry, that of wallaby shooting. A bit of a 'one street wonder' was Waimate, but a decent pub gave us all that we needed before bedding down in our cabin bunks.

The day of April 1st dawned. For the last three days' riding we had battled against driving rain to arrive at a swamp. We had ridden 248 miles in New Zealand and in total 6,861 miles. Fools indeed, but we were happy fools and so once more set out knowing not what might befall us. But we did have a plan and we had come to the first turning point. The plan was to execute a figure of eight on the South Island, with the bottom loop of the 'eight' in the south of the island and the top loop in the north. We were just about to turn inland towards the 'waist' of the 'eight'. New Zealand is a mountainous country, as those of you who have seen 'Lord of the Rings' will know, and now we were heading towards the hills.

The steep hillsides of the Waimate Gorge crowded in on us, its slopes covered in low bush and stunted palm trees. It soon opened out into spacious pastures cutting a broad swathe through rolling hills rising to soaring, mile high mountains. An isolated schoolhouse had been converted into a café, its owner full of sadness at the recent death of her husband. It was a remote spot. Whilst we sat, no traffic passed and only one vehicle came by in the three hours it took us to reach our overnight stopping place of Kurow ('the place of many mists').

We were deep into the ranges of the Hawkdun and Kirkuston mountains. This was hunting, shooting and fishing country, Kurow being a centre for such activities. A community of five hundred souls, its main claim to fame is that it lies on the 45th parallel, exactly halfway between the equator and the South Pole. A friendly and helpful place though. The bank had no money – just think about that, would you ever find a bank in comfortable Surrey with no money? So they sent us to the garage across the road. We were given cash on our credit card, a fictitious purchase being invented to save us an interest payment. A hunting lodge provided our night's accommodation, where we were given an eight-bunk room to ourselves. We slept well that night.

We awoke to a heavy frost beneath a clear blue sky. Mountains pressed in on both sides of the sun-dappled waters of the Waitaki River. We had been climbing steadily to reach the Waitaki Dam. Completed in 1934, it was the last of the 'pick and shovel' dams and the platform for the world's first social security system. The local doc provided health care in return for the workers chipping in to a common kitty. Steeper climbing took us past the Aviemore and Benmore dams. The beauty of this mountain valley fastness seemed beyond the power of any words: literally breathtaking. Not that we had any breath left as we struggled to the 1,700-foot summit of the Ahuriri Pass. A sweeping descent took us along the southern shore of Lake Benmore, the Barrier Range of mountains in purple distance ahead. At the confluence of three valleys lay Omarama 'place of light' and our stopping place for the night.

The Lindis pass lay ahead, well over 3,000 ft and steep. Mary was concerned that we might be forced to push our loaded bicycles, an exercise that gave her much back pain. She decided to take the bus over the pass, an easy process in New Zealand, as the buses are equipped for taking bikes and just require a phone call in advance. So it was that I flogged over the pass amidst stark mountain scenery before a blood-tingling descent of twenty-five miles in less than and hour. (Well, I had to beat the bus, didn't I?) A garage, a store, tearooms and a school, the playground of which doubled as a campground – this was Tarras. The bus turned up and, reunited, we pitched our tent by the school swimming pool and spent a night of utter tranquillity.

We had entered Central Otago, the dry interior of central southern New Zealand. The sheep men came first to open up the region. Hot on their heels were the gold men and today the area thrives on the riches of its orchards, vineyards and flocks of another kind, the tourists. Bare brown hills sloped down to the shores of the blue ribbon of Lake Dunstan. Approaching the town of Cromwell, we passed the 7,000 mile mark of our journey.

Twenty years ago the building of the Dunstan River Dam left the old town of Cromwell beneath the rising waters. Built on higher ground, the new town is a somewhat dreary modern place which we soon quit to continue to the historic gold-mining town of Clyde. The old road too had vanished below the waters. The new one was a spectacular feat of engineering clinging to the steep rockbound side of the Clutha Valley. It is the most expensive per mile in the country. It seems the engineers chose to ignore the wisdom of the local folk and built the road on unstable ground which is ever propelling the road into the lake, thus costing millions of dollars in maintenance. To make matters worse the dam, towering above Clyde, is built on an earthquake fault. The design apparently makes allowances for this. Needless to say, the local residents are hoping that the engineers did a better job on the dam than they did on the road.

Clyde is an attractive place, owing its existence to the 1862 gold rush which brought ten thousand miners to this region. At the head of the Clutha valley a bronze plaque details the exploits of two miners who, in two months, gathered eighty-seven pounds of gold here. At today's value this is £0.33 million, equivalent to an annual salary of £2 million – a rich strike indeed. Stone and wooden buildings, dating back to the 1860s, still line the streets of Clyde. It seemed a place to tarry awhile.

Whilst we were pitching camp in steady rain, welcome tea and chocolate Hobnobs were produced, as if by magic, by a couple who were camped nearby. They were Bob and Janet from Christchurch. They had come to New Zealand some thirty years ago and, by double coincidence, had lived not two miles from my boyhood stamping ground on a lane named after their adopted country. Kind folk they were too, continuing to ply us with fruit and other goodies during our brief stay and inviting us to stop with them should we happen by Christchurch again.

Introducing ourselves to a nearby solo cyclist, we discovered that he had left his home country of Germany some two years ago. He had ridden some twenty thousand miles through Europe and the Middle and Far East. After New Zealand, he intended to ride from South Africa back again to Europe – all in all a three-and-a-half year journey of some thirty thousand miles. His trip made our little jaunt look like a Sunday afternoon fun ride, but he was distant and uncommunicative. We wondered if solo travel had taken its toll on his social skills.

The weather dogged our stay at Clyde. A trip to the nearby town of Alexander took place in a shroud of rain, road-flanking fruit farms and vineyards dripping moisture as we passed. The rain continued as we returned through the Clutha valley to Cromwell on our way towards Queenstown. A roadside fruit vendor displayed an amazing variety of produce, and we ate plum/apricot and peach/ nectarine hybrids topped off with chocolate peanuts.

From Cromwell the highway passes through the Kawarau Gorge. Flanked by four thousand feet high mountains, the Kawarau River falls one thousand feet in its twenty-five mile length and we were going upstream. Its rugged beauty certainly helped to divert our thoughts from a stiff climb through the gorge. At the sound source of a deafening roar of water, a dizzying viewpoint revealed the terrifying sight of 'Roaring Meg' below. 'Meg' is a set of violent rapids and through them, as we watched, shot a group of undoubtedly insane belly-board rapid riders. Apparently one 'Mad Dog Ged' started this trend back in 1985. We thought we might stick to our bicycles.

The Gorge opens out into the Gibbston Valley. Numerous vineyards line the road. Mary counted their number as thirty-one. The wine industry is big business in Central Otago, the climate hereabouts is the hottest and driest in New Zealand and is ideal for grape-growing. It was a fertile and tranquil valley, so why then the blood-curdling screams drifting on the sun-warmed breeze? Yet another roadside adrenaline trip in the form of bungee jumping from the Kawarau River Gorge Bridge. Here people, apparently voluntarily, are tied to a rope, leap into an abyss and fall at terminal velocity until stopped with a violent jerk just before certain death. This seemed another good reason for sticking to the bicycles.

We decided to stop short of Queenstown and divert to Arrowtown, another settlement founded on the prosperity brought by the 1860s' gold rush. A comfortable cabin on the town domain was to be our lodging for the night, but first an exploration of the place. Trees from Europe, the Americas and Australia have been planted all around Arrowtown. It was now early autumn and their leaves were turning to a thousand shades of russet and gold. Low sun lit the scene with a kaleidoscope of shimmering colours and original shops, houses and civic buildings from the days of the gold rush gave an attractive glimpse of the past.

The town is built on the banks of the Arrow River. This river is said to have been one of the richest sources of alluvial gold in the world and is still a site for casual panning of that precious metal. Within five years the best of the gold rush was over. By then most Europeans had left for richer pickings elsewhere so the Government invited Chinese gold miners to the area to make the best of what was left. They lived in shanties, ostracized by the local white community. Such men as Kung Hai from Mongolia remained until his death in 1922, the last Chinese settler dying in 1933. Tough gold they may have won, but they were never able to win the acceptance of the citizens of their host nation. Their village has been reconstructed and is a poignant reminder of this sad incident in the history of gold mining.

Queenstown is said to be 'the Action and Adventure Capital of the World'. The approach was certainly adventurous, for the road was narrow and busy with only an occasional hard shoulder. Spectacular views across Lake Wakatipu to the soaring snow peaks of the Remarkables Range of mountains were a constant distraction. Eight kilometres of urban development led to the centre, a throbbing nucleus of activity dedicated to the adrenalin rush. The area boasts the residence of no fewer than thirty-one still living world champions of exotic sports, ranging from sky-surfing to sheep-shearing. Glitzy sales offices hawk everything imaginable by way of contrived adventure. Approaching the crowded booking desks of these establishments needed the brute strength of a rugby international prop forward. So we gave up and cycled back to Arrowtown, dreaming of the adventures we had so narrowly missed.

The major proportion of the population of the southern half of the South Island lives in the cities of Invercargill and Dunedin. Apart from the fabled Foirdland in the west, the countryside thereabouts is mostly farmland and a large proportion of the interior is a barren, stone-covered wasteland. With this in mind we decided to hire a RV (recreational vehicle) for a week, to cover the ground through the less interesting sections and take day rides on our bikes in the choice parts.

Our first stopping place was Te Anua, standing on the shores of the lake of that name. Lake Te Anua is the largest lake in the south island and the town a sprawling resort with the splendid backdrop of the Murchison Mountains and the towering bulk of Mount Luxmore. We took a ride for a day along the eastern shore of the lake, the views of the mountains on the opposite shore whetting our appetites for the scenic wonders that local travel brochures told us we would encounter, for we were now at the gateway to Fiordland.

Scenic wonders indeed, our arrival at our next destination of Milford Sound leaving us literally stunned into an awed silence. Let the words of James Hingston, writing in 1883, do the job:

"For thousands of feet upwards the eye looks upon straight cut rocky frontages, not worn smooth by time, or by wind or water, but as sharply defined and as fresh looking in all respects as if riven asunder but yesterday by the stupendous wedges of Titanic Masons."

The next day we took a ride on a traditional schooner along the ten-mile length of the sound to its ocean mouth. In 1770 and 1773 Captain Cook sailed past the hidden entrance to Milford Sound. It was not charted for another hundred years. The upper reaches of this mysterious ocean cleft are dominated by the vast six thousand foot bulk of Mitre Peak which plummets, almost vertically, into the one thousand feet deep black depths of the fiord. It is a magnet for photographers, artists, sightseeing cruisers and rain. The region records the highest rainfall in the world, all of twenty-five feet per year. By comparison, the English county of Norfolk receives an average of twenty-five inches. This is serious rain and a pretty forbidding prospect for most tourists', hell bent on acquiring a nice holiday tan. However, according to our guide for the day, all this water just adds to the beauty of the place, producing a million cascades, swirling mists and coruscating rainbows. We had to take his word for it, for it had not rained in the area for some time and we were there on a perfect blue day. Normally huge waterfalls roar down from the mountains above, one of them five times higher than Niagara. On this day most of them had been reduced to a trickle, only three retaining any watery appeal at all.

Bare rock ribbons cut vertically down through the dense rainforest covering the mountains. These are the result of a cycle of growth and collapse taking some one hundred to one hundred and fifty years. Starting with naked rock, lichens take hold, then mosses and small plants. Bushes and trees follow, all of this living on the rich fertiliser of annual decay and all interlinked by a tangle of root systems. Eventually the whole lot becomes too heavy for its own good, one root fractures, then another and another and so on, until the forest avalanches into the waters leaving behind, you guessed it, a ribbon of bare rock.

A layer of peaty water, about thirty feet thick, floats upon the salt water of the sound and thus cutting out the light. This allows deep water species of ocean life, normally found three hundred feet deep or so, to live near the surface. You can visit this ecosystem (and we did) by taking a spiral ladder down a steel tube with windows and there wonder at gorgonians, black coral and sundry deep-water fish species of the sort not usually seen at your local 'undersea world'.

It was a fabulous trip. At the mouth of the sound we were told the nearest land to the south was Antarctica and in the other direction, a small island to the north of New Zealand called Australia. Our guide had a sense of humour, which is just as well, for in groping for a lost mooring rope when we were berthing back at the head of the sound, he fell into the sea.

Travelling south through rolling farmland, we arrived at Tuatapere, the westernmost town in New Zealand and also the self-styled sausage capital of the country. A local sausage factory apparently turns out no less than a ton of sausages a week. By my totally trivial calculations, a year's production, if laid end to end, would stretch the length of the south island of New Zealand. A scattered collection of clapboard ranch-style buildings was about the extent of Tuatapere, with a rugby ground doubling as a camping domain.

We were in search of rare wildlife and so took a day's ride around the sweeping arc of Waewae bay to a ten mile stretch of silver sand called Bluecliffs Beach. Approached by a dirt road, it was totally deserted and had the kind of magnificent beauty guaranteed to cause holiday property developers to drool into their wallets (place names have been changed to protect the environment). Such was the firmness of the sand that we were able to ride the length of the beach and we did, stopping regularly to scan the ocean for a glimpse of our quarry of the day, hectors dolphin. This is the world's rarest and smallest cetacean, found only off the coast of New Zealand and known to frequent the waters of Waewae Bay. They grow to about the size and weight of an average human being and are particularly spectacular aerial leapers, but on this day they were nowhere to be seen. However, we did make the acquaintance of a much more ubiquitous creature, the sand-fly. And the sand-fly won the day, as halting for more than thirty seconds gave these beasties all the invitation they needed to eat us alive and so we fled.

Moving eastwards along the south coast of the South Island, we came to Invercargill, the southernmost city in New Zealand. Settled in the 1850s by people from the nearby Scottish community of Dunedin, Invercargill retains its Celtic sense of identity. Whilst we had no burning desire to delve into the Scottish past of the city, it was quite impossible to ignore its manifestations in the somewhat unexpected form of men walking about in kilts and showing no embarrassment at all.

Our interest in Invercargill was in the Tuatarium in the city museum. This houses a live colony of tuatara, a throwback to the age of the dinosaurs, which looks like a lizard but isn't. As a species, the creatures are halfway between a reptile and a bird. However they are generally described as reptiles although they are very different in that they like cool weather, have three eyes and hibernate. They have lifespans of between sixty to a hundred years and a few venerable specimens are housed in their glass-fronted rainforest home in the museum. However, on the day of our visit Henry, Mildred, Lucy and Albert were not coming out to play.

We thought we had seen the last of Invercargill but on the way to Dunedin our RV broke down. Almost a day's bike ride to the nearest farmhouse to use the phone brought a rescuing mechanic. However, when he arrived he was unable to repair the vehicle and we were towed back to Invercargill to await the delivery of a replacement. This came on the back of a lorry the next day and carried us safely to Dunedin.

Dunedin was established by Scottish immigrants in 1848. It is New Zealand's oldest city and one of the grandest, with many fine Victorian and Edwardian buildings and splendidly set in the arc of a sweeping crescent of hills. The Presbyterian Scottish origins of the city are today swept by 21st century winds of change. The Doric-columned magnificence of a former bank is now a strip club and the variety of the city's shops and restaurants are a testimony to multi-ethnicity. The city's Baldwin Street, at a slope of thirty-eight degrees, is said to be the world's steepest. Needless to say, it had to be tackled on our bikes but we might as well have attempted the north face of the Eiger. It was quite beyond our capabilities so we set out to ride the twenty-mile length of the Otago Peninsula to the east of the city.

The peninsula road clung ingeniously to the side of steep rocky slopes arcing down to the turquoise waters of the Otago Harbour. Sheltered inlets held scattered mosaics of moored sailing craft whilst islets of golden sand appeared to float in the blue offshore distance. We stopped to marvel at the sight of a yellow-eyed penguin darting hither and thither beneath the clear water in search of a fish dinner. At the end of the road the windswept heights of Taiaora Head reared above the marching waves of the Pacific Ocean. In 1885, this remote headland was fortified against Tzarist Russia. Unbelievably, it seems someone considered the Russians a threat at the time. Today it is home to the only mainland colony of breeding royal albatross in the world and as such, enough of a tourist magnet to bring in the crowds and drive us down from the headland to the refuge of the nearby Pilots Beach. We were not the only ones to shelter from the tourist hordes in this secluded haven. Languishing on the beach there was a small group of southern fur seals, quite unconcerned by our presence and hauling out of the sea to rest within touching distance. One, a bit of an acrobat, attempted to mount Mary's bike. Another, clearly a bit of a show-off, posed for photographs, right and left profiles and simpering full frontal in the manner of any self-adoring fashion diva. He or she then spoilt it a bit by farting loud and long, at which we quickly headed for our bikes and the clear air of Dunedin.

We were now heading back to the 'waist' of our planned 'figure of eight' route in the south island. Wuthering Heights had nothing on the rock-strewn and unpopulated country which took us through the Umbrella and Knobby ranges of mountains to Alexander and on once again to Queenstown. From there, back on our loaded bicycles, we rode in a downstream direction, returning through the Kawarau Gorge to Cromwell, this time to stay for the night in a student hostel cabin.

The early morning light of a low sun fashioned diamonds in the frost-painted trees of an Otago dawn. We were riding north along the western shore of Lake Dunstan. Across its dark waters we could see the white snake of road we had ridden south some two weeks ago. All around us were vineyards and orchards. The vines heavy with soon to be picked grapes, the fruit trees denuded of their crop. We were riding to Wanaka, passing on the way through the scattered settlements of Queensberry and Luggate. A dazzling white clapboard church with a bright blue tin roof stood by the roadside. Its spire formed a vertical pointer to sky-divers, spinning earthwards from above as we came to our destination of the day.

Wanaka is another centre for those addicted to the adrenaline rush but claims to supply its thrills more sedately. Certainly the pumped-up atmosphere of Queenstown was not so much in evidence here although a 'Lord of the Rings Bus Tour' would surely satisfy the cravings of the most hardened thrill seekers. Child-laden pedal boats splashed around the margins of the eponymous Lake Wanaka whilst parents watched reclining on shoreline lawns. Southward across the lake, smooth and rounded hills drew the eye to the ten thousand foot heights of the snow-capped Mount Aspiring. It seemed to be a place for relaxation but this was not to be. Our night on the local camping domain was to be rendered sleepless by carousing fellow campers. In the morning a young man, unsympathetic to this crowd, told us they were "shit-head petrol-heads", in the locality to charge about the hills in four-wheel drive vehicles. A bad night and a cold one, the inner skin of our tent was covered in a layer of ice in the morning as we shivered to pack up and take to the road.

It was one of those "buggered if I know" starts to the day as we pedalled uphill out of town to take the highway north between the glaciated valleys of Lake Wanaka and Lake Hawea. It was not long before the road levelled out and the sun climbed higher in the sky of a magnificent blue day. As the sun rose, so did our spirits and soon we were bowling along, the misery of the previous night quite forgotten. We were riding the western shore of Lake Hawea, its cobalt blue waters framed by the soaring peaks of six thousand foot high mountains. A one thousand four hundred foot high shoulder of land had to be crossed before we could descend back to the shores of Lake Wanaka. A viewpoint gave us the opportunity to chat with a couple of Aussie truckers on a bus-man's holiday. They were enjoying the sedate driving in New Zealand, a welcome release, they told us, from the amphetamine-fuelled turmoil of their working lives. A quartet of our compatriots from Berkshire arrived, and it gave them such pleasure to patronise us.

A comfortable descent to Lake Wanaka and an easy ride northward along its eastern shore took us to Makarora, the extent of which was an airstrip, souvenir and supplies shops and campground. This was a damp place, mist swirled around afforested hills and there was an unfamiliar lushness about the local vegetation. We were approaching the rainforests of the west coast, just one mountain pass stood between us and a landscape dominated by the power of water-laden winds blowing from the far reaches of the great southern ocean.

The Haast Pass, at 1,847 feet, is the lowest route over the 'main divide' of New Zealand's Southern Alps. Until 1922 it was a bridleway, the present highway only receiving a coat of tarmac in the early 1990s. In the fifty-five miles between Makarora and the town of Haast there are no settlements. It is then a remote place and tough to ride on a loaded bicycle. The ascent was hard and the descent awkward, with diagonally placed animal barriers and many ominous gravel traps for runaway vehicles. Flashing past lush rainforest, cut through by roaring glacial torrents, we emerged onto easier ground to pass by the mouth of a broad valley, the soaring snow-peak of Mount Cook standing sentinel its head. At 12,300 feet, it is the highest mountain in the country. Riding now in the valley of the Haast River, we came to the town of that name.

Haast is split into three bits: the township, the junction and the beach. The landscape's roundabouts are a mixture of rainforest, sand dunes and shingle beaches. We found a backpackers' hostel in the township. The owner 'Ollie' was busy meeting and greeting and the place was almost full but he found us a closet and a slab of foam rubber to place on the floor. Ollie had a colourful vocabulary, describing the keeper of a hostel next door as a "fucking tosser". We were to leave the next day to the continuing strains of Ollie cheerfully cursing all and sundry.

Crossing the Haast River on Highway 6, we plunged into dense rainforest. A riot of trees, ferns, creepers, mosses and lichens surrounded us. Plant architecture beyond the imagination formed a richly embroidered canopy of a thousand shades of verdant green. A five hundred foot climb took us to a coastal lookout with a south-westerly prospect towards the faraway continent of Antarctica. At Lake Paringa we pitched our tent for the night in the grounds of a motor-camp and dined on a takeaway from the camp café.

The countryside hereabouts is home to the kiwi, the national emblem of New Zealand and a quite extraordinary bird. Often described as an 'honorary mammal', it has hair-like feathers, heavy bones and external nostrils, giving it a keen sense of smell. It is a nocturnal bird, living in burrows and about the size of a chicken but, poor thing; it lays an egg as big as that of an ostrich. They are not rare yet few New Zealanders have ever seen one and neither did we, despite hanging hopefully around the local rainforest as darkness fell that night.

The next day we laboured to cross the shoulders of the Fox and Franz Josef Glaciers. Both glaciers have their attendant townships, neither of which would exist were it not for the tourist industry. Guided glacier walks, scenic flights by helicopter and light plane, exploration trips, kayak safaris, wildlife tours and many more – all were available here and the streets lined with bucket shops selling their wares. We settled for a rainforest campground on the edge of the township of Franz Josef, there to arrange a helicopter flight over the summit of Mount Cook. It was not to be, for the west coast weather intervened, a steady rain set in and, after a two-day wait, we gave up.

As we rode north the rain began to relent, leaving the Mount Cook Range clothed in vestments of billowing white cloud. On this occasion, as close as we would get, but the ethereal beauty of this scene haunts us still. A climb of six hundred feet took us over the flank of Mount Hercules then gave us an easy freewheel into the township of Harihari – one street, a pub and a motel with cyclists' cabins at $40 a night (about £15).

The following day a light tail-wind took us past peaceful Lake Ianthe and on to the settlement of Pukekurg. Here the 'Bushman's Café' displayed a giant plastic sand fly to remind all of a potent local hazard. Across the road there stood a pub, a busload of backpackers heading for the bar. The name of this establishment, perhaps prophetically, was the 'Puke Inn'. Halting for lunch, we were joined by two cyclists from Baslow in Derbyshire. Having backpacked in South America, they had flown to New Zealand, purchased bikes and gear and were riding happily towards the coming winter of the south. They were hardy souls indeed. At Ross we stopped for coffee. In 1907, the largest gold nugget ever found in New Zealand was discovered near to the township. Weighing in at ninety-nine ounces it has been named 'The Honourable Roddy' and today graces a hall of Buckingham Palace as a table decoration. There is still gold hereabouts; the only open cast alluvial gold-mine in the country still operates at Ross.

Hokitika was our next stopping place, a township where craft shops, full of greenstone trinkets, lay thick on the ground. Our next objective was Greymouth, the home town of two friends of Jimmy of Christchurch and with whom we hoped to stay. On arrival, a quick phone call, a set of directions and we soon found the house of our hosts, Ben and Grace, there to receive the warmest of welcomes.

Ben, an American, had little affection for the country of his birth. A mining engineer, he had moved into farming in Zimbabwe but had been dispossessed of his farm and had come to New Zealand to join up with his partner Grace, who is Irish and had been teaching in Africa when the couple met. She now teaches in a local school and Ben seemed to be the local odd-job man. This was their first venture into joint domesticity, despite having known each other for many years. We were to stay for a couple of days with these worldly and kind people, there to give our legs a rest, and our hearts and minds to exchange the gifts of friendship.

It is said of Greymouth that it is 'grey by name and grey by nature'. This is probably because the west coast rain doesn't often allow the township to be seen in sunshine. A cluster of central shops, a cinema, a bank and a few eating houses, it didn't seem too bad to us but it did bring us problematical news. An email from Mary's son announced the sudden ending of his long-term partnership, and his forthcoming marriage, in Sri Lanka, to his new partner, whom he had known for some six weeks. Mary, a profoundly committed parent, was presented with a deep dilemma: to complete our journey or fly back halfway around the world, the timing and logistics of which meant that she would not cycle across the whole of Canada as planned. She was to wrestle with this agonizing decision for some weeks to come.

Sunshine was to lighten our time in Greymouth. Ben lent us his four-by-four and we set out to do the touristy thing. First was a trip to a reconstructed gold town called Shantytown and beautifully done it was too. There amidst the rainforest stood a recreated pioneer town of the 1880s' gold rush. There were period buildings, rail track and operational gold workings and the opportunity to pan a few specks of gold. Perhaps the gold panning was a little contrived, for the gravel used was laced with the precious metal. No matter, we had gold fever.

Ben, recognising the madness in our eyes, sent us off the next day with all his gold fossicking gear to a remote, and definitely not contrived, river site hidden deep in the rainforest. So it was that, burdened down with picks and shovels, sieves and pans, we laboured in a remote river bed to make our fortunes. Hours later, our backs racked with pain, we were cured of the fever. A single speck of gold was all we had to show for our efforts, but we did own the riches of an unforgettable experience.

It was time to leave Greymouth; a notorious local wind called 'The Barber' carried a cascade of cloud, like an avalanche of snow, flowing from the hills inland to the beaches below. It was a cold uphill slog until the countryside levelled out to take us easily to the township of Reefton. This was the first town ever in the southern hemisphere to have its own electricity, supplied by a local hydro-electric scheme. A gradual downward incline for twenty miles took us to the tiny settlement of Inangahua Junction. Little more than a convenience store, a couple of farmhouses and a splendid farm backpackers hostel which was to be our exclusive accommodation for the night. Mary was appointed milkmaid but might have achieved more production by squeezing a stick of rhubarb.

A tranquil night saw us receive a cheery morning greeting from the farmer's wife, who brought with her our breakfast of muesli (and fresh milk). Riding north-easterly on Highway 6 we threaded our way through dark, mist shrouded mountains, their summits seeming to float above swirling garlands of cloud. Squalls of rain drove past as we climbed through the Upper Buller Gorge. Surrounding peaks swam in and out of our vision as though a giant celestial hand was attempting to bring them into focus. We passed the forest covered site of an earthquake which, in 1898, destroyed the township of Lyell taking many lives. Reaching the town of Murchison we decamped for the night to a holiday park cabin.

We were heading towards the north coast of the South Island with one hundred miles of sparsely inhabited mountainous terrain between us and the City of Nelson. In addition there was the two thousand, one hundred foot height of Hope Saddle to climb. This was a lot for us to cover in a day but there was no indication of any accommodation along the way. We would have to take pot luck. Our spirits were low, the climbing was relentless and the landscape about us obscured by the grey curtains of a merciless rain. This was not a day for travelling with the possibility of no bed for the night.

At thirty-five miles a farm hostel stood by the roadside. It was closed for refurbishment but sounds of activity came from within. Bedraggled and cold, we rang the bell and were received with unhesitating hospitality. We were given an unfinished bunk-room for the night and invited to use the family's own cooking facilities. Later, more cyclists turned up and were accommodated in a tent on the lawn. These were a young couple from France, one pulling a trailer in which rode their three-year-old son. They had been travelling for two years, with eighteen months to go. The family gave us a sense of unease. The parents seemed driven, their infant son deprived of the company of his peers, drawn along in a capsule of friendless instability.

More rain, dense fog and unremitting climbing were to be our lot the next day. Enveloped in mist, we might have been traversing any mountain range in the world until we sped downwards and broke out of the cloud to roll easily into the port of Richmond. A winding bike path took us along the shore of Tasman Bay, the limpid ochre glow of an evening sun adding drama to a magnificent vista of mountains across broad waters. At Nelson we found our way to the 'Green Monkey' Backpackers' Hostel, there to be greeted by the English proprietors, Charley and his partner Di – jolly souls both and full of helpful information about the area, this leading to Di booking a place for me on a kayaking expedition along the shores of the Abel Tasman National Park. We were then ferried to a recommended Thai restaurant, there to eat a splendid meal. How quickly forgotten were the trials and tribulations of the previous few days.

Nelson lays claim to being the driest place in New Zealand. Mountains shelter the city giving a climate in the Mediterranean style, thus enabling the cultivation of olives, citrus fruits and the inevitable grapes. A large community of artists lives here. They support a café society almost reminiscent of Monmatre but without the moustaches. Clean cut activity dudes stalk the streets with thousand mile stares on their faces and everywhere the sweet smell of the tourist dollar. It is the gateway to the Abel Tasman National Park. 22,500 hectares of upland wilderness and tomorrow I was to canoe its wild coastline.

Six-thirty am, and a minibus to Motueka, where the voyage was due to commence. I was teamed with Brunhilde, a young Dutch woman and a prime example of the horizontally challenged. She and I clambered into a tandem kayak of long and slim proportions, not easy for Brunhilde, and were instructed to follow our guide for the day. Easier said than done, for Brunhilde was supposed to be operating the foot steering but seemed to be something of a slow learner. Round in circles we went as the rest of our party disappeared into the distance. Eventually beginning to get the idea, Brunhilde then decided that she wanted to talk about sex. Not in any suggestive way, you understand, but rather from an academic point of view. Tandem kayaking is perhaps not the ideal forum for such a discussion, the dramatic coastline, the languidly waving fin of a sunfish and the occasional passing dolphin being much more to my taste.

Well, somehow we made it to our lunch spot, a devastatingly beautiful crescent of beach with a golden halo of sand adorning the emerald waters of a tranquil bay. Here we played frisbee and ate Pavlova. This, unbeknown to us, had been hidden beneath the deck of our kayak. Just as well we hadn't run on the rocks and sunk! Twenty odd kilometres and we came to a broad bay. Here there were log cabins on the beach and just offshore, a floating backpacker's houseboat, complete with bar. Brunhilde was beside herself with excitement for she was staying the night and hopeful of turning academic issues into real ones. It was with some relief that I boarded the speedboat back to our starting point, but also with great delight at the experience of a never-to-be-forgotten day.

Whangamoa Saddle, a lung-bursting climb of one thousand three hundred feet followed by a plunge back to sea level before another climb of eight hundred feet over Rai Saddle. This was proving to be a tough day and I was tackling it alone, as Mary had opted for the bus. Her morale was low and her motivation drained as she struggled to choose between loyalty to her family and commitment to our journey. Following the mountainous section, I too hopped on the bus to complete the last few miles of this day's travel along the coastal flats. Darkness was falling when we arrived at our destination of Picton, there to keep what was for us a deeply significant rendezvous.

At Arras, in Northern France and just two days and ninety miles into our journey, we had met Peter and Jane. Now, over ten months and eight thousand miles later, we had reached their home town. During this time we had made an inner journey from self-doubt to self-belief; now the value of friendships was to be reaffirmed and with luck we would enjoy the luxuries of a bath and a bed. And we did, but not before an evening of excited swapping of travel stories.

Picton is the service centre for visiting yachties and the home of our friends was built on a hillside overlooking the yacht harbour. Like many of the homes we had visited in the Antipodes, it was of timber construction with utilities and bedrooms on the lower floor and daytime living space above. A spacious glass fronted lounge opened out onto elevated wooden decking, giving a splendid view of the harbour below. It seemed to us to be a very practical and comfortable arrangement and here comes the really impressive bit: it had been constructed from a kit, single-handed, by Peter.

Peter and Jane, although retired, were working at the local green mussel plant for a few extra dollars, so we had the day to ourselves. Picton stands at the head of Queen Charlotte sound, part of a labyrinth of waterways known as the Malborough Sounds, one thousand miles of bays, inlets and richly afforested hills. Many of its small communities have no road access. Goods, supplies, post and people, all travel by water and we were taking a trip on the delivery boat, a chugging diesel craft about the size of a corporation mini-bus. Most of the settlements visited were geared to tourism in a restrained 'outdoorsy' manner and many others little more than a few 'batches' (holiday homes). Fifty miles of cruising took us to the mouth of the sound and Ship Cove. Here Captain Cook landed on four occasions in the 1770s. Vegetables were grown and pigs reared to provide snacks for the crew, turning the cove into a veritable home from home. On the way back we chugged into Resolution Bay and Endeavour Inlet. Cosily sheltered by tree covered hills, you could easily see why an early ocean explorer would name them after his ships, and certainly admire his skill in navigating this watery maze.

It was a day to remember and an evening never to forget, with a riotous pub session and sad farewells, for our hosts were off to work at the crack of dawn and we were off to catch the ferry to the North Island and the capital city of Wellington.

CHAPTER ELEVEN
TWO GEEZERS TO THE GEYSERS

The month of May was passing by and our time in New Zealand was limited by the need to reach Canada and cross its 4,500 mile width before winter set in. We had made a couple of hard decisions. We had by now ridden 1,380 miles in the South Island. Christchurch lay 150 miles to the south. It would not be possible to ride this distance to complete our planned 'figure of eight' and our time spent on the North Island would have to be limited to a few selected areas. We were not too disappointed, as word on the travellers' grapevine was that the North Island did not match the pedaller's paradise of the south. These limitations could not dampen our excitement as the ferry from Picton crossed the Cook Straits to enter the broad expanse of Wellington harbour, heading for the capital city.

New Zealand has a population of four million. Two thirds of them live in the North Island and it might therefore be expected that a fair proportion of them would be living in the capital. This is not the case; most folk live in the Auckland region in the north, just one third of a million live in Wellington and hardly anyone more than three kilometres from the sea. It is a compact place and looked it, with dark hills seeming to herd the city buildings towards the waiting shoreline.

We must have looked bemused standing on the dockside, for a sports car drew to a halt beside us and out stepped John from Northampton, cultured and urbane and a resident of New Zealand for some thirty years. He gave us directions to the information centre and sent us there by the waterfront scenic route. Wooden staging a bit like a zoo penguin run took us past the occasional museum and art gallery and across an elegant square to our objective. Helpful staff soon found us a room for the night at the local YHA. They too were pleased to assist and arranged a bus ride for us to leave the next day for the township of Stratford, on the western side of the island.

The bus left early and so it was that we visited the capital city of New Zealand but saw very little of it. We were heading for the region of Mount Taranaki, a dormant volcano eight thousand feet high, there to circle the mountain in a ride of three or four days. As we approached, the vast bulk of Taranaki reared mistily skyward, a plume of cloud streaming downwind and a white lace collar of snow encircling the summit. The bus dropped us in the shadow of the icon of the district, the mock Tudor clock tower of Stratford. The streets, as we rode them, had such names as Romeo, Juliet, Cordelia, Portia and Hamlet. In fact sixty-seven streets in Stratford pay homage to twenty-seven of the bard's plays, one of those quaint statistics which perhaps says as much about Stratford as anyone needs to know. On second thoughts, it was still preferable to its money-grubbing counterpart in England.

The city of New Plymouth was our next destination and soon attained after thirty miles of easy riding through the rolling green pastures of cattle and sheep country. It is the west coast's only deep water port, with an attractive waterfront and neat grid of central streets. The foremost of these is Devon Street, a collection of shops and cafés known as the 'Devon Mile'. We were soon established at the 'Shoestring Backpackers', the prices fully living up to the name and our room good enough. We had read of 'Pukekura Park', first opened in 1876 and reputedly having the finest gardens in the country. On the way there, chatting with a young aboriginal man, we learnt of his relief that the actor Tom Cruise has just quit the city after making the film 'The last Samurai'.

"At laarst the bladdy prysus are bick ter norrmul!" he celebrated

The park gardens fully lived up to their reputation. There were moist fern plantations and woodland bog gardens surrounded by banks of camellias, rhododendrons, azaleas, pinetum, aloes and many more. A puriri tree, over two thousand years old, stood close by a three hundred foot high ginkgo tree and in a clearing, an aviary where free-flying parrots, parakeets, lorikeets and other such members of the avian species, flew kamikaze missions around our heads. The *pièce-de-résistance* was a tree-shaded lake with a visitor operated fountain. In 1954, in great tribute to the locality, Queen Elizabeth and Prince Phillip came all the way here just to switch it on.

Strenuous undulations in the highway and a crossed head-wind hampered our progress the next day as we headed south, now on the western side of mount Taranaki and following the coastline. The peak itself was shrouded in rainstorms; you have doubtless heard it before. "If you can see it, it's going to rain, if you can't, its already raining" and it was. Approaching a place called Opunake we spotted a conglomeration of huge steel tanks amidst a forest of pipe work. A short diversion and we came to the Maui Gas and Oilfield Terminal. A helicopter landed nearby and the pilot obligingly took us into a visitor centre where an astounding scale model of the plant and rigs and a video docu-speak enlightened us. The Taranki Basin, twenty-five miles offshore, has been the site of gas and oil exploration since the 1960s and now accounts for most of New Zealand's oil and gas production. It could soon be depleted but the oil giants are there drilling frantically for there is thought to be more and the country needs it.

At Opunake we were soon ensconced in a rusting relic of a caravan on the local, somewhat rundown, holiday park. On the beach we conducted a research project into the phenomenon of one-legged seagulls. Only eight out of twenty-seven of the local population had two legs. No competition at all for the members of the town surf-club, who were holding a celebration, rendering most of them legless. However, they could still sing and this, along with the drumming of heavy rain on the roof of our rusty refuge, did not make for a good night's sleep.

In the morning, tired and a little low in spirits, we gave up on our circuit of Taranaki, still invisible, and continued south along the aptly named 'surf highway'. The road parallels a coastline of exceptional surf beaches and a strong wind was whipping up a dramatically breaking sea and speeding us southwards. The township of Manaia allowed us a coffee stop and a chance to admire gigantic plastic models of bread loaves, apparently celebrating the place as the 'Bread Capital of South Taranaki'. Twenty-five miles per hour cruising in a howling tail-wind carried us rapidly to Hawera from whence we planned to take the bus the next day to the central volcanic area of the North Island.

Hawera was something of a backpacker's way station and even laid on the odd activity or two. Dam Dropping was one of them (sliding down the concrete face of a dam on a plank) and if that became too much then there was always the Elvis Presley Memorial Room to visit. Two thousand records and memorabilia of 'the King' are collected together here.

We were en route by bus to Turangi and crossing the Central Volcanic Plateau on Highway 1, called by the bus driver 'the desert road'. Aptly named, for there was little to be seen but vast tracts of lifeless volcanic ash, with just the occasional tussocks of grass and patches of heather, clinging to life. Cloud capped peaks to the west of the road were the volcanoes of the Tongariro National Park. Two of them, Ruapehu and Ngauruhoe, are the most active of their type in the world, Ruapehu having erupted in 1995 and again in 1996. Eventually the highway descended into Turangi, a township of but forty years standing and a burgeoning centre for mountain activities as well as the self-styled 'Trout Fishing Capital of the World'. Turangi lies at the southern end of Lake Taupo, an inland sea created in 181 AD by the world's biggest ever volcanic eruption and Australasia's biggest lake. This was landscape on a grand scale and tomorrow we would be riding the shores of this vast tract of water.

The nine thousand feet heights of the snow-capped summit of Mount Ruapehu seemed to float in the sky above the blue waters of the lake as we rode north the next day. Wind-whispering pine forest clothed the countryside to the east, whilst wavelets chuckled on the lakeshore stones and the sun shone kindly from a cloudless azure sky. Drifting effortlessly along the highway in a cyclist's balmy reverie, we savoured a passage of pure enchantment to Taupo.

Taupo did not disappoint, with a stylish lakeside and an easily accessed grid of shopping streets with many eating houses and pubs. We were soon settled in at the YHA and began seeking to explore further the intriguing geothermal landscape of this region.

Our budget did not run to a scenic flight into volcanic craters so we settled for a bike ride to the nearby 'Craters of the Moon', these having the irresistible attraction of free entry. Worth every penny, when we eventually found them after a grinding uphill bike ride. There, hidden in the forest, we were allowed to wander in the bowels of a simmering amphitheatre of boiling mud-pools, hissing fumaroles and belching steam vents, all lit by the lurid glow of the late afternoon sun and stinking to high heaven. It was a visit that would linger in our minds and nostrils for a long time to come.

A freezing fog cloaked the pine forest and chilled our bones as we rode towards Rotorua. A passing motorist stopped to warn us of the danger of riding in such conditions but there was little more that we could do for we were wearing our bright yellow overtops and had clipped flashing red rear lights to our cycle panniers. Grim cycling indeed until we reached the small settlement of Reparoa where a convenience store cum café furnished us with a late breakfast of bacon and egg butties, washed down with steaming hot coffee. A weak sun began to burn off the fog as we continued and revealed a surrounding landscape of verdant cattle meadows, scattered clumps of vegetation and meandering streams. A rural idyll but with a difference, for the streams were steaming hot and rich clumps of vegetation indicated the presence of seething fumaroles. A brooding sense of deep down elemental forces pervaded the air and grew ever stronger as we rode into Rotorua, a township steeped in the sulphurous smell of its many spewing vents and geysers. Our home for a couple of nights was the Spa Lodge Backpackers, where the energy of the core of the earth was harnessed to provide a steaming hot spa pool, Nirvana to a weary cycle traveller

After a day of rest in Rotorua, servicing our bicycles and our bodies, we caught the bus to Mangapere, a southern suburb of Auckland. Our quarters for a couple of nights were a backpacker's lodge with a regime so controlling that we quickly christened the place 'Colditz'. It was our intention whilst we were here to find the airport and sort out conditions for the shipping of our bicycles. We would then explore an area north of Auckland imaginatively called 'Northland', before returning and flying out to Canada. Well, the best laid plans, for although we found the airport, the information we required was much more difficult to come by. Do we box the bicycles or don't we? If we do, where do we find boxes and how do we get them to the airport and so on?

We escaped from 'Colditz' to the Queen Street Backpackers, commonly abbreviated to the QSB. Now located in the centre of the city, we hoped our problem solving would become a little easier. But not so. Seemingly endless shipping hassles continued, by now we both had steaming colds and an unyielding rain was falling. Eventually we made some progress but the effort required had sapped our motivation to explore New Zealand any further. We just wanted to get out and Air New Zealand were able to oblige by bringing forward the date of our flights by a few days to the 22nd of May.

Our stay in Auckland was not all self-pitying doom and gloom. Occasionally the sun shone and we were able to visit the harbour area where smart cafés, restaurants and knick-knack shops lined the very quayside where the French Secret Service blew up the Green Peace Warrior. The City Museum had a spectacular collection of Maori artefacts but also a seriously naff performance of Maori folk dance and music. The high spot was an evening's ride up the Sky Tower, a slender concrete construction, one thousand feet tall. From its dizzy heights, the terminally insane could overdose on adrenaline with a bungee jump. Quite sufficiently thrilling for me was to stand jelly-legged upon a glass-floored observation gallery, sweating with fear whilst Mary remained the very epitome of cool. Perhaps we were not in our most positive frames of mind to enjoy to the full the delights of 'The City of Sails'. Our focus was the city of Vancouver, the western gateway to the vast country of Canada.

CHAPTER TWELVE
THE ROCKIE ROAD TO THE PARTING OF THE WAYS

We were taken to the airport by minibus, our boxed bicycles in a towed trailer. It was still raining, the driver was grumpy and so were we, for our colds persisted and our spirits were low. For the very first time in our journey we did not feel charged with excited anticipation at the prospect of entering a new country. The journey across the Pacific Ocean promised to be an arduous one, for the whole trip would take some twenty-four hours and necessitated a change of aircraft at Los Angeles. Well at least we would pay a flying visit to The United States of America.

The passage through Los Angeles Airport was chaotic. America was deep in the throes of coming to terms with 9/11. Security procedures, although appearing to be effective, were far from slick. There was no holding in transit. Passengers went through the full disembarkation procedure, even though not formally entering America and there then followed the complete boarding procedure. Packing and unpacking boxed bicycles, panniers and undergoing searches, was a demanding business and at one point quite worrying for Mary. She was taken to one side by a female airport official who disappeared to return with one of those kidney bowls associated with an internal search. Fortunately she was spared. However, the tense atmosphere in the airport had rubbed off on us, only to be relieved when the dramatic landscape below was revealed through the window of our aircraft to Vancouver.

Great mountain ranges with processions of ragged brown peaks, resembling the scaly backs of giant lizards, stretched to the North and South. To the East a vast expanse of trackless wilderness bore the random, dirty white stains of salt pans, like fungus on old leather, whilst from above a blazing sun appeared to drain all life from the surface of the earth below. It was the Great Central American Basin Desert which, unbeknown to us, stretched a long withered arm into the Canadian Rockies, the burning finger of which would later point our way through their mountain fastness.

Our first day and night in Vancouver were spent in our bed at The Village Backpackers. Our colds were still troublesome and our body clocks woefully awry. Later, feeling better, we ventured out. Our accommodation was situated in a street of strip joints, porn shops and sleazy bars. All sorts of dodgy-looking people lurked in dark corners and beggars lay thick on the ground. A guide book, with delicate discretion, described this region as 'an unfortunate area of the city'. Sleaze we had expected, for this seems to be a feature of all cities, but not the beggars. Our vision of Canada was of a country with very little poverty or homelessness. We were to learn that social problems of this sort are all but restricted to the Vancouver area and the reason is the weather. Warmed by the Pacific Ocean, this region of Canada does not have the cold winters experienced throughout most of the country. Winters of fifty below are simply not conducive to living on the street.

Not ten minutes' walk from this area is the heart of the city, a neat grid of boulevards where stand elegant sky-scrapers, stylish shopping malls, cafés, restaurants, chic boutiques and banks. Many of the downtown buildings are heated by an underground system of steam pipes. In the somewhat prosaically named district of Gastown, these pipes are put to the appealing use of powering a steam clock. Steel balls are raised by steam to the head of the clock and dumped on a chain, which is driven downward by the weight of the balls and so turns the hands of the clock. Constructed in the style of a grandfather clock, about twelve feet high, it stands on the sidewalk belching steam and simpering magnificently for the cameras of the tourists.

Downtown Vancouver and the major precincts are situated on a peninsula. Water surrounds the city on three sides whilst the Coastal Mountains form an imposing landward backdrop to the city-scape. We found it an easy place in which to meander and soon procured maps and guides for route planning.

We would not, however, be crossing Canada together. After much agonising thought, Mary had decided to attend her son's wedding in Sri Lanka. But there was a month left before she needed to leave, which left time for us to cross the Rocky Mountains, after which Mary would depart from Calgary and I would continue the journey alone. Neither one of us could find words to express the mixture of emotions we both felt at our impending parting. We had shared a multitude of joys and a few sorrows on our quest to reach Canada. This was to have been the final leg of our journey and soon we would be together no more. Sadness consumed us but an email from our cycling friends in Australia did the trick:

"Your son's wedding will happen but once whereas Canada will be there for a long time to come."

Some kindly cyber-counselling and all was OK. We would have a good crack at the Rockies together and let the future take care of itself.

Route planning had taken us all of five minutes, for there are very few alternatives available for crossing Canada by road and for much of the way just one single option, that of the 'Trans Canadian Highway'. It is the world's longest highway, effectively the country's main street and, from coast to coast, stretching some four thousand and five hundred miles.

Leaving Vancouver, we rode the Fraser River Canyon. At first the valley was broad and flat, the river alongside was a mile wide and host to many rafts of floating logs. Sawmills lined the shore, their activities lacing the air with the fresh clean odours of pine and spruce. The riding was made easy with very little in the way of gradients, a broad shoulder to the highway and 'saintly' truck drivers. Slowly the mountains began to close in around us. Stopping at a roadside store for coffee we chatted with the owner and other coffee drinkers. Stories were told. We heard of elk, blocking the road, their horns wider than a four by four. Tales were related with relish, of campers (like us), their food devoured by marauding chipmunks and racoons and, just occasionally, a raiding bear. We were advised not to store provisions in our tent but to hang them on a rope in a tree. Even allowing for a degree of line shooting, cycle touring in Canada was clearly a little more hazardous than anywhere we

166

had yet experienced. Here the power lay with the animals. It was their territory and we would pass safely through only by affording them respect.

Approaching our objective of the day, a roadside hoarding announced the township of Hope as the 'Chainsaw Carving Capital of Canada'. This seemed to hint at an even greater prospect of danger than marauding bears. But no, this peaceful mountain township turned out to be graced with street decorations of a unique kind. Huge wooden statues of bears, an eagle, pumas and many others, all were carved with unbelievable intricacy, using nothing more than a chainsaw. Hope was once a thriving fur trade and gold-rush Township but now stands sleepily on the shores of the Fraser River. Rising to the south are the snow-capped Cascade Mountains and to the north stand the rugged peaks of the Coastal Mountains. With stories of wildlife raiders in our minds we decided to forgo the local campground and settled for a room in a cheap and cheerful motel.

The Trans Canadian Highway was not the only form of arterial transport used in this region. The Fraser River alongside is the longest in the province of British Columbia. It rises near to Mount Robson on the Alberta border and flows for some one thousand miles to the Pacific Ocean. It was the main means of transportation for the Hudson Bay Company until the mid 19th century gold rush motivated the building of a road. And what a road it is today. Its course follows the river gorge above roaring waters, it clings to the valley sides, here and there plunging in tunnels through mountain buttresses and dizzily skirting the headwalls of rock-bound subsidiary canyons. The tunnels were well lit with designated paths for cyclists and pedestrians. Safe but alarming, for the echoing noise of passing trucks was deafening and together with the pounding rush of their bow-waves of air, combined to create a very intimidating atmosphere. A long one thousand foot climb took us to Hell's Gate summit, so named because of its proximity to a thirty yard wide defile, through which the Fraser River hurls three times the amount of water passing over the Niagara Falls. A cable car lowers visitors to view what the brochures describe as an 'awesome sight'. Perhaps so, but by now we had learned to take 'brochure speak' with a pinch of salt and therefore decided to give Hell's Gate a miss.

Resting at the roadside, we met a young woman from the island of Jersey. Travelling with her was a recently acquired companion, an uncommunicative man from Germany. Dismissing her friend, she told us her story. She had left her home two years before and had since cycled across Europe, Thailand, India and Laos. America followed, where she had worked to raise money to finance her trip, but her employer had welshed on her wages. She seemed to be deeply disillusioned with the US of A and so had opted to cross Canada – and all on $10 a day. It was a very limited budget, necessitating wild camping and only the barest minimum of food. She seemed to be a very resilient young woman indeed.

It was all downhill to the Township of Brandon. Whilst shopping for food we met yet more Trans Canadian Cyclists. Two men from Toronto, they were riding lightweight touring bicycles and towing sleek 'Bob-Yak' trailers. They were in a hurry, planning to ride the four thousand miles or so to Newfoundland in two months. When not riding bicycles, they were driving dog-sleds, making their living from teaching their skills to others whilst escorting them through wilderness areas, of which Canada has plenty.

We were entering the area where the Great Basin Desert extends a long finger into Canada. Local topography is responsible for this. An interior dry belt lies on the landward side of the Coastal Mountains which collect all the rain carried by the Pacific Winds, leaving warm dry air to descend into the valleys inland. Locals affectionately refer to it as the 'Pocket Desert', the only desert in Canada. The highway was now traversing hot and arid country and the going was hard. Two climbs, in the region of a thousand feet took us across the flank of Jackass Mountain. At a viewpoint a group of passing women told us it was so named because its steep and rough terrain had caused many deaths by falling of pack-asses belonging to early prospectors, bound north in search of Klondike gold. Far below, another form of Trans Canadian Transport was travelling north, a freight train on the Canadian Pacific Railroad. With one hundred and fifty wagons, we calculated it was approaching three thousand yards long and took some ten minutes to pass by.

We were now losing height and passing through a starkly beautiful landscape of bare hills supporting nothing more than scattered sage brush and the occasional lone pine. At the small settlement of Spencer's Bridge we took a cabin on a roadside RV station. The owner was the great-grandson of a Klondike gold-rush prospector and the absolute spitting image of Alan Alder of 'Mash' fame. That evening, in the local log cabin saloon, the lady saloon keeper treated us to a diatribe on the shortcomings of the Canadian Government, something to do with idiots and taxes and so on. Her words had a very homely ring to them.

The Highway had quit the gorge of the Fraser River and was now following upstream along the course of the Thompson River. Barren country continued until, just when we needed it, we came upon a timely place of comfort. It was Ashcroft House, built in 1862 as a way-station for weary gold prospectors trekking northwards to the Klondike. It is today a very English tea house complete with lace tablecloths, silver service and chock-a block with antiques. The owner was a cyclist and a lover of all things historical. In his shed he had a twenty-seven-year-old Italian racing cycle, a Cenelli, on which he still rode fast time trials.

Armed with useful information about the road ahead, we continued easily to the village of Cache Creek. This too was once a stopping place on the gold trail and is now a collection of motels, fast food outlets and gas stations. It is a dry and dusty place, receiving an annual rainfall of only ten centimetres. Standing at the junction of two valleys, surrounded by sagebrush and cactus covered hills; it was easy to imagine the early prospectors and their pack animals passing through in search of a fortune in gold. Few of them succeeded and many died in the attempt.

The highway now turned east, still following the course of the Thompson River through semi-arid desert country. We were heading for the community of Savona, described in a tourist blurb as 'picturesque'. Stretching the term to its limits was our view when the massive dump of rusting heavy plant machinery that seemed to be Savona came into view. The town stands where the Thompson River flows out of the western extremity of Lake Kamloops. By the lakeside there was a ribbon of development, making a half-hearted attempt at being a place for people to live. Even the attendant at the provincial campground felt obliged to apologise for the frowsy state of her site, which had been wrecked following a three month rental by a film crew. They must have been filming some post nuclear disaster type of production. However, there was a pleasant view to hills across the lake.

Lake Kamloops was to be our constant companion the next day as we rode steeply undulating country along its southern shoreline. Here and there ginseng farms stood by the roadside. This plant is native to Eastern North America and Canada is the world's largest grower, even exporting to China. We could have used some of its reputed energy boosting qualities, for it was a hard days riding before we reached the heights above Kamloops. Here, a thousand feet below, the buildings of the city stood upon a flat plain about the confluence of the North and South Thompson Rivers. A brake-burning descent took us to a street of hotels and motels and a bed for the night.

The following day, a friendly tail-wind allowed us to bowl easily along the valley of the South Thompson River towards our next objective, the township of Chase. On the way the countryside had begun to change from semi-arid in character to a fertile region where irrigation enabled the growing of fruit and luxurious crops of hay. At Chase we pitched our tent by the riverside, on a 'Lions' campground. Set up by the Lions charity, these campgrounds were to be found all along the highway. Run by volunteers, they have basic facilities, always clean and usually relying on honesty boxes for payment of their minimal fees.

This one was in an idyllic meadow setting where the Thompson River flowed out of the Little Shuswap Lake. As we sat, leaping salmon described glistening arcs of silver above the sparkling waters of the river whilst clouds of apple blossom were courted by shimmering golden humming birds.

Hoping to share our feelings of benign contentment we approached a fellow cycle traveller attempting to pitch his tent nearby. He turned out to be German. From the uncomprehending look on his face, our efforts at communication were a failure but we were full of nodding comprehension when he pointed at the ground and, smiling ruefully, said "shite", for he had picked a wet spot. We helped him move his tent and made him a brew for he had no 'Gaz' for his stove.

We were joined by another camper, a young English woman who was a summer resident on the campground whilst working as a driver for a local trucking company. She now lived in Canada, spending her winters in a cabin on the lakeshore.

"Do you know the best kept secret in Canada?" said she.

"No, what's that?"

"The summer in British Columbia."

We had no reason to disagree, for as yet we had seen nothing but unbroken sunshine.

From Chase, undulating afforested hillsides took us along the shores of the Shuswap Lake until arriving at the community of Salmon Arm. This stands on one of four arms, roughly in the shape of an 'H' that constitutes the Shuswap Lake System. This area is a holidaymaker's paradise, if you like boats that is. With a thousand kilometres of shoreline and a veritable armada of floating caravans, it styles itself the 'Houseboat Capital of Canada' and indeed is thought to have the largest fleet of such craft anywhere in the world. Now there's a record to be proud of and it is an attractive place, a leisurely world of slow waters amidst sleepy mountains.

We continued to ride this area of watery recreation for another two days until the range of the Columbia Mountains began to fill our field of vision ahead. Prominent amongst these snow giants was the peak of Iconoclast Mountain. At 10,700 feet, it stands guard above the giddy heights of Rogers Pass, over which we would soon have to climb.

A roadside museum caught our attention, if only to buy an ice-cream. It turned out to be a place of deep significance to all Canadians, for it was the site for the driving of 'The Last Spike'. Here, at Craigellachie, on the 7th of November 1885, the last spike was driven in the completion of three thousand miles of steel rail across the country. With the last blow of the hammer, the provinces of Canada were linked and unification of the country began. Photos of hammer-wielding dignitaries in heavy cut suits and bowler hats were on display and by a stone monument stood a Caboose, the last carriage and home to the guards and crew of the early Trans

Canadian trains. The sun shone benignly on this place of pilgrimage as visitors strolled around or sat in quiet contemplation of the moment that brought their country together, and the ice-cream was good too.

Riding on, we stopped to chat to a young Canadian couple who were cycling across their country from Vancouver to the capital of Ottawa. Unremarkable except that they were on their honeymoon. A steady upward gradient and strengthening head-wind were to oppose us until we arrived at the township of Revelstoke, the home of our Canadian motorcycling friends whom we had first met in Istanbul nearly eight months before. An answering machine responded to our phone call so we found ourselves a room in a 'backpackers' hostel. Later that night Peter turned up. He had scoured the town's accommodation to find us and tomorrow we would join him at home, Carol being away visiting her family.

We were to remain for four days at Revelstoke. The first of those were spent driving with Peter to collect Carol from Kelowna Airport, situated in the fruit and vineyard region of the Okanagan. Family visiting in Canada is a little more demanding than in England, for Carol had flown a round trip of some four thousand miles to visit her relatives and thought nothing of it.

Peter and Carol were both at work so during the daytime, we were left to occupy their sprawling ranch-style bungalow complete with an outdoor hot-tub on the veranda, with a view across the valley of the Columbia River to the Monashee Mountains. A fishing trip on Lake Revelstoke in our host's cabin cruiser occupied one evening, only low cloud preventing a flight in Peter's private plane on another. They enjoyed a prosperous life-style yet both had ordinary jobs. They are typical of many people in Canada, for theirs is an affluent, hi-tech industrial society with one of the highest living standards in the world. Like many Canadians we met, they had concerns about the economic might of America and the seepage of American culture across the border. Carol quoted us some statistics which revealed that only ten per cent of Americans ever own a passport and that fifty-five per cent of them did not know the location of Canada. These hinted at levels of insularity and ignorance which she did not wish to be exported to her country. Peter and Carol were thoughtful and worldly people and their kindness gave us a precious respite before we tackled the rigours of the lofty Rogers Pass in the crossing of the Columbia Mountains.

It was a cool and cloudy day as we began the climb out of Revelstoke. Giant peaks swam in and out of our vision as the cloud rolled about the mountain tops. The gradient, although not steep, required a consistent head-down work rate. Suddenly we were not alone; there by the roadside stood a black bear, turning its head from side to side and cautiously sniffing the air. We halted, frozen on the spot. The bear spotted us, stared suspiciously for a while then ambled into the forest. We had seen our first bear. It was a heart-stopping moment. The bear was very close and very big and we were fresh meat on wheels, for it is well documented that encounters between humans and these animals can have a lethal outcome.

With hearts pounding, we continued to climb and a cold rain began to fall as the highway traversed snow covered slopes. It seemed an eternity before the buildings at Rogers Pass loomed out of the mist. We were wet, cold, tired and hungry and the only accommodation available was an up-market motel. Needs must and having fed and watered ourselves, we reflected back on a tough day. In very adverse weather conditions we had climbed in the region of four thousand feet, over a distance of some forty-two miles. It cannot be said that such experiences are fun. Neither of us was above weeping in misery or quietly cursing at our situation and circumstances, despite knowing full well that we alone were responsible for being there. And yet, at the day's end, the sense of achievement derived from such experiences always far outweighed the discomforts of the journey. Now we felt that nothing could prevent us from crossing these great mountain ranges.

Chief Engineer A.B. Rogers was an employee of the Canadian Pacific Railway. His bosses had obviously attended one of those management courses and dreamed up an ingenious incentive scheme to get the best out of their staff. Immortality was to be the bonus for Rogers were he to meet the designated target. "Find the pass," said they, "and we will name it after you." Well he did, in 1881, and from 1885 until 1916, Rogers Pass formed a crucial link in the transcontinental railway. The route was treacherous, steep and swept by avalanches. The 'White Death' claimed the lives of two hundred and fifty railroad workers until the opening of a railroad tunnel in 1916. It was 1962 before a road was constructed over the pass. Avalanches remain a hazard, requiring the largest mobile avalanche program in the world to keep the road open. Even so seven young people had been swept to their deaths less than four months before our crossing. It is a wild and sometimes dangerous place and it looked it, the road a fragile ribbon of tarmac cut between forbidding ice-bound rock faces and menacing snow fields. Swirling cloud clothed the slopes in grey and the air around was thin, damp and cold.

Freezing rain stung our faces as we rode downhill the next day. Five long avalanche sheds, unlit and wet, had to be negotiated before the wild and rugged terrain began to soften and the sun began to shine. The air grew warmer and our noses ceased to run, perhaps mountain cycling was OK after all. Undulating hills of spruce forest led the eye to serried ranks of snow peaks, etched with piercing clarity against an azure sky. A black bear ambled across the road ahead but this time at a distance to delight rather than dismay and soon came our destination, the happily named township of Golden.

We were back in the valley of the Columbia River, which loops two hundred and fifty miles to the north through the Columbia Mountains between Revelstoke and Golden. Six National Parks surround Golden. Avoiding tedious name-dropping, let us just say that they are Alpine wilderness for which the locally much over-used adjective of 'awesome' is a feeble description, and now we were about to take on our last great challenge together, that of the Rocky Mountain Range. To the North stood Mount Robson; at 12,972 feet it is the highest in the range. Ahead, mountains of well over ten thousand feet stood sentinel over the heights of the Kicking Horse Pass. It was not going to be the cyclist's equivalent of a stroll in the park.

Steep climbing and strenuously undulating terrain took us ever deeper into the heart of the mountains until reaching the small community of Field. This was a neck-ache place, the eye being constantly drawn to the gigantic peaks which crowd in upon it.

Amazingly, far above on the slopes of Mount Field, there lies the Burgess Shale, a fossil site of such importance as to be designated a World Heritage Site. Why? Because it is stuffed with the fossils of soft bodied marine animals that swam in the Cambrian Seas, five hundred and fifteen million years ago. No big deal you might think except that the site is high up on the side of a two mile high mountain that was once a part of the sea bed. Well we were impressed and our three-roomed apartment was good too.

Field stands on the Kicking Horse River at the foot of the pass of the same name. It seems that a surgeon on an expedition in 1860 was kicked by his horse, an event which inspired the naming of the pass. We could think of other names for it as we flogged towards its lofty summit on a hot day. But there were compensations, a coyote wandered across the highway and a bull elk posed for photographs by the roadside. A little further on, we came upon the 'Spiral Tunnels'.

The Canadian Pacific Railway has found a way over this pass since 1884. The slope was dangerously steep, resulting in many runaway trains and the deaths of many railroad men. In 1909 the Spiral Tunnels were constructed. The railroad now corkscrews through the mountains, increasing the distance and thereby lessening the gradient. From time to time it emerges into daylight, thus producing the astonishing sight for the observer, of the head of a train overtaking its own tail as it winds through the tunnels.

Highway construction works near to the summit of the pass were an obstruction to traffic but not so to cyclists, for radio-equipped marshals, perhaps out of sympathy, allow such two-wheeled travellers to jump the queue. As we passed a smiling and waving marshal, she spoke into her radio:

"We have two pedestrians on bicycles coming through!"

And so we rode, happy and sad, on to the summit of our final pass together.

We had entered the Banff National Park within the Province of Alberta and an easy descent alongside the pine-fringed Bow River took us to the community of Lake Louise. At the campground, regulations demanded that our food be concealed in a locker room and the site itself was protected by an electrified fence which certainly wasn't there to keep us in. If ever evidence were needed of the dangers of bears, then this was it. But it was a beautiful place to camp by the riverside and that evening we were able to cook our sausages on an open wood fire, secure in the knowledge that we would be eating and not eaten.

Intent on a day of rest, we decided to ride our unladen bicycles to Lake Louise itself, as distinct from the village of the same name in the river valley. Some rest, for despite the lack of weight, it was a strenuous ride to the lake, which is cradled high up in the mountains above.

"Jumping Jackasses, if you've ridden up here you can enter for free!"

With these words, a smiling attendant waived the National Park entry levy. Well we did look a bit scruffy and poor amongst droves of tourists clad in brightly coloured outdoor designer gear. Not that it would do them much good, for prominently displayed signs announced the mortal danger of walking this area due to the presence in the surrounding forest of a grizzly bear and her two cubs. Nevertheless, a convenient viewpoint gave access to the most beautiful photographic opportunity ever to be had. We stood before a landscape almost dream-like in its perfection. A truly astonishing vista across the turquoise waters of the lake to ice-covered peaks reaching so high as to merge with the sky and draped in hanging glaciers like the ballet skirts of colossal snow dancers.

Given energy by this inspirational place, we rode the opposite side of the valley to a cable-car lift up Mount Whitethorn, the scene of past Winter Olympic skiing epics and a true animal kingdom. Only a cordoned-off area was available to visitors, for this was the haunt of grizzly bears, black bears, coyote, mule deer, marmots, ground squirrels, wolves and many others. It was also the haunt of the Japanese Tourist, all of them in groups and chattering like flocks of starlings whilst firing off veritable fusillades of camera shutters. Stereotyping! You accuse and you are right, but you can only tell it like you see it.

The valley of the Bow River was to lead us out of the mountains to Calgary, on the way taking us through the Alpine resort of Banff. We were traversing the Banff National Park, this too named after dignitaries of the Canadian Pacific Railway. Wildlife Park Managers from around the world come to Banff to learn how to do it, for it is arguably the best. The animals have their own private bridges across the highway and to prevent them coming to harm, or from doing harm to the humans, the park is fenced. Re-assuring to vulnerable cyclists but only to a certain point and, rounding a bend, we reached that point. There by the fence was a bear as big as the fence itself. We had seen a model of this animal at Mount Whitethorn. This one was the same characteristic brown, with a long nose and it was big, very big. It was a grizzly and a little way into the forest there were two smaller versions. The grizzly can weigh up to nine hundred pounds and stand twelve feet tall on its hind legs. Most bears do their best to avoid human contact but the grizzly will hunt people for a meat dinner and it doesn't like you anywhere near its offspring. At this moment a thin wire fence looked very flimsy and we knew that if this creature decided to take a dislike to us, we were in big trouble. So what did we do? We stopped to watch it and it stopped to watch us. Fascination and fear fought for ascendancy in our feelings and perhaps the bear was just as mixed up, but soon became fed up and ambled into the forest followed by its family. We ambled along the highway to Banff.

Banff and the National park came into being as the result of an accident. Here, in 1883, railway construction workers stumbled across a mountainside cave containing hot springs. As we all know, the Victorian gentry couldn't get enough of this sort of thing. Grand Hotels were built and they flocked here in their hundreds to drink in the scenery and give themselves a soothing soak in the sulphur springs. The grand hotels are still here along with lots of modern stuff associated with mountain sports. As mountain resorts go this one was a humdinger and we spent a very pleasant day meandering about the streets of Banff.

Gradually there was a transformation in the landscape. Mountain grandeur gave way to bare hillsides rolling downward to softly undulating grass plains. We were leaving the Rocky Mountains and entering the wide open spaces of cattle country. It was hard going. The expansive countryside deceived the eye. Seemingly gentle slopes were a lung-bursting climb and it was raining an old grey rain, devoid of any life-giving energy. We could find nowhere to stop. We were in the middle of nowhere and it was my 64th birthday. Surely there were better things to do on such a day? But long-distance cycling gives you no choice. Each day, once you have started, you have to finish.

And finish we did. After eighty grinding miles, we arrived at the outskirts of Calgary and collapsed into the nearest motel, there to celebrate with a pizza delivery and a can of coke. We had ridden a distance of 820 miles across the giant mountain ranges of Western Canada. It was a year since we left England, during which time we had cycled more than 9,000 miles together. Within a week we would be parting.

"This is not the place to be, Ma'am."

It was the laconic drawl of a traffic cop, speaking to Mary. Somehow we had contrived to ride along the course of an urban tramway in downtown Calgary whilst seeking more central accommodation. In delightful contrast we later rode a bikeway alongside the Bow River to a convenient motel. The city has a network of bikeways second to none and we were to spend several days exploring them whilst in the region.

Calgary is a very people friendly place. The tramway on which we had trespassed provides free city transport. A central shopping boulevard is ablaze with flowers, planted in beds and baskets. Old and new buildings stand in easy companionship with one another whilst musicians and street theatre players provide entertainment for passers by. A five minute stroll leads to the south bank of the Bow River. A restored covered market is surrounded by a collection of original buildings, now serving as cafés, bars and restaurants. Running through this area, in testament to the energy of humans, is the Bow River bikeway. Following the winding course of the river for many kilometres, it provides arterial transport for self-powered commuters and strolling and rolling recreation for all.

There were the usual practicalities to take care of but each step taken was a step closer to our coming separation. We had shared life-space with a rare intensity for one year and a week. During this time, we had ridden a distance of 9,100 miles through eleven countries. We were a team. Yet our impending parting was an event that neither of us was able to confront. Intense feelings of sadness stood between us in a mute grey fog of cheerless silence. We rode to the airport together, each of us wrapped in our own thoughts and wondering how we would deal with the moment of parting. Wearing the protection of brave faces was our defence and so it was with determined grins but grieving hearts that we kissed and waved each other goodbye.

It was the 1st of July and Canada Day, a national holiday. The Bow River bikeway took me eastwards until joining Highway 1a. A strengthening south-west wind aided progress through gently undulating countryside, vast tracts of young green wheat stretching to the horizon. Birds were swooping and calling and ground squirrels cavorted amongst roadside carpets of flowers. Joining Highway 1, I rode easily to the township of Strathmore where the Municipal Campground was basic but quiet and free. Retiring to my tent to sleep, I felt satisfied with my first day of solo riding but ill-at-ease with the space beside me.

This was the region of the Canadian Prairies, the northernmost branch of The Great Plains of North America. Ahead of me lay nearly one thousand miles of flatlands through the provinces of Alberta, Saskatchewan and Manitoba. The Canadians had been liberal with their jokes. To do with prairie farmers not knowing how to turn corners in their station-wagons and dogs you could see running away for three days. Couldn't see the funny side myself, especially when battling against a head-wind the next day to arrive at the frowsy village of Bassano, there to spend a restless night listening to the roar of passing trains on the Canadian Pacific Railroad.

The uniformity of horizon-to-horizon grasslands was gently broken the next day when Candice from Vancouver rode alongside me. It was her first ever cycle tour and she was hoping to make it to Winnipeg before flying home. She had legs just made for cycling and a mouth just made for smiling. Like many young Canadian women, she wore braces on her teeth. Studded with semi-precious stones, these braces turn a potential blemish into a thing of beauty. We rode together chatting, not noticing a growing wildness in the wind until almost too late. Coming up to our rear was the menacing spiral of a tornado. With nowhere to hide, we decided to make a dash for it. No need to pedal: a roaring tail-wind propelled us along at speeds in excess of thirty miles an hour for a distance of some twenty miles before abating.

Still in a good blow, we amused ourselves by rigging sails with ground mats and tent poles, flying wildly along the highway shoulder until a puncture halted my progress. Candice rode on while I stopped to effect a repair before continuing to Medicine Hat, having ridden a distance of 106 miles in less than six hours.

The danger of tornadoes was not something considered in our planning, for these tend to occur in the more turbulent atmospheric conditions of late spring and early summer and are largely thought of as a phenomenon confined to the USA. A mistake, for in 1987, on the 31st of July, a tornado hit the city of Edmonton just to the north, killing twenty-seven people and causing $330 billion worth of property damage. What we had seen as an amusing game had in fact been a lucky escape.

According to legend, Medicine Hat was so named after an Indian Medicine Man who lost his hat here. Believe this if you will but it is today a prosperous place deriving its riches from the oil industry. It sports the tallest tepee in the world, over two hundred feet high. This is no rustic construction of wooden poles and animal skins but a tracery of steelwork giving the thing the appearance of an experiment in scaffolding gone wrong. My motel resembled a set of chicken sheds and every bit as uncomfortable. However it was cheap and so was the local cycle shop. They fitted my bike with new tyres and self self-sealing inner tubes at cost, threw in a full service for free and as much coffee as I could drink.

Prairie lands continued with flat going and a tail-wind giving my daily mileage figures a very healthy look. An average of over ninety miles a day, with a record day of one hundred and fourteen miles, took me through the Townships of Maple Creek and Swift Current to Moose Jaw. This was big country indeed, at Swift Current the highway passing by the historic '76 Ranch', once covering an area of 160 square miles.

Immense brackish lakes with dazzling white fringes were a haven for many species of water-birds, seeming to share their home quite happily with the bulldozers and plant of a thriving Sodium

Sulphate Industry. This area is one of the most important sites for migratory birds in North America. Half the world's population of sanderlings use this site as a bed and breakfast stop-over on their way to the Artic. But it is under threat, the lakes are drying up. However, for once human commercial activity is helping to preserve the environment, for the sulphate extraction process involves water management to keep it wet. This area had the grandeur of seemingly limitless space, a dazzling blue harmony of water and sky, the timeless abode of wheeling and calling birds.

The distinctive name of Moose Jaw apparently bears no relationship to a moose or a jaw but is said to be derived from the Cree word *moosegaw*, meaning 'warm breezes'. Here, in 1882, a lonely trading post was overnight transformed into a thriving prairie town by the coming of the railroad. A coming to Moose Jaw of another kind is commemorated in 'The Tunnels'. The railroad was built by the muscle of Chinese immigrant labour. They were shipped here in the late 19th century, having been sold dreams of prosperity in Canada by unscrupulous Chinese people traders. They were not well treated, being regarded as sub-human and therefore expendable. When no longer needed to construct the railways, and with nowhere to go, they became the victims of vicious and often violent racism. They literally went underground, constructing workshops, laundries and living quarters in a series of tunnels and cellars beneath the city. It is said that people were born and raised without ever seeing the light of day.

I joined a party of visitors to the tunnels. We were asked to endure a role-play where we took the parts of a group of 'coolies' and our guide that of a bullying Scottish foreman. In this dark and oppressive place, cringing at the roaring voice of our 'foreman', we were given a vivid lesson in the evils of racism. How precious the fresh air and freedom of the streets seemed after this unnerving experience. The story of Chinese immigrant labour doesn't end there. A 'Head Tax' was imposed, applicable only to the Chinese. New immigrants were forced to pay $50 a head to enter Canada. Still they came, for opium wars and dire government made life in their own country close to unbearable. The tax was increased by increments, eventually reaching the sum of $500, a fortune to the poverty stricken Chinese. At the very same time British immigrants were being given a free passage to the country. This was discrimination on a grand scale. It was not until 1947 that Chinese Canadians were finally allowed to become Canadian citizens. A hard-won acceptance indeed.

I was now in the Province of Saskatchewan and approaching the capital city of Regina. However, rain and a murderous head-wind slowed my progress and left me with no desire to explore. So I took the orbital road to camp to the east of the city. Nearby were a party of Trans-Canadian cyclists from Quebec. They were riding to raise money for charity. No doubt they were an interesting group but I was too far gone to be sociable and just flopped exhausted into my tent.

Rain in the face, pain in the bum and no-one to moan to except you, dear reader, it was not a good day, but succour was on hand. The support team for the charity riders from Quebec must have thought I looked pitiful and plied me with food and drink as I passed their supply stations at the highway-side. At the 'Shady Hollow' campground near the town of Wolseley, we swapped our stories whilst I gratefully drank their cold beer. They were crossing Canada in an impressively organised charity ride. One of their members was a profoundly unsighted athlete of sixty-seven years of age, who rode on the back saddle of a tandem. Like most Quebecois, few of this party spoke English. "Enchanté!" was the greeting I received from the blind rider and "Quelle courage!" when he heard of my trip. Well, hardly, when compared with the extraordinary bravery required for an unsighted man to cycle 4,500 miles across Canada. I was to meet up with this party on a number of occasions and was invited to become an honorary member of their group. I declined, wishing to retain my independence but becoming an informal member by virtue of regularly ending up on the same campgrounds. This had its advantages for they were being donated free camping and their support vehicles carried ice cool beers. We even had the odd impromptu race whilst on the road, but I never stood a chance, for they were unloaded and I was not.

The Quebecois were riding to 'Mile Zero' at Halifax in Nova Scotia, the easternmost point of mainland Canada. Studying their itinerary, it was becoming clear to me that my own goal of Toronto was too easily attained and I began to think of extending the distance of my trip, perhaps also to Halifax. This decision would have to be deferred to my arrival in Winnipeg, a city big enough to sport airline offices.

Prairie towns were 'ticked off' one by one as I made excellent wind assisted progress. At one place I spent a lively evening with a couple of Trans-Canadian bikers riding gleaming chrome machines of the motorised variety. Theirs was a one week excursion, covering a daily distance of some seven hundred miles. We drank cans of Bud and swapped stories far into the night. In another township I met a couple of superhuman cyclists who were riding in the region of 300 (yes, 300!) miles per day. They went to bed early. The mileage was eaten up as I passed through the communities of Indian Head, Moosomin, Virden, Brandon and Portage-la-Prairie to reach Winnipeg, the capital city of the Province of Manitoba.

I found a middle-range hotel near to the city centre. A few home comforts seemed justified after the long days on the prairie and I needed time and space to consider the options open to me. A hot bath and burger with fries were all it took. The next day I headed for the offices of Air Canada and changed my objective to Halifax, Nova Scotia. The die was cast; I had committed myself to a further 2,500 miles of travel. It was time to explore the city. Close by the hotel I came to a somewhat ordinary junction of roads. Two young women were sitting on a bench eating their lunch. My request as to the whereabouts of the city centre was met with gales of laughter.

"This is just about it," said one of them. I was standing at the famous junction of 'Portage and Maine' said to be the "windiest corner on the continent" – a place blasted by howling winds and seared by winter temperatures of fifty below. To me it was the familiar city scene of high rise offices with the occasional colonial style building thrown in. It seemed to be a rather characterless spot but perhaps my eye was becoming a little jaundiced by the dreary uniformity of such places.

The next day I made an early start but not early enough to escape the presentation of a commemorative mug and mini Canadian

Flag, they probably gave them to all their guests. Outside the city environs, flatlands continued but now the cornfields were dotted with clumps of trees which quickly thickened into dense spruce forest supporting swarms of monster black-flies. These could easily fly at the pace of a passing cycle traveller and were a torment until the forest began to thin and with it the flies.

My stopping place was the hamlet of Prawda. The local campground appeared to be deserted but I eventually found an extremely horizontally challenged man tinkering prone in his garage. He was as tall lying down as when he stood up and declined my offer of payment as he couldn't find his pocket. I had the place to myself and luxuriated in rustic silence before strolling to a nearby gas-station-cum-café. It was time for a celebration, for I had passed the 10,000-mile mark. Lacking Champagne, a can of Coke had to suffice.

Back at the campground, I had companions. The site, a field the size of Trafalgar Square, was empty except for me and a family who were pitched within spitting distance and had stacked most of their gear on and around my tent. The place resembled a car boot sale on a summer Sunday. Worthless junk was strewn all around and the air was vibrant with lyrical cursing. My new neighbours were Jimmy, a Nova Scotian man and his partner Alice, a lady so fat she could hardly stand. An equally rotund grand-daughter loafed around stuffing chocolate into her face as if her life depended upon it. They were refugees from city living in Winnipeg, planning to begin a new life in a tent and quite indifferent to the coming winter of fifty below. Small trees were felled and a roaring fire was lit, upon which coffee was brewed whilst Alice regaled me with stories of encounters with angels. We spent a most convivial evening together, sharing our life experiences but, needing to rise early, I was forced to decline the bedtime offer of sharing a joint. Perhaps I should have accepted, for a drugged coma might have spared me the nocturnal sounds of explosive snoring and farting from the tent next door.

The character of the countryside was beginning to change. The plains were quietly folding into gentle hills wearing a dark green cloak of mixed conifer trees. Granite outcrops stood like watchtowers in the forest, mirrored in the unruffled surfaces of cobalt coloured

184

lakes. It was a delight to feel the rise and fall of the land beneath my wheels and to ride towards a horizon that could be attained in hours rather than days. Seeming to respect this transformation wrought by nature, the workings of man had found a fitting harmony with the landscape. The highway became a broad passage of graceful curves and inclines with an easy rolling smoothness until, by the wayside, there stood the elegant timber and glass structure of a very posh Tourist Information Centre. I had entered the Province of Ontario.

Furnished with free issue maps, I rode on towards my goal of Kenora, where I sought directions to a campground. I first spoke to a Canadian man who turned out to be a Tour-de-France enthusiast. He knew lots about cycling but nothing about campgrounds. Next I buttonholed a kindly-looking woman, who told me she lived nearby, about 250 miles off-route, and invited me to visit her and her family should I fancy a bit of a diversion. With her help I found the campground and later followed my nose to 'The Whistling Monkey Saloon' for evening refreshment.

Kenora is one of a number of resorts standing around the shores of 'The Lake of the Woods'. This is 1500 square miles of glacially formed lake with 65,000 miles of shoreline and no less than fifteen thousand islands. Some municipal boating lake and a good place for a day's rest.

At the campground I met Daniel, a salesman from Toronto with a salesman's facility for words. He was cycling back to his home city from Vancouver. He had met up with Louis and Frances, whose home was near to Quebec. They were cycling across Canada. Louis spoke no English; his partner Frances had a smattering whilst Daniel and I spoke some French. We soon contrived a working Franglais and with it the instant camaraderie that seems to come so easily between long-distance cyclists. Louis and Frances believed in comfort and were carrying a mountain of gear. Between them they had eight panniers, two bar-bags and a trailer for Louis. He had the thigh muscles of a rhino and neck to match and was one of those riders who disdained the use of the 'Granny Ring'. Well, we all have our own riding styles but Louis's was costing him a fortune in broken chains, to say nothing of his gonads and the amount of earache he got from Frances. In the manner of Trans-Canadian cycling, we were to meet again, both on and off the Highway.

Meetings were becoming a daily feature. A young Montreal man travelling west was embarrassingly reverential of my trip to date but an older man travelling east was less easily impressed when I caught up with the Quebecois charity riders at the next overnighter. He was Pierre from Quebec. He had answered an advert and somehow found himself a member of the charity ride. Now retired from a very lofty post with an international aid agency, he had seen it all and done most of it. He had a well-developed sense of the ironic. He too was to become a regular companion on the journey eastwards and offered to be my guide if and when I arrived in Quebec.

Companionship on the road is a transient thing. No-one ever actually rides with anyone else. There is common recognition that each rider has their own pace and rhythm. Thus most time on the road is spent alone. No arrangements are ever made to meet again, for it is in the nature of cycle travel that you may well not do so. And yet you do, for stopping places in Canada are often the only one within a day's ride. A day's rest may be taken but inevitably others must rest also and so there is a delightful randomness yet inevitability that somewhere, someplace, sometime, old friends of the road will meet again. And we did.

But at the next place I slept alone and nervous on a rustic campground where the previous day a raiding bear had been captured, one of several pestering the area. I was told not to pitch my tent near the garbage cans and it was suggested I run for the laundry if I heard any snuffling in the night. Somehow I managed a good night's sleep. The tiredness resulting from riding 97 miles of moderately undulating terrain had been sleeping pill enough.

Steady climbing and light rain born on a hampering head-wind, not a day likely to bring much joy to the heart. The highway was a puny mark on a wilderness landscape that stretched 2000 miles to the north and reaching ahead, a seemingly endless corridor through dense and dark forest. But there was life. Far enough away to excite and not alarm, a solitary black bear loped across the highway. Close by the dark waters of a lake stood a moose, watching alertly from the forest fringe. Further on, eating a road-kill on the grass shoulder of the highway was a grey wolf. Raising its head from its meal, it studied me carefully for a moment then walked casually into the forest. Nature had come to the rescue and made for a special day. Tired but satisfied, I rolled into the small community of Upsala. The Quebecois were there, giving the bonus of good company, free camping and free beer.

Upsala boasts the dubious distinction of being the home of the largest and most voracious mosquitoes in the world. In their honour a twenty foot high welded steel model of the insect stands menacingly by the campground but we needed no reminder for they were out in force and we were cowering in our tents.

In the morning, plagued by these pests, we all rushed to be away, heading for the city of Thunder Bay which stands at the north-western extremity of Lake Superior. It is the home of the largest community of Finnish nationals outside of Finland, attracted to the area by the lumber industry. My acquaintance with the city was brief for it had too much of a dockland aspect to it to attract me and so I passed quickly through to call at an Information Centre to be directed to a Big 4 campground beyond the environs of the city.

The Information Centre had, standing in its grounds, a bronze statue of a runner. Being tired, I had paid it scant attention but the wall of the campground laundry was covered in newspaper cuttings about the man represented in the statue. He was Terry Fox. Bone cancer in his right leg had led to its amputation six inches above the knee and he was equipped with a prosthetic. On April the 12th 1980, he set out to run across Canada to raise money for cancer research. Starting from St Johns, Newfoundland, he ran a Marathon a day for one hundred and forty-three days, covering a total distance of 3,400 miles. At Thunder Bay he was forced to stop, for cancer had appeared in his lungs. He died ten months later. One of Canada's greatest heroes had gone but he left an astonishing legacy. He himself had raised $24 million by his efforts. The first run in his memory took place in Canada in the year of his death. Today, Terry Fox runs are held all over the world and to date have raised over $360 million for cancer research. When Terry Fox died, he was aged just twenty-two.

"Howdy, care to join us for coffee?"

The invitation came from Byron and Carmel, who were staying in a cabin close by my tent site. He was from Regina and she came from Chicago. They had made contact through the internet and this was the very first time they had met face to face. Theirs was evidently a passionate liaison, for Carmel bore the marks of Byron's affection upon her neck like a garland of red roses. Both were sweetness personified and sent me to my tent that night with a whole new perspective of cyber-romance.

For seven days I rode the north shore of Lake Superior. It was tough going, for the route of the highway resembled a fairground big-dipper as it followed the serrated coastline of headlands and bays. The aesthetic in me was constantly in conflict with the physical. No doubt these coastal hills rolling majestically down to the lakeside had grandeur. Like a beautiful dominatrix, they gave both pleasure and pain (or so I have been told). This was riding as hard as any I had yet encountered but the addictive reward of mileage covered had me in the irresistible grip of 'road fever'.

There were diversions.

"At last I've caught up with you, you must be the Englishman."

This was Don, a retired teacher from British Columbia, fulfilling his lifelong ambition to cycle across Canada. The highway 'grapevine' had put him on my track and shortly afterwards Pierre, Louis and Frances arrived. We five were to encounter each other over the course of the next few days, bringing happy companionship to evenings which might otherwise be spent in solitude.

Place names intrigued and amused. Three lakes of unequal size were named 'Dad Lake', 'Mum Lake' and 'Baby Lake'. 'Rabbit Blanket Lake' and 'Pancake Lake' could surely tell their stories. White River had a tale to tell, for in 1914 this community supplied a bear mascot to the Royal Canadian Army Vetinary Corps. It was later donated to London Zoo, where Winnie the Bear became a major attraction. One A.A. Milne was apparently in the habit of hanging around the zoo and was inspired by the bear to write *Winnie the Pooh* – a matter of civic pride in White River and marked by a giant plastic model of the bear sitting in the fork of a giant plastic oak tree.

The township of Sault-Saint-Marie provided the opportunity for a day's rest and bike maintenance. At the local bike-shop, I was again greeted as 'The Englishman'. It was a title I was beginning to enjoy. The campground saw a gathering of Trans-Canadian cyclists. Two supported groups, the trio from Quebec and Don from B C, made for a veritable cyclist's jamboree and much telling of stories of the type which involve a great deal of talking but very little listening.

Quitting the shores of Lake Superior, I rode alongside the St. Mary's River to join the north shore of Lake Huron. The terrain was flatter here with numerous condominiums and fishing lodges by the lake shore. Leaving the lakeside the highway cut north-eastward through open bush country, here and there breached by cleared ground cradling smart villas amidst well manicured lawns. For the next few days the countryside was characterised by occasional small towns standing in river valleys. Undulating tracts of spruce forest between townships had to be crossed before reaching the valley of the Ottawa River. During this time I had encountered Don, Pierre, Louis and Frances on occasion, but the three from Quebec had the scent of their home territory in their nostrils and sped on ahead whilst Don and I had taken different routes. None of us were to meet again but I did encounter the Quebecois charity group, their numbers depleted for various reasons but still going strong.

A long day's ride of ninety-nine miles took me to the outskirts of Ottawa, the capital city of Canada. It was the 6th of August. I had now cycled 3,189 miles in Canada and 11,415 miles in total. Falling into a cheap motel, I began to hatch plans for yet another change of destination. A few days before I had chatted with a pair of young women cyclists who were crossing Canada to finish at St. Johns, Newfoundland. It too had a mile zero, this one situated on the easternmost extremity of the Canadian Federation and the easternmost point of the North American continent. It was the closest point on land to home. Tomorrow I would explore Ottawa and take the opportunity to change my final destination. It meant another 1,300 miles to be covered in just over a month but I was feeling fit and confident and, barring accidents, should make it.

I took the bus into downtown Ottawa, not expecting anything very much for I had been told by Canadians that it was "just another capital city". Something of an understatement, for the administrative heart of the city had a spaciousness and graciousness as good as it gets. The main drag of Wellington Street runs parallel to the Ottawa River. A broad concourse between the road and the river is the setting for imposing Victorian stone buildings. Standing mightily at the highest point are the Houses of Parliament, a Westminster look-alike in a perfect position towering above the Ottawa River. I ambled along traffic free boulevards lined with everything the strolling visitor could wish for and soon found the offices of Air Canada to change my Trans-Atlantic departure point to St. Johns, Newfoundland. The route ahead would now take me through the cities of Montreal and Quebec and the Maritime Provinces of New Brunswick and Nova Scotia.

An early morning mist hung over the Ottawa River. The city was still sleeping, the parliamentary square empty of people and the roads easy to ride in scant traffic. Bowling along I was stopped by a friendly policeman who told me that bicycles were not permitted on four lane highways and directed me to the old Montreal road, a carriageway of two lanes. At the Township of Hawkesbury a two mile long bridge took me over the Ottawa River. Broad waters glistening in the summer sun bore sailboats, tacking hither and thither between distant shores. I stopped at an information centre to ask directions to a campground.

"Voulez vous parlez français?" said the assistant, forcing me to use my halting French. I had entered the Province of Quebec where French is the spoken language. I was directed along the north shore of the river to a municipal campground charging an extortionate fee for a lone cyclist ($Can27, about £12). It was, however, beautifully situated on the broad grassy bank of the Ottawa River.

I continued to ride alongside the river the next morning before re-crossing by ferry at the hamlet of Carillon. Now on the south shore of the river, the highway meandered pleasantly through wooded hills and fields of corn until the signs of urban development began to appear. I was drawing near to Montreal and riding the north shore of the mighty St. Lawrence River. A local cyclist gave me directions to a dedicated bike-path along the course of the Canal de Lachine. The waterway cut through a landscape of gigantic slab sided factories, their chimneys soaring above skeletal networks of steel and pipe-work, smoke darkened remnants of the industrial revolution. This was the cradle of Canada's industrial history and not the prettiest of approaches to a city centre but nonetheless powerful in its expression of past industrial might.

Even more imposing dereliction loomed in the buildings of the old docks. These are no longer used for shipping but on my arrival were a hive of activity. It was a Saturday and all around stood the stalls of traders, surrounded by prospective buyers and those who had just come to look. The dockland area adjoins Le Place Jacques Cartier, a market place standing in a three-sided square of restaurants, cafés and shops. Street traders displayed their wares whilst street performers displayed their skills amidst throngs of meandering people, the whole combining to create a colourful kaleidoscope of human activity. It seemed a good place to stop but the cost of downtown hostelries was way beyond my means and so I quit the heart of Montreal to ride on to find a cheap motel on the eastern outskirts of the city.

For two days I rode the north shore of the St. Lawrence River. Dreaming villages were a visual feast of pastel coloured clapboard villas and tiny bistros, watched over by lofty stone churches. The arty and crafty set had made their homes here but I doubt they made much of a living. Sculpture was greatly in evidence but I have seen better, steaming on the floor of a zoo elephant house. Approaching the outskirts of Quebec it became a navigational nightmare to find the way ahead. At various junctures, progress was obstructed by un-named roads, miss-directions from well meaning Quebecois, roads barred to cyclists, and a bike-path blocked by construction. There is a problem inherent in the way information services seem to be located in most cities. They put them in the centre. For an approaching traveller this means that the place you are trying to find is the very same place that holds the information to lead you to the place you are trying to find, if you get my meaning. Well, eventually I found it, by following the course of the St. Lawrence River on whatever road or path I could discover. Not that the river was easy to miss for it is going on two miles wide and on the north side fronted by very steep ground, forming a natural passage for traffic by the riverside.

Approaching downtown, I rode a bike-path beneath a wooded cliff positively bristling with elegant churches and sumptuous

191

chateaux. To my right, the south, lay the broad expanse of the St. Lawrence River and to the left the imposing buildings of the city centre. At last I found an information office where the staff booked me a room in a cheap motel just a short distance along the bike-path. Exploration would have to wait until tomorrow.

Quebec has a long history and it shows. Indians and Inuit had been here for thousands of years before the Europeans arrived nearly four hundred years ago. The French were the first to move in on the people already living here and set up home. The English turned up a hundred and fifty years later, laid siege and defeated the French. For once it was not just the ordinary soldiers in the firing line, for both commanding generals were killed in the action. The British took over, which sparked a flood of immigrants from England, Ireland and Scotland. Good sense seems to have prevailed and it was not many decades before the Canadian Confederation became established, allowing everyone to rub nicely along with each other. Quebec is the capital of that chunk of Canada which is mostly French, to the extent that ninety-five per cent of the population speak only the French language.

You could be forgiven for thinking you were in France in this city. The Petit Champlain Quarter is a maze of narrow alleyways, lined with boutiques and bistros and echoing to the agreeable sounds of spoken French. MacDonalds and KFC are nowhere to be seen but *nouvelle cuisine* is found aplenty. It is the only fortified city in North America and The Old Port is old. Towering above the port area is a chateau as grand as grand can be and the winding streets around bring surprise views of architectural gems at every corner. Always the wide blue waters of the St. Lawrence River attract the eye as sailboats tack in search of clear water amongst the bustle of international shipping. For two days I wandered entranced around this gem of a city. It is a place where the old and the new worlds come together in true style.

Slumbering cities in the light of dawn are atmospheric places. Friendly echoes dance about the streets and long shadows grow shorter, shaping a prologue to the story of the rising sun. It was with such poetical musings or whatever, that I rode to the port to catch the early morning ferry across the St. Lawrence River. A strong tide was running, forcing the ferry-boat to sail crabwise to the opposite shore. Eastward progress was made easy by the presence of a fine bike-path, running parallel to the broad waters of the river. It was good to be on the move again but not for long, for suddenly the path ended, forcing me to push up the steep grass bank of a park into a confusion of housing estates. Escaping this dormitory maze was not easy but eventually I found my way to the highway going east and with a friendly tail-wind rode easily to Riviere Ouelle. The campground was a holiday site set in woodland on the south bank of the St. Lawrence River, which here was so wide as to render the opposite shore a thin purple line on the horizon. That evening the setting sun lit the waters in reflections of fire and the whole campground turned out to watch.

Early morning rain made for a wet and grubby start to the day and the mosquitoes were out in force. The rain persisted and with it a gloomy mist. Somehow I managed to miss the way and had to retrace wheels. The small coastal township of Riviere de la Loups confronted me with the steepest hill of the whole journey. Pushing three steps at a time was the only way to surmount this obstacle although, when I could find the breath, a liberal sprinkling of cursing seemed to help. The owner of a hilltop convenience store directed me to a bike-path which made its way for eighty miles over the afforested Appalachian Mountains to the Township of Edmunston. Once committed to it, there was to be no leaving this path. This would have been fine were it not for the rain which had turned it into a cyclist's nightmare. Compacted crushed gravel became a very effective grinding paste in the wet and where the gravel had been washed away, the mud did its best to halt progress altogether. The cycle transmission became clogged on more than one occasion. In clearing it, I managed to leave behind the essential tool of my Swiss Army knife. This was a near life-and-death mistake, for no food was to be had for two days. I had only canned supplies and the knife had my only can opener. I was forced to return to retrieve it.

This stretch had become a catalogue of mishaps. The trail climbed relentlessly, the lowest cycle gears would not function and it was growing dark. I would have to camp wild, despite the danger of bears. A patch of grass in the forest had to suffice. It was still raining and my already wet gear grew wetter as I made camp in a plague of mosquitoes. In a wet tent, wearing damp underwear and shivering in a damp sleeping bag, I yearned for the comforts of home but the lack of them could not prevent me from drifting into an exhausted sleep.

Putting on wet clothing the next morning and once again devoured by mosquitoes, I began to reflect that long-distance cycling might not always be fun and just then it wasn't, for the going became no better and the bike and I were both suffering. What had I done to deserve this misery? Was it a payback for all those sins of the past or was life a cosmic set of scales, good fortune on one side, bad fortune on the other and was I now due to cop for some of the downside? Can this kind of mental masturbation ever be at all helpful when all that is needed is just to get on with it? And anyway, what choice is there? Well, none, and so I flogged on and the sun came out, I began to dry out and eventually broke out of the forest to spend the night on a splendid lakeside campground at the small community of Notre Dame du Lac.

Drier conditions made the trail a little easier to ride but a drifting mist limited visibility to a few yards and the bike transmission remained troublesome. Good enough to reach Edmunston where the sun came out and I was able to find a bike shop. There I was able to buy a new chain and fit it by the roadside. It was a relief to ride on a hardtop road along the valley of the Saint John River. I was now in the province of New Brunswick, the river alongside forming the border between Canada and the USA. However the bike transmission was delivering an occasional but very ominous clonking and would clearly need further attention. Close by the township of Grand Falls I came upon an idyllic campground set in a sheltered hollow in the bend of a chuckling river. The owner was chuckling too for she was a jolly French/Irish lady with a keen sense of the ridiculous. Perhaps this was a quality she saw in me and maybe, after three days of fighting my way over the Appalachian Mountains, there was just a touch of hillbilly madness about me. That day I had passed the 12,000-mile mark. My steed was faltering and I was coming out in sympathy, but failure was a zero tolerance issue and tomorrow always another day.

Something to do with raining and pouring but the next day the front tyre of my bike disintegrated, covering me and the bike in a layer of luminous green self-sealing goo from the burst inner-tube. All was not lost, for the past fourteen months I had carried a spare folding tyre and always had inner-tubes and so was able to carry out a roadside repair. However the transmission problem had become so severe that I was forced to take a small round file to the chain-wheel and reshape the teeth. This was a desperate measure but it seemed to work and enabled me to reach the township of Woodstock. More tinkering aided by a smattering of gentle profanity apparently enamoured me to a couple seated outside a nearby RV, who invited me to join them.

They were Gregoir and Val. Greg was a French-Canadian from New Brunswick and Val a Newfoundlander. They had purchased a parcel of land nearby and were planning to build on it. Val had the musical lilt of an Irish accent to her voice and Greg the seductive cadence of a Parisian night-club crooner. To hear them was to hear the vocal equivalent of a lyrical cello and violin sonata, but with the added cadences of Molson's beer, Canadian whisky and chicken stew. I remember little of the rest of the evening but I will never forget the kindness of Val and Greg.

The valley of the Saint John River gave bike-riding of the kind that touring cyclists dream of: quiet roads, not monotonously flat but interestingly undulating and with cheerful villages appearing at convenient, thirst-quenching intervals. I was almost disappointed to reach Fredericton, the capital city of New Brunswick, but also relieved, for here I should be able to find the means of sorting out my bicycle. The local information office directed me to a cheap motel, told me where I could find a bike shop and gave me a plethora of tourist information.

The first priority was my machine and the next day I rode to the bike-shop where, without a moment's hesitation, they set out to fit a new front chain-set, as the old one had been practically worn away. It was time to explore. Tourist hot-spots in a city wouldn't be such if they were not interesting but they tend to be hyped-up places which give no impression of ordinary day to day life. Hence I have a leaning towards throwing away the brochures and just wandering around.

The residential norm in Fredericton seemed to be broad avenues graced with an abundance of trees and lined with elegant Victorian villas. I came across two art galleries and two universities. One of the galleries was called the Beaverbrook, apparently a gift to the city from his lordship, who was raised around here. A brightly painted wooden lighthouse stood by the river, unique in its inland situation. Hard to say what purpose it might have served for ocean mariners but it looked good. A very functional looking military barracks had a guard of soldiers dressed in kilts and busbies all tricked out with much gold braid. Here was one of the most charming things. Every now and then, to no timetable as far as I could see, squads of these men marched around the city and occasionally a piper and drummer would trot along and stop to do their stuff. There seemed to be no system. No chance for crowds of shutter clickers to gather at any time or place. Pot luck was the order of the day.

Fredericton, then, gave the impression of comfortable living for its folk. They must be people with a great commitment to education and the arts, a well developed sense of the city's military history, a love of spontaneity and a keen eye for the tourist dollar. Just my impression, for what it is worth, and they did a great job on my bike, which ran like a Rolls Royce thereafter.

The early morning forest was cloaked in a delicate tracery of silken webs hung with beads of dew, shining like diamonds in the light of the awakening sun. The highway climbed gently but persistently alongside the placid Canaan River. I drifted through no-name villages and passed by scattered farms, standing on the edge of hayfields hacked from the bush. At a roadside coffee-house there were people wandering around wearing kilts, a reminder that the Province of Nova Scotia was close by. At Moncton, outside the information office, I met a Canadian couple, both of whom were cyclists.

"Are you planning to visit PEI? You just have to go there, it's one of the most beautiful places in Canada."

I had to ask what was meant by PEI. Prince Edward Island. The name had appealing ring to it and sounded worth a visit. OK, PEI it would be. It meant something of a diversion but I was making good time and could not resist the lure of an island.

Moncton has a renowned tidal bore, anything from six inches to six feet. That evening saw a gathering of the hopeful, waiting by the riverside. A six foot wall of water roaring up the river promised to be an exciting sight. It was not to be, we got the six-incher. That man who went walkabout with his donkey wasn't far wrong when he wrote "to travel hopefully is a better thing than to arrive", for the air was pregnant with the excitement of the waiting crowd but when it arrived the bore was... well, a bit of a bore. I was hoping this didn't also apply to Prince Edward Island.

As I rode towards my next objective, the surrounding spruce forest began to open up to give tantalising glimpses of wide blue water. It was Shepochy Bay which lies off the Atlantic Ocean. I was drawing ever closer to home. Warning signs began to appear which marshalled cyclists into a pull-out and led to a building giving a welcome to those crossing the Confederation Bridge. Leaning outside was a fully loaded touring bike.

"Howdee aahhm Eric, goldarn ut effun yew aint thet thur Englishmairn aahh bin orn the trayul of fer a darn larng tarm."

Sitting in a waiting room was Cedric, an American (did you spot the accent?) crossing Canada and positively pulsating with New World charisma (he talked a lot). On the advice of Cedric, I called the bridge authorities on the land-line provided to tell them of my presence. Transport was already on its way, for cyclists are not allowed to ride the bridge and are given a free passage across. Very soon a 4WD towing a purpose made trailer turned up. The driver quickly and efficiently loaded up the bikes and on the way across the bridge gave us the low-down. This mighty structure is eight miles long, stands two hundred feet above the water and is bristling with all sorts of electronic sensors, for it has to withstand more stresses and strains than most and needs constant monitoring. It is the longest bridge in the world over ice covered waters and is subject to gusts of wind up to speeds of 140 mph. No place to be riding a bicycle.

The bridge led to a purpose built 'gateway' village with a central square where we were just in time to catch a performance of a posse of The Royal Canadian Mounted Police dancing their mounts to music. Horsemanship of the highest order was on display and the performance rightly received a rapturous round of applause from a large crowd of spectators. Cedric and I took lunch together in a nearby café but we conversed little for he was busy on his mobile phone arranging what sounded to be a hot date. He took off towards a friendly bed for the night and I took off for a night in my tent on the local campground.

Prince Edward Island was living up to its promise. The countryside was a patchwork quilt of gently undulating fields, many given over to the growing of crops, whilst others supported herds of grazing cattle. This was a very agricultural landscape but everywhere in a tender partnership of ocean and land gently embracing in a coastline of bays, inlets and river estuaries. Fishery too is a major industry, lobsters, mussels and oysters are harvested in great quantities. And if you fancy a round then this is the place to come, for there are more golf courses per head here than any other place in the world. Tourism is high profile and if the exorbitant cost of camping at the township of Cavendish is any guide, is a big money spinner. Throwing thrift and gastronomic caution to the winds, that night I ate a dinner of clams in the campground restaurant.

The next day I rode to Charlottetown, the provincial capital. The usual approaching sprawl of fast food outlets, gas stations and motels did not look too promising but soon gave way to a gem of a downtown. Sleepy avenues of brightly painted clapboard and shingle houses lay between a lively waterfront and a collection of civic buildings. In a prominent position stood Province House, an imposing pile constructed of sandstone with an arresting columned portico. This was the birthplace of modern Canada.

Back in the mid 19th century, a handful of bright sparks from the Maritime Provinces gathered here and came to the conclusion that something needed to be done to preserve their laws and customs in the face of pressure from the USA. In 1864, the 'Founding Fathers', as they are now called, came up with the idea of the Canadian Federation. Not a single document was signed but it worked and so the foundation for modern Canada was laid. In Province House I watched a filmed recreation of those historic events but although the history is fascinating, the film was not and I fell asleep.

I had to ride hard the next morning, for to leave the island there was a morning ferry to catch at Wood Islands some forty-five miles from Charlottetown. It was a close call but I made it in time and after a fourteen mile crossing, landed at Caribou in the Province of Nova Scotia. A hard east wind was blowing and I was going east. Resting at a road junction, I was joined by Donna and Leonora, two young women I had first met on the road weeks before, and who had set me on course for Newfoundland. They too had been to PEI but had caught an earlier ferry. Having swapped stories and photos, we went our separate ways but, heading for the same destination, we would doubtless meet again.

Tough going continued. An uphill flog into a tearing head-wind just about brought me to my knees until I was able to stagger into a roadside motel near the township of Westville. It was a three day ride to North Sydney the departure point for the ferry to Newfoundland. It was necessary to phone to make an advance booking. I was to leave mainland Canada on Monday the 1st of September and the time, 5-00 am. A bright and early start was that. Something to do with the rhythms of the sea, I supposed.

The highway was heading due east and crossing numerous ridges and valleys holding swift rivers feeding into the Atlantic Ocean. This was brutal terrain to ride, for the ridges were high and the valley sides steep. Place names gave testimony to the region's Scottish Heritage. St Andrews, Knoydart and Arisaig, the early settlers had comforted themselves with these reminders of home. Perhaps not Barneys River Station but a comfort to me, for here the hills became gentler and a helpful tail-wind set in. At Linwood I left the highway to take a minor road leading to a rustic campground standing on the shore of St. Georges Bay. The owner was a friendly and helpful chap. In the absence of any nearby shops he drove to the nearest one available and brought me back bananas and beer. I would not go hungry or thirsty that evening. Later, looking very tired and weary, Donna and Leonora turned up and quickly disappeared into their tent.

I took a walk along the beach. The evidence of human habitation was nowhere to be seen. A boulder strewn shore, backed by a dense forest of conifers, stretched out towards the mouth of the bay. The waters of the bay were mirror calm and over this pristine landscape there hung a profound silence. Here was a vision of how unspoilt the world must have been before we humans got busy. This was a place seen only in dreams. Deep in a rustic reverie I meandered back to my tent, there to fall into a dreamless sleep.

Looming ahead lay the blue-green bulk of the Cape Breton Highlands. The explorer John Cabot landed here in the late 15th century. When he brought back news of his discovery to England, King Henry (him of the many wives) bunged him an award of £10. Perhaps encouraged by the king's generosity, he tried a repeat performance but was never seen or heard of again. I had thought of exploring the region myself but it is a very mountainous place and I had the scent of home in my nostrils. The easier option was to stick to lower ground surrounding a series of inland seas known as the Bras d'Or Lakes.

There was no escaping the influence of the early Scottish settlers on this region. By-passing Dundee and Aberdeen I was heading for Iona and could easily have been in Scotland, amidst the landscape of Ocean, Loch and Mountain. Iona turned out to be a touristy re-creation of a Nova Scotia highland village, complete with piped music and costumed staff. This was situated on the north-western shore of a slender neck of water called the Barra Strait. Across the strait stood the village of Grand Narrows marked by the prominent three storey wooden structure of the Grand Narrows Hotel. It was the only available accommodation. The 'Canada Select Four Star Rating' of the hotel gave me some concern about damage to my wallet as I entered to seek a bed for the night. I need not have worried; the place was full, but in the accommodating manner I had become used to with all Canadians, I was allowed to camp on the front lawn and use the hotel facilities, all for free. Never before had I pitched my tent in so elegant a setting on immaculate hotel grass by the shore of a mountain-fast lake. That evening, as I watched a blazing sunset across the Lakes of the Arms of Gold, I would not have swapped my sleeping bag for a grand four-poster for all the pebbles on the beach before me.

I awoke to torrential rain born on a howling wind. Well at least it was blowing eastward and sped me along the shore of a lake, inexplicably called St Andrews Channel, for it was wide enough to render the opposite shore invisible. Who needed a view, progress was all, for today was my last day of riding on the Canadian mainland. I soon reached the Sydney area which proved to be a somewhat spread out urban region with various districts surrounding a broad ocean inlet. My destination of North Sydney was soon found, as was my bed for the night, in a traditional Bed and Breakfast establishment, complete with a menacing landlady and aspidistra.

North Sydney is one of those 'just passing through' places. No-one would ever boast the township as their dream holiday venue. This is not to say it isn't a pleasant place, with a harbour-side roadway not short of places to shop, eat or stay. It just cannot escape its basic and very important function. It is a docking place for shipping with a whole string of wharfs and landing stages for cargo and passenger vessels with an attendant sprawl of service buildings. It is a very practical place but, with a morning call of 4-00am, not one to keep me out of bed for long.

After a DIY breakfast, I rode in darkness to the ferry terminal. Donna and Leonora were there and together we boarded the 'MV Joseph and Clara Smallwood'. Doesn't really have the ring of an ocean greyhound to it, does it? But perhaps you have to immortalise a former premier and his wife somehow.

Bikes firmly lashed to an aft bulkhead, we repaired to the outside decking to watch the dawn. And what a dawn it was. If the sky could burn then on this morning it was ablaze with the fire of a billion flaming torches. Slowly the heavens turned to a burnished gold, then suddenly the sun leapt over the horizon and consumed all traces of its fiery coming in its own white hot intensity.

Two hundred and eighty miles of open sea lay between us and our Newfoundland destination. For a time I dozed in a passenger lounge but the call of the ocean was irresistible and I sought the foredeck. A school of dolphins swam alongside, leaping in graceful arcs above the waves. Hump-backed whales were blowing and showing their dark rounded topsides and all around passengers were busy marvelling at this abundant freedom of ocean life as they imprisoned it with their cameras.

Life of another kind was gravitating towards its fellow species on the foredeck – that of the long-distance cyclist. There were seven of us in all, most of whom were on the last leg of their journey across Canada. You have probably had your fill of cycling stories by now so I will say no more. None of us had any arrangements for sleeping on our night-time arrival at the port of Argentia. Alighting, we made our way to a convenient patch of rough grass to pitch our tents. Across the departure area, an official in bright yellow uniform came towards us. Could this mean trouble? Just the opposite: he guided us to a manicured lawn adjacent to the ferry terminal, complete with picnic tables, and a terminal building exit door was jammed open to give us access to the public facilities. Newfoundland promised to be a hospitable place.

During my last day's riding I had somehow picked up a companion. This was Josie, a student from Montreal, who was riding to St Johns to pick fruit before completing her degree in ecological studies at the University of St Johns. She was short of funds and had therefore been camping wild by the roadside – an interesting experience by her account, involving several police visits. These were not to arrest her as a vagrant but to check that she was OK and, more than once, to supply her with food and beer. She must still have been hungry for when we stopped at a roadside diner, she circulated around, collecting leftovers. After eating her fill she proceeded to demonstrate her satisfaction by rattling off a series of appreciative belches. She was definitely an individual who marched to the beat of a different drum.

We rode on, but not for long, as Josie was still hungry and stopped to pick blueberries before needing relief and shamelessly squatting to bare her bottom. Suddenly, the bleak tundra around us became a beautiful sight.

Somehow we made it to St Johns and to the city's campground, but not before sinking a pint or two in O'Reilly's pub, whereupon the last of Josie's natural inhibitions melted away as she shared her pungent symptoms of wild camping with all in the bar:

"I fucking stink!"

I knew what she meant, and her ribald presence had brought energy and laughter to a day which I might otherwise have spent in lonely contemplation of the end.

The end was not yet nigh, however, for although we had stopped for photos at City Hall, there was still ground to be covered. The next morning, Josie and I set out to ride to Cape Spear, together with Donna and Leonora, who had also turned up. Cape Spear is the easternmost point of land of the Canadian Confederation. It is as far as you can go without falling into the Atlantic. Without panniers we soon made it. I had half expected a 'Lands End' type theme park but Cape Spear was mercifully uncluttered, simply a big finger of rock with a lighthouse on top. Here a bike ride of fifteen months and twelve thousand seven hundred and fifty-three miles came to an end. But it is never over until the fat lady sings, as they say, and that night she sang loud but not very clear. Josie had been donated some left over beer from departing campers and was in the mood for serenading her fellow travellers.

The time had come to beat a retreat and so the next day I moved to a downtown backpackers' hostel, there to better explore the city of St Johns. Picture a child's drawing; see how the houses seem to be suspended in impossible positions, sometimes crowded together, other times standing apart. Marvel at their colours and wonder at the steepness of the winding streets. This is downtown St Johns. Steep hills slope down towards the harbour-side. Parallel streets of shops, pubs and eating houses follow the course of the quayside. Everywhere there is the sound of the traditional music of Newfoundland, drifting through the doorways of Irish bars or dancing on the air from the tin whistle of a busker. Walk the harbour-side and wander through the alleyways of a traditional 'Newfie' fishing village until you reach a winding path through rock and heather to the summit of Signal Hill. Here the first radio signals to bridge the Atlantic were received. Surely there is only one harbour and headland walk in the world more beautiful than this, and that is the walk back. Everywhere there are smiles and hellos and there is time to stand and chat or just watch the world go by. And it does, for shipping from all over the globe docks at St Johns to re-provision. But they are not the only visitors, for now and then, sailing southwards on a drifting iceberg, there comes the occasional polar bear to liven up the city life, whilst hump back whales patrol the waters outside the harbour mouth.

This remote northern outpost of the Canadian Federation is the end of the road for travellers of all kinds, as it was for me. The journey by cycle was over.